THE COMPLETE
TAX PLANNING
HANDBOOK FOR
EDUCATORS

1984-1985 EDITION

Prepared by
RALPH GANO MILLER, CPA, JD, MBA
WILLIAM D. HOSHAW, JD, LLM

UNITED RESOURCES PUBLISHING
NEWPORT BEACH, CALIFORNIA

This book reflects the tax laws in effect on July 18, 1984, (including the changes made by the Tax Reform Act of 1984).

Printed in the United States of America

First printing, 1985.

Library of Congress Cataloging in Publication Data

Miller, Ralph Gano, 1926-
  The complete tax planning handbook for educators.

  Includes index.
  1. Teachers — Taxation — Law and legislation —
United States. 2. Income tax — Law and legislation —
United States. I. Hoshaw, William D., 1951-
II. Title. III. Title: Tax planning handbook for
educators.
KF6369.8.E3M55   1985   343.7305'2'024372   84-26409
ISBN 0-932307-00-0 (pbk.)   347.30352024372

United Resources Publishing
1100 Quail Street, Suite 100
Newport Beach, California 92660-2701

C O N T E N T S

"Anyone may arrange his affairs that his taxes shall be as low as possible. He is not bound to choose the pattern which best pays the treasury. There is not even a patriotic duty to increase one's taxes....Over and over again, courts have said that there is nothing sinister in so arranging one's affairs as to keep taxes as low as possible. Everybody does so—rich or poor; and all are right; for nobody owes any public duty to pay more than the law demands. Taxes are enforced exactions, not voluntary contributions."

— Judge Learned Hand
U.S. Court of Appeals, 1934.

ABOUT THE AUTHORS

Ralph Gano Miller, a senior partner with the San Diego law firm of Miller, Ewald & Monson, has been practicing law since 1958. He specializes in income, gift and estate tax law and estate planning, in addition to employee benefit planning. He is a Certified Specialist in taxation law as provided by the California Board of Legal Specialization.

He was educated at Stanford University, where he was awarded his BA in 1949 and an MBA cum laude in 1951, and at University of San Diego, where he was awarded his JD summa cum laude in 1958. He also was awarded Certified Public Accountant credentials in 1956.

He has authored numerous publications and journal contributions in the fields of his specialties—taxes, pensions, estate planning, and employee compensation. He also served as a member of the Board of Regents, University of San Diego Law School, and as lecturer and professor on subjects of taxation, real property, probate and trust law at California Western Law School.

He is a member of, and has held section chairmanships for, the American Bar Association, the State Bar of California, and the San Diego County Bar Association.

William D. Hoshaw, a partner of the Miller, Ewald & Monson law firm in San Diego, has practiced law since 1978. He earned his BA at University of Arizona in 1973, was awarded his JD in 1977 and an LLM degree in taxation in 1983, both from University of San Diego.

He is a member of the State Bar of California, where he is a member of the tax section, and the San Diego County Bar Association.

HIGHLIGHTS OF 1984 TAX LAW CHANGES

On July 18, 1984, President Reagan signed the Tax Reform Act of 1984. While most of that law's provisions do not take effect until 1985, some important changes became operative in 1984. Each of those changes, as well as previously enacted amendments, which will affect the 1984 income tax returns of educators, are analyzed in this handbook and summarized below.

☐ **Rate Reduction** The final part of the three-year reduction in tax rates has been phased in. For 1984, the tax rates are 5 percent less than the 1983 rates.

☐ **Social Security Benefits** Up to 50 percent of all social security benefits you received in 1984 may be subject to tax.

☐ **Reduction Of Long-Term Holding Period** The long-term capital gain/loss holding period has been reduced from one year to six months. This change applies to assets purchased after June 22, 1984.

☐ **Individual Retirement Accounts** All IRA contributions must be made by April 15, 1985, even if you were granted an extension to file your return.

☐ **Income Averaging** The tax benefits derived from income averaging have been reduced.

☐ **Estimated Taxes** The IRS may now waive an underpayment penalty if, during this year, the taxpayer retired after reaching age 62 or became disabled and the underpayment was due to reasonable cause. There are also new rules regarding 1985 estimated tax payments.

☐ **Contribution Deductions For Taxpayers Who Do Not Itemize** The maximum deduction allowed has increased to $75 for most taxpayers. For married taxpayers who file separate returns, the maximum deduction is $37.50.

☐ **Self-Employment Tax** For 1984, the self-employment tax for social security is effectively 11.3 percent.

☐ **Medicines And Drugs** Only prescription drugs and insulin can be deducted. And the old 1 percent limitation rules no longer apply.

☐ **Medical Care** Upon your arrival for medical treatment away from home, lodging expenses of up to $50 per night for each individual can be deducted.

☐ **Loans With Below-Market Interest Rates** Loans with below-market interest rates may generate income and/or gift tax consequences to the lender and borrower, depending on the type of loan involved.

☐ **Transfers Of Property In Divorce** Transfers of property made after July 17, 1984 and incident to a divorce will not result in taxable gain or loss. If both spouses agree, this favorable tax treatment will apply to property transfers made after December 31, 1983.

☐ **Disability Income** The disability income exclusion, which was available in prior years, has been repealed. There is now a new tax credit for taxpayers who are permanently and totally disabled.

☐ **Business Use of Automobiles, Home Computers And Other Property** With respect to purchases of "listed" property, e.g., automobiles, home computers and certain other property used for business, after June 18, 1984, there are special depreciation and investment credit eligibility rules. These new rules consider whether the "listed" property is used more than 50 percent for business purposes and whether such use is for the convenience of the employer and required as a condition of employment. If you plan to depreciate an asset which you purchased in 1984, you should consult Part III.

☐ **Real Property Depreciation** The ACRS depreciable life of real property other than low income housing has been increased from 15 years to 18 years. This change applies to property purchased after March 15, 1984.

INTRODUCTION

This book is intended to provide educators — at all levels of the profession — with enough information about applicable tax laws to enable them to prepare their individual tax returns. Written in straightforward, basic English, this handbook provides only what is necessary and omits confusing legal jargon and burdensome details.

The book's five-part format follows a logical progression, beginning with initial taxpayer considerations, followed by the steps involved in completing a 1984 tax return, and continuing through tax planning considerations for 1985 and beyond. The component parts of the handbook are:

Part I Before You Start On Your Tax Return
Part II Step-by-Step Through Your Form 1040
Part III Specific Tax Laws Affecting Educators
Part IV Tax Planning For Educators
Part V Sample, Filled-In Tax Forms And Schedules

A key feature of this handbook is its emphasis upon tax provisions that are particularly applicable to educators. Among these are deductions for education expenses incurred to retain one's salary, status or position as an educator, and expenses incurred by college professors while lecturing, writing and publishing. And not to be overlooked is the deduction available exclusively to employees of public school systems and tax-exempt educational organizations for qualifying contributions to Tax-Sheltered Annuities (TSAs).

This unique tax guide also features scores of specific examples and real-life situations which illustrate important tax issues. These examples should help to make the more difficult tax concepts understandable. Because most topics are not treated in overwhelming detail, however, the examples and other explanations should not be viewed as a substitute for competent tax advice. Rather, they should be used as an aid in seeking advice.

This handbook has been researched and written to achieve two principal goals. The first is to enable educators to efficiently and accurately prepare their tax returns for the current year. The second is to provide guidance in the important area of tax planning so that they can minimize their tax liability in future years.

1 BEFORE YOU START ON YOUR TAX RETURN

Today's tax laws are extremely complex. Although Congress has considered proposals to make the system more comprehensible, no such legislation has been enacted. As a result of the complex nature of tax laws, regulations and court decisions, two taxpayers reading the same provision of the Internal Revenue Code are likely to make different interpretations. Throughout this handbook, these ambiguities have been interpreted in a manner which will minimize your tax liability.

THE IMPORTANCE OF SUFFICIENT RECORDS

If you keep good records, you will never forget to include a deduction on your tax return and you will be able to substantiate your income and deductions if you are audited by the IRS. The extent of your record keeping efforts will depend upon your employment, business activities and investment portfolio. Some general record keeping guidelines for educators are:

☐ Retain your cancelled checks.
☐ Record all tax deductible cash expenditures in a diary.
☐ Obtain written receipts whenever possible.
☐ Save all home improvement receipts.
☐ Keep track of transportation mileage.
☐ Record all travel and entertainment information in a diary at the time expenses are incurred.
☐ For items used for both business and personal reasons, keep a record of the time the item is used for business.

When Records Required

Technically, you must keep sufficient records to enable you to prepare a complete and accurate income tax return. With respect to travel expenses, entertainment expenses and business gifts, the tax code requires that deductions be substantiated by adequate records which corroborate the oral statements of the taxpayer. The corroborating records must set forth the amount of the expense, the time and place of travel, the business purpose of the expense and the business relationship of the taxpayer to the persons entertained.

Beginning in 1985, tax records must be maintained contemporaneously, i.e., prepared at the time of the expense for which a deduction is claimed. Additionally, such contemporaneous records must indicate the business use percentage of "listed" property that is used both for business and personal reasons. [See Part III, "Depreciation And The Section 179 Deduction."]

Procedure When Records Inadequate Or Nonexistent

If you don't have any supporting records, but you incurred a tax deductible expense, you should still take the deduction. It is quite possible that you will never be audited by the IRS. And if you are audited, you may be able to convince the IRS agent that you incurred these expenses. In addition, the courts have allowed, on occasion, a deduction even though the taxpayer had no receipts.

Example During 1974 Alice, a public school teacher, spent $125 for educational supplies which she used in the classroom. Even though Alice did not save her receipts, the Tax Court still allowed her to take the deduction. The court stated that, although Alice provided no documentation, her testimony as to the amount and its reasonableness was credible enough. [Gudmundsson, 37 T.C.M. 1249 (1978).]

THE BENEFITS OF PREPLANNING

In order to maximize your deductions and correspondingly minimize your tax problems, it is important to preplan your transactions. Although you make transactions for economic reasons, you should always consider the tax consequences. Once you have completed a transaction, there are very few instances when you can reverse the tax consequences.

REDUCE THE CHANCES OF AN IRS AUDIT

Approximately one out of 60 1984 income tax returns will be audited. While there is no way to guarantee that your return will not be included among that number, here are some suggestions to minimize the chances of your return being audited.

Avoid Common Tax Return Errors

Before mailing your return you should carefully review it. The return should be dated and signed by you and your spouse if you are filing a joint return. The social security numbers of all parties signing the return should be included. You should check to see if you used the correct tax table or tax rate schedule.

You should double check your arithmetic and note whether all information is set forth on the proper line.

All W-2 forms and required schedules should be enclosed. If you are unable to include your W-2 form, you should attach a statement explaining its absence.

If you have a ''balance due,'' you should enclose a check. If your tax return shows a balance due and no check is enclosed, the IRS will contact you immediately. If your tax return shows a balance due and you are unable to pay it, you should contact the IRS. They may be able to arrange a payment schedule.

Report All Income

If you intentionally omit salary, interest or dividend income on your return, you are breaking the law. Through its enormous computer system, the IRS matches the salary, dividend and interest income listed on your return with W-2 forms and 1099 forms supplied directly to them by your employer and financial institutions. If the IRS list doesn't match the income reported on your tax return, you will be contacted immediately.

Compare Your Deductions With The National Average

Occasionally, the Treasury Department releases the average itemized deduction dollar amounts claimed by taxpayers throughout the nation. [See table below.] If your itemized deductions are substantially higher than the national average, the IRS may scrutinize your return and contact you.

This table is included only as a guide. If you have valid deductions higher than the national average, you should

Average Deductions Claimed By U.S. Taxpayers In 1981				
Adjusted Gross Income	Medical and Dental	Taxes	Contributions	Interest
20,000-25,000	$756	$1,718	$ 670	$2,887
25,000-30,000	672	1,983	697	3,122
30,000-40,000	605	2,496	834	3,483
40,000-50,000	553	3,211	1,079	4,282
50,000-75,000	676	4,400	1,567	5,586
75,000-100,000	859	6,636	2,512	8,312

claim your higher amounts. On the other hand, if your legitimate deductions are lower than these averages, you should not randomly increase them.

Avoid Round Number Deductions

A contribution deduction of $619 looks, on the surface, less suspicious than $600. If you must estimate a number, do not use a round number.

Select Your Paid Preparer Carefully

If you use a professional tax preparer, your return could be audited simply because that preparer's name is included on a list maintained by the IRS. This list includes the names of preparers who consistently prepare inaccurate tax returns. Because these preparers do not follow the rules, the IRS is forced to audit many of their clients when it otherwise would not do so.

Explain Large Deductions

You should attach additional statements to your return to explain relatively large deductions. For example, if the illness of your spouse or child necessitated constant medical treatment in 1984, you should attach a statement to your return to apprise the IRS of the reasons for your unusually large medical deductions.

Avoid Abusive Tax Shelters

The IRS has been very aggressive in its pursuit of ''abusive'' tax shelters in recent years. If you have invested in a tax shelter which the IRS has deemed ''abusive,'' you can be sure it will come calling. [See Part IV, ''Negative Income.'']

While these precautions can substantially reduce your chances of being audited by the IRS, there are other factors that could trigger an audit. Generally, your chances of being audited are increased if your income level is comparatively high, your tax return is complex or if you reside in a densely populated metropolitan area.

A final factor which may increase your chances of being audited is the IRS Taxpayer Compliance Measurement Program (TCMP). TCMP was developed by the IRS to measure how taxpayers are complying with our nation's tax laws. Under TCMP, the IRS computer randomly selects a limited number of taxpayers for audits of their entire return. Since this is a random selection, you simply cannot reduce your odds of a TCMP audit.

PENALTY PROVISIONS

A number of tax code provisions authorize the IRS to impose penalties upon taxpayers. These penalty assessments are expensive and nondeductible. You should avoid them.

Failure To File A Return

If you fail to file your return by its due date (including approved extensions), you will be subject to a penalty equal to 5 percent of the tax not paid on time. The penalty is calculated for each month or part of a month the return is late. Generally, this penalty cannot exceed 25 percent of your tax. However, if your tax return is more than 60 days late, the penalty will not be less than $100 or 100 percent of the amount required to be shown as tax on such return, whichever is less.

If you will not be able to file your completed tax return by April 15, 1985, you should file Form 4868 and pay the expected tax balance you owe. If you file Form 4868, you will then have until August 15, 1985, to file your completed Form 1040 without a penalty, provided your April 15 payment was sufficient.

If your return shows that you are due a refund, there is usually no failure to file a return penalty if your return is filed within 60 days of April 15. If you do not file your return within this 60 day period, the penalty will be the lesser of $100 or 100 percent of the tax shown.

Failure To Pay On Time

This penalty is one-half of 1 percent of the tax not paid on time. It is calculated for each month or part of a month the payment is late and may be as much as 25 percent of the tax paid after the return due date. This penalty can be waived by the IRS if you can show that you had a good reason for not paying your tax on time. And if you are subject to both the failure to file a return penalty and the failure to pay on time penalty, the combined penalty is limited to 5 percent of the unpaid tax for that month. The total cannot exceed 25 percent of your tax.

Filing A Frivolous Return

You will be subject to a $500 penalty if you file a "frivolous" return. A "frivolous" return is defined as a return that does not include enough information to enable the IRS to calculate the amount of tax due. Accordingly, you should not file a tax return with no information and a statement that all tax laws are unconstitutional. If you do so, the IRS will quickly hit you with this $500 penalty.

Failure To Supply Your Social Security Number

By failing to include your social security number on any tax return or statement when required to, you could be subject to a $5 penalty for each failure. If you refuse to give your social security number to a bank or any other person or entity when it is required on a tax statement, you could be subject to a $50 penalty.

Substantial Understatement of Tax Liability

You could be subject to a penalty of 10 percent of any underpayment of tax you owe if you file a return which "substantially" understates your actual tax liability. "Substantial" understatement occurs when your actual tax liability, as redetermined by the IRS, is more than 10 percent of the tax on the Form 1040 you originally submitted, and the understatement exceeds $5,000.

This penalty may be waived by the IRS if you attach a statement to your return which "adequately" discloses the relevant facts and how you treated them on your return. (e.g., "I have NOT included funds I received from ABC Corp in this return because ...").

Overvaluation of Property

Various rates of IRS penalties can be imposed if your tax is understated by at least $1,000 due to your overvaluation of property. The penalty rate applies to the underpayment of tax and is determined as follows:

If the valuation claimed is the following percent of the correct valuation . . .	The applicable percentage is:
150% or more but not more than 200%	10
More than 200% but not more than 250%	20
More than 250%	30

Underpayment Of Estimated Tax

If you did not pay at least 80 percent of the actual tax on your return, either through payroll withholdings or by making estimated tax payments, you may be subject to a penalty. However, you will not be subject to this penalty if any of the following conditions apply to you.

- ☐ Your 1984 payments are equal to or greater than your 1983 tax, including self-employment tax.
- ☐ Your 1984 payments are equal to or greater than what would have been due on your 1983 income, if you had figured it at 1984 rates, including self-employment tax.
- ☐ Your 1984 payments are equal to or greater than 80 percent of the tax, including self-employment tax, on your annualized taxable income for certain dates during 1984. [See IRS Form 2210 for specific details.]
- ☐ Your 1984 payments are equal to or greater than 90 percent of the tax, including self-employment tax, on your actual taxable income for certain dates during 1984. [See IRS Form 2210 for specific details.]
- ☐ The adjusted amount of tax you owe is less than $400. [See IRS Form 2210 for specific details.]

If you are subject to an underpayment penalty for 1984, the IRS may waive it if you retired after reaching age 62, or became disabled and the underpayment was due to reasonable cause rather than willful neglect. The IRS may also waive the penalty in the event of a casualty, disaster or other unusual circumstance where it would be inequitable to impose the penalty.

1985 ESTIMATED TAX PAYMENTS

If you have income that is not subject to federal withholding, e.g., interest, dividends, pension benefits, or if your withholdings are not enough to cover your tax liability, including self-employment tax and alternative minimum tax, you may be required to make estimated tax payments for 1985. If you expect to have underpaid your tax liability for 1985 by less than $500, as a general rule, you do not have to make payments. However, you must be careful because there are penalties if you are inaccurate.

SAVE MONEY BY SELECTING THE MOST APPROPRIATE TAX FORM

Since doing so can save you a great deal of money, you should be careful to choose the correct tax form. The three forms from which you may choose are 1040EZ, 1040A and 1040 ("Long Form"). Even if you meet the requirements for filing 1040EZ or 1040A, you may save money filing 1040. This is true because Form 1040 allows you to reduce your tax liability by itemizing your Schedule A deductions and taking various adjustments to your income. None of these tax saving advantages are available on Form 1040EZ and only limited adjustments are available on Form 1040A.

Form 1040EZ

As its name suggests, this is the shortest and simplest form available. You qualify to use 1040EZ if (1) your filing status is single, (2) you do not claim exemptions for being 65 or over, or for being blind, (3) you do not claim any dependents, (i.e., you claim only one exemption), (4) your taxable income is less than $50,000, and (5) your income consists only of wages, salaries and tips, and interest income of $400 or less.

You should not use Form 1040EZ if (1) you want to itemize your deductions, (2) you want to take an IRA deduction, or (3) you want to obtain tax credits for child care expenses or residential energy conservation.

Form 1040A

You qualify to use Form 1040A if your taxable income does not exceed $50,000, and your income consists only of wages, salaries, tips, interest, dividends and unemployment compensation. Form 1040A differs from Form 1040EZ in several ways. First, 1040A allows you to make adjustments to your income for payments to an IRA, and if your spouse also teaches or has other wages, you may be entitled to the working married couple deduction. Secondly, Form 1040A allows you to obtain credits for a portion of your political contributions, for child and dependent care expenses and for the earned income credit.

Form 1040A has only one schedule (Schedule I) on which you enter information about interest and dividends received in excess of $400 and any payments made to an IRA. Schedule I must also be completed if you claim the deduction for a working married couple and the credit for child and dependent care expenses.

Form 1040 ('Long Form')

Form 1040 is commonly called the "long form." As stated above, you may be able to save money by filing Form 1040 rather than Form 1040A or Form 1040EZ. You should file Form 1040 if your itemized deductions exceed $2,300 for single persons, $1,700 for married couples filing separate returns, and $3,400 for married couples filing joint returns. You should also note that, in order to deduct your Schedule A itemized deductions in excess of the zero bracket amount, you must file Form 1040.

If you moved in order to take a teaching job in a new location, travelled or took a course in order to improve your teaching skills, contributed to a Keogh plan, incurred a penalty on an early savings withdrawal or paid alimony, filing your return on Form 1040 will save you money.

Example George, a professor at a college in an eastern state, accepted a position at a California university. George then moved his wife, Susan, and infant son out to California the summer before school was to begin. Even though George and Susan's itemized deductions did not exceed $3,400 and they otherwise qualified to file Form 1040A, they should file Form 1040. Many, if not all, of the expenses associated with their move to California can be deducted from their gross income as adjustments to income.

STEP-BY-STEP THROUGH YOUR FORM 1040

Beginning at the heading of your tax return and ending with the calculation of your tax due or the amount of your refund, this part contains line-by-line instructions for completing Form 1040. You get plain English explanations of taxable and non-taxable income, itemized deductions, credits and scores of other tax-saving measures.

Easy to follow instructions explain what must be entered on each line of your tax return. And extensive cross-references guide you to detailed explanations of various tax law provisions, enabling you to research any part of the tax code. Since each subject area begins with the applicable section of Form 1040, you can make your computations right on the pages of the handbook.

The IRS requests that you affix to your return the printed mailing label on the tax booklet that you received in the mail. This will speed up the processing of your return and help avoid key punching errors that can cause you future headaches when you try to straighten them out. The IRS

has also indicated that the labels do not affect your chances of being audited. If there are any corrections necessary, you should make them directly on the printed label. If an IRS forms booklet was not mailed to you, you should simply fill in the requested information directly on the tax form.

PRESIDENTIAL ELECTION CAMPAIGN FUND

Congress has established a fund which provides financing to presidential candidates meeting specific requirements. You may indicate on your return that $1 (or $2 if both spouses designate) of your tax is to go to this fund.

The decision whether to check "Yes" or "No" is strictly up to you. If you check "Yes," the amount of tax you pay or the refund you receive is not affected (i.e., your refund amount is not reduced).

HEADING OF RETURN

Form **1040**	Department of the Treasury—Internal Revenue Service **U.S. Individual Income Tax Return**	**1984**	

For the year January 1-December 31, 1984, or other tax year beginning	, 1984, ending	, 19 .	OMB No. 1545-0074

Use IRS label. Other-wise, please print or type.	Your first name and initial (if joint return, also give spouse's name and initial)	Last name	**Your social security number**
	Present home address (Number and street, including apartment number, or rural route)		**Spouse's social security number**
	City, town or post office, State, and ZIP code	Your occupation	
		Spouse's occupation	

| **Presidential Election Campaign** ▶ | Do you want $1 to go to this fund? . . . . | Yes | No | **Note:** *Checking "Yes" will not change your tax or reduce your refund.* |
| | If joint return, does your spouse want $1 to go to this fund?. . | Yes | No | |

FILING STATUS

Filing Status

Check only
one box.

1 ☐ Single

2 ☐ Married filing joint return (even if only one had income)

3 ☐ Married filing separate return. Enter spouse's social security no. above and full name here. _____

4 ☐ Head of household (with qualifying person). (See page 5 of Instructions.) If the qualifying person is your unmarried child but not your dependent, write child's name here. _____

5 ☐ Qualifying widow(er) with dependent child (Year spouse died ▶ 19___). (See page 6 of Instructions.)

Basic Considerations

Your marital status will dictate the tax rates that are available to you. For tax purposes, your marital status is determined on December 31 of each year. However, if your spouse died during 1984, you can still file a 1984 joint return.

Joint return rates are the lowest tax rates. These rates are available to (1) married taxpayers who elect to file a joint return and (2) certain qualifying widow(ers) with one or more dependent children. However, there are some instances when it will not be to your advantage to file a joint return. If you fit within more than one filing status category, you should calculate your taxes under each status and select the filing status that will save you the most money.

If your marriage has been dissolved or you were separated pursuant to a court order on December 31, you generally must use the single filing status. However, you may qualify for the more favorable head of household filing status. Also, a qualifying widow(er) with one or more dependent children is entitled to use the most favorable joint return filing status.

HEAD OF HOUSEHOLD RATES

Head of household rates are lower than single rates, but not as low as joint return rates. You may qualify for head of household rates if you were unmarried (including certain married persons who live apart) or legally separated and: (1) contributed more than 50 percent of the cost of maintaining a principal home for your parents and declare them as dependents (they need not live with you) or (2) contributed more than 50 percent of the cost of maintaining a home for certain individuals who lived with you for the entire taxable year.

Individuals who would qualify you under the second option include your unmarried child, adopted child, stepchild or grandchild; your married child, adopted child, stepchild or grandchild who is your dependent; or any other close relative (as defined in the Form 1040 instructions) whom you claim as a dependent, except those who are claimed as a dependent under a multiple support agreement.

You need not be single to qualify for Head of Household tax rates. For example, if you are married with a child you can qualify for Head of Household rates if you satisfy these four tests:

(1) You do not file a joint return;

(2) You contributed more than 50 percent of the cost of maintaining your home;

(3) Your spouse did not live with you at any time during the entire year; and

(4) One or more of your children or stepchildren whom you can claim as a dependent established a principal home with you for the entire year. If your child lived with you for more than six months, but less than the entire year, you cannot file as a head of household. However, you can file as a single person rather than as a married person filing a separate return.

SPECIAL RATES FOR QUALIFYING WIDOW(ERS)

If you are a widow(er) with one or more dependent children, your spouse died in 1982 or 1983, and you did not remarry, you can qualify to file as a qualifying widow(er). If so, you can use the lower joint return rates on your 1984 return if the following requirements are met.

First of all, you must have been eligible to file a joint return for the year in which your spouse died, regardless of whether or not you did so. Secondly, your dependent child, stepchild, adopted child or foster child must have lived with you during 1984 And finally, you must have paid more than 50 percent of the cost of maintaining your home for the year.

WHETHER TO FILE A SEPARATE OR JOINT RETURN

If you are married, you have the option of filing a separate or joint tax return. Generally, you will save the most money if you file jointly, since the joint return rates are lower than the rates for a married individual filing a separate return. And where both spouses are employed, filing a joint return will enable you to take advantage of the married couples deduction.

A number of factors should be considered before you decide whether to file a separate or joint return. For example, community property jurisdictions commonly require community income and obligations to be reported equally by each spouse, even if separate returns are filed. The states which have adopted a system of community property are Arizona, California, Idaho, Louisiana, Nevada, New Mexico, Texas and Washington. You should also be aware that, if you file separately, you lose the deduction available to two-earner married couples, the credit for child and dependent care expenses and the credit for the elderly. Additionally, even if you decide to file separately, there is a limitation imposed on your freedom to decide whether or not to itemize. If your spouse claims the standard deduction, so must you. And if you elect to deduct your excess itemized deductions, your spouse must do likewise. Finally, if your spouse's deductions do not exceed the zero bracket amount, a por-

Example Janet's husband, a retired school principal, died in 1983 and she has not remarried. Janet has a 9-year-old daughter. Due to her circumstances, Janet can choose to file as (1) a single taxpayer, (2) head of household, or (3) a qualifying widow with dependent child. She should choose to file as a qualifying widow, however. By doing so, she can use the lower joint return rates to compute her tax.

EXEMPTIONS

Exemptions

Always check the box labeled Yourself. Check other boxes if they apply.

6a ☐ Yourself   ☐ 65 or over   ☐ Blind   } Enter number of boxes checked on 6a and b ▶ ☐

b ☐ Spouse   ☐ 65 or over   ☐ Blind   }

c First names of your dependent children who lived with you_____   } Enter number of children listed on 6c ▶ ☐

d Other dependents: (1) Name	(2) Relationship	(3) Number of months lived in your home	(4) Did dependent have income of $1,000 or more?	(5) Did you provide more than one-half of dependent's support?

Enter number of other dependents ▶ ☐

e Total number of exemptions claimed (also complete line 36). . . . .

Add numbers entered in boxes above ▶ ☐

---

tion of that zero bracket amount will go unused.

Despite all of the advantages of filing jointly, separate returns may be desirable in several situations. In states where income from separate property remains separate income, for example, you may save money in taxes if one of you has a casualty loss attributable to separate property which would be nondeductible on a joint return because it does not exceed the 10 percent adjusted gross income floor.

It may also be advantageous to file separately if one of you incurs substantial medical expenses which would be nondeductible on a joint return because they do not exceed the 5 percent adjusted gross income floor. And if one spouse had a substantial increase in income during the year, you could probably benefit more by income averaging on a separate return rather than filing a joint return.

In addition to the preceding monetary reasons, there may be other reasons for electing to file a separate return. Since both spouses are liable for the taxes shown on a joint return, as well as any additional taxes, penalties and interest that may be assessed, you may decide to file a separate return if you suspect that your spouse is understating his or her income.

A decision to file a joint federal tax return does not necessarily mean that filing a joint state return is advisable. You should carefully examine your state's tax rate schedule to determine if (1) the rate schedule for single returns is the same as the rate for joint returns and (2) if your income is taxed at progressively higher rates. If income is taxed at progressively higher rates and the same rate schedules apply to single and joint returns, you can probably save money by filing separate state tax returns.

Every exemption that you claim results in a $1,000 decrease in your taxable income. It is to your advantage to carefully examine the rules governing personal and dependency exemptions and, if at all possible, do the planning necessary to enable you to claim additional exemptions.

'Personal' And 'Dependency' Exemptions

If you file a joint tax return, a personal exemption of $1,000 is allowed for each spouse. If you are single or married and file separate returns, you will generally be entitled to only one exemption. However, if you are married and file separately, you can claim an exemption for your spouse if he or she (1) will not file a return, (2) had no income for the year, and (3) was not claimed as a dependent on the return of another taxpayer.

Additional personal exemptions are available if, as of December 31 of the year, one or both of you is 65 or older and/or is blind. You are considered to be blind for tax purposes if you cannot see better than 20/200 in your better eye with correcting lenses or if your field of vision is less than or equal to 20 degrees.

If your spouse died during 1984 and you did not remarry before the end of the year, you can file a 1984 joint return. Also, you can claim all exemptions to which your deceased spouse was entitled upon the date of his or her death.

In addition to the personal exemptions, you may be entitled to dependency exemptions for children, relatives and certain other individuals whom you support. You may claim a dependency exemption, and thereby reduce your taxable income by $1,000, for any individual who meets the following five tests:

(1) The person received less than $1,000 of gross income during the tax year. (An exception is recognized for a child under 19 or a child over 19 who, for five months of the year, is a full time student.);

(2) You must have furnished over one-half of the dependent's support or be treated as having provided over half of the support;

(3) The person supported is a U.S. citizen or resident, a resident of Canada or Mexico or an alien child adopted by and living with a U.S. citizen living abroad;

(4) The person must not have filed a joint return with his or her spouse; and

(5) The person supported was a close relative, child, grandchild, parent or grandparent, sibling or child of sibling or, if not a close relative, was a member of your household for the entire year in a living arrangement that does not violate local law.

CLAIMING DEPENDENCY EXEMPTIONS BY DIVORCED PARENTS

As a general rule, the parent who has custody for a majority of the year will get the exemption. This rule will apply, however, only if both parents together provided more than one-half of the child's support during the year. If you are the non-custodial parent, you can claim the exemption if a written agreement awards the exemption to you and you contribute at least $600 per year to each child's support. You can also claim the exemption if you provide at least $1,200 per year for each child's support and the custodial parent cannot prove that he or she provided more. Starting in 1985, the exemption will generally be awarded to the custodial parent unless he/she agrees in writing to waive the exemption, where prescribed conditions are met.

For purposes of claiming dependency exemptions, support includes social security and welfare benefits. Support also includes food, shelter, clothing, medical and dental care, and the fair market value of any goods provided. Money from a scholarship or fellowship, however, is not treated as support for this purpose.

Example Jim gives his ex-wife, the custodial parent, $1,000 per month for the support of their only child. Unless his ex-wife can prove that she provided more, Jim will be entitled to claim the dependency exemption because he paid more than $1,200 in support for the year.

Example Your aged mother receives $3,400 in social security benefits which is her only annual income. You contribute $4,000 toward her support. Even though social security benefits are treated as support provided by your mother, you still contributed more than one-half of her

---

INCOME

Income

Please attach Copy B of your Forms W-2, W-2G, and W-2P here.

If you do not have a W-2, see page 4 of Instructions.

7	Wages, salaries, tips, etc.	7
8	Interest income *(also attach Schedule B if over $400)*	8
9a	Dividends *(also attach Schedule B if over $400)* _____ , 9b Exclusion _____	
c	Subtract line 9b from line 9a and enter the result	9c
10	Refunds of State and local income taxes, from the worksheet on page 9 of Instructions *(do not enter an amount unless you itemized deductions for those taxes in an earlier year—see page 9)*	10
11	Alimony received	11
12	Business income or (loss) *(attach Schedule C)*	12
13	Capital gain or (loss) *(attach Schedule D)*	13
14	40% of capital gain distributions not reported on line 13 (see page 9 of Instructions)	14
15	Supplemental gains or (losses) *(attach Form 4797)*	15
16	Fully taxable pensions, IRA distributions, and annuities not reported on line 17	16
17a	Other pensions and annuities, including rollovers. Total received **17a** _____	
b	Taxable amount, if any, from the worksheet on page 10 of Instructions	17b
18	Rents, royalties, partnerships, estates, trusts, etc. *(attach Schedule E)*	18
19	Farm income or (loss) *(attach Schedule F)*	19
20a	Unemployment compensation (insurance). Total received **20a** _____	
b	Taxable amount, if any, from the worksheet on page 10 of Instructions	20b
21a	Social security benefits. (see page 10 of Instructions) **21a** _____	
b	Taxable amount, if any, from the worksheet on page 11 of Instructions	21b
22	Other income (state nature and source—see page 11 of Instructions)_____	22
23	Add lines 7 through 22. This is your **total income** ▶	23

Please attach check or money order here.

support. Thus, you are entitled to claim an exemption for your mother. However, if you had provided only $3,000 of support to her, you would not have been entitled to the exemption.

TAXABLE AND NON-TAXABLE INCOME

Income is reported on lines 7 through 23 of Form 1040. If you are like most educators, the bulk of your income will be in salary. This is set forth on your W-2 form provided by your employer. You should review this form carefully. If you do not receive your W-2 form within two or three days after January 31, you should contact your employer. You should bear in mind that you must still report your income to the IRS, even if your employer fails to supply you with a W-2 form in a timely manner.

You may also receive Form 1099 from different individuals or entities that made payments to you during the year. This income should also be included on your return, unless a portion is specifically identified as being non-taxable.

As a general rule, all income is taxable, unless specifically exempted by the tax laws. Although there may be some exceptions, the following lists include those items which constitute taxable and non-taxable income, respectively.

W AGES, SALARIES AND TIPS

On line 7 of Form 1040 you will report the total amount you received during the year for wages, salaries, tips, bonuses and other employee compensation. This amount is usually shown on the W-2 form sent to you by your employer.

Exclusion For Foreign Income

There is an exclusion available if you earn income while

Non-Taxable Income
Accident and health insurance premiums paid by employer
Accident and health insurance proceeds
Bequests and devises
Board and lodging on premises and as condition of the job
Carpool receipts by auto owner
Child support payments
Damages for personal injuries
Disability payments, limited in some cases
Dividends from U.S. companies under a certain amount
Dividends paid in stock of the corporation
Dividends paid by public utilities reinvested in utility
Fellowship and scholarship grants — limited as to amount and time
Gifts
Group life insurance (non-permanent type) - cost paid by employer for coverage of $50,000 or less
Income tax refunds (federal and sometimes state)
Inheritances

Interest on certain stock and municipal bonds
Life insurance proceeds, paid on death of insured
Lodging furnished for convenience of employer
Meals furnished for convenience of employer
Medical care payments, employer financed plans
Old age, survivor and disability payments under Social Security Act or Railroad Retirement Act, limited as to amount
Pulitzer Prize and similar awards
Scholarship and fellowship grants (limited as to amount and time)
Social security, limited as to amount
Unemployment benefits, limited

Taxable Income
Alimony and separate maintenance payments
Annuities — limited
Armed forces pay
Bad debt recovery
Back pay
Bartering income
Bequests, income from

Board and lodging
Bonuses
Business expense reimbursements in excess of your expenses
Capital gains
Christmas bonus
Commissions
Director's fees
Distributions from an IRA or other pension plan
Dividends from U.S. companies over a certain amount
Executor's fees
Gains from sale or exchange of property
Group term life insurance, cost paid by employer for coverage in excess of $50,000
Health resort expenses paid by employer
Income distributed from trust or estate
Interest received, excluding municipal bond interest
Jury duty fees
Life Insurance proceeds from a policy you cashed in if proceeds exceed premiums you paid
Lump sum distributions
Moving expenses of

employees if reimbursed by employer
Notary public fees
Original issue discount
Partnership income
Pensions
Premiums on ordinary life insurance paid for employee if latter may name beneficiary, except those paid for certain non-permanent group insurance
Prizes in contests
Profits from your business or profession
Refunds of state and local taxes if you deducted as an itemized deduction in an earlier year
Rental income
Retirement pay
Rewards
Salaries
Social security, limited as to amount
Tips
Tuition paid by employer in excess of $5,000
Unemployment benefits, limited
Wages (i.e., gross wages). This includes amounts withheld from your salary for social security and income taxes.

working in a foreign country. The rules are fairly strict. However, if you are planning to work abroad for a significant period of time, it is well worth your time to review these rules and plan your journey or sabbatical so that you will qualify for the exclusion. For the 1984 tax year, you may exclude up to a maximum of $80,000 of earned income. An additional exclusion or deduction is available for housing costs.

You may exclude income earned while working in a foreign country if your income consists of wages, salaries or professional fees received as compensation for personal services performed while abroad. This includes self-employment income to the extent produced by personal services and not capital investment. Qualification for the exclusion also requires that the income is received for services performed while you are a bona fide resident of a foreign country for an uninterrupted period that includes a full tax year, (generally January 1 through December 31). Brief trips elsewhere for vacations or business will not compromise the exclusion. Alternatively, you must have spent at least 330 full days out of any period of 12 consecutive months outside of the United States. Under this test, vacations or other nonemployment time in a foreign country count toward the 330 days. In addition, if you were required to leave the foreign country because of war, civil unrest or other adverse conditions, and you would have otherwise met the 330 day test, you can still qualify.

The exclusion is not available if you were employed by the U.S. government or one of its agencies. Thus, if you teach in a school operated by the U.S. government you will not be able to exclude your income.

In order to qualify for the foreign income exclusion, it is imperative that you plan ahead. When making preparations for your sabbatical abroad, you should take steps to ensure that all payments by your school in the U.S. are clearly paid for work performed while you are gone. Since the exclusion is dependent on the income being earned while abroad, payments received by you that are characterized as compensation for past services, or to aid in your personal growth, will not qualify and the exclusion will not be available.

You can claim this exclusion by filing Form 2555 with your return. Because of the obvious benefit of the exclusion, there are certain trade-offs. If you elect to exclude your foreign income, you will not be able to claim any deductions attributable to the excluded income. Therefore, you will not be able to deduct any travel expenses related to your foreign employment or claim the two-earner married couple deduction.

Example Joyce lived in France from January 1 through December 31. She worked on writing a book and various newspaper articles during that time. Joyce can exclude royalty income since payments under a personal service contract to write newspaper articles and a book are earned income. Thus, Joyce had earned income while working in a foreign country. [Rev. Rul. 254, 1980-2 C.B. 222.]

Scholarships And Fellowships

As a general rule, scholarship and fellowship grants are exempt from income and social security taxes. The exemption covers not only the value of services and accommodations contributed, but also any payments covering expenses for incidental travel, research, clerical help or equipment, so long as the amounts received are actually expended for these purposes.

In determining the availability of these exemptions, you must remember that, generally, amounts paid as compensation for services (e.g., teaching, research or other part-time employment) or amounts paid primarily for the grantor's benefit cannot be excluded. For example, an employer-employee relationship will frequently result in a presumption that amounts received as a summer grant or sabbatical pay are either compensation or for the grantor's benefit, and thus are not excludible. However, if (1) you are a degree candidate and the same teaching, research or other type of services are required of all degree candidates, regardless of whether or not they are recipients of scholarship or fellowship grants, or (2) the grant is a federal government grant which fits all other requirements except that it requires future services to be performed as a federal employee, compensation or grant funds so received may be excluded.

Those educators who are not degree candidates may still be able to exclude the scholarship or fellowship grant, if the grantor is a tax-exempt organization or governmental unit. However, the exclusion is not without some restrictions. You are limited to a lifetime exclusion of $300 per month for 36 months. Although the months need not be consecutive, the 36 month time period begins when you start to receive the funds, regardless of whether you elect to exclude them. The $300/36 month limitation does not apply to amounts specifically designated for expenses, if the money is actually so expended.

In some cases it may be beneficial for you to forego the exclusion for scholarship and fellowship grants. For example, if the grants are not particularly substantial and will not result in a large current tax, it may benefit you more to forego the exclusion and income average. Income averaging requires that you must have provided 50 percent or more of your support for a specified period of time. The key questions are whether fellowship and scholarship grants count as part of your support and, if they are support, whether they are support from an outside source that will jeopardize a finding that you provided more than 50 percent of your support. The amount you save through income averaging may outweigh the benefits of excluding a small amount of income now. [See the income averaging discussion in Part II and complete Schedule G to make your decision.]

Example Carl received a post-doctoral fellowship grant in 1984. The total amount of the grant, which covers a nine-month period, is $4,500. It commenced on September 1, at which time Carl began receiving monthly installments of $500. During 1984, the first year of the grant, Carl can exclude $1200 (4 x $300), and thus should include the remaining $800 in his income. During 1985, Carl can exclude $1500 (5 x 300) and will include $1000. [Treas. Reg. §1.117-2(b)(3).]

Prizes And Awards

Prizes or awards which you receive may be tax-free if (1) the award was made primarily in recognition of religious, charitable, scientific, educational, literary or civic achievement, (2) you were selected without any action on your part, and (3) you are not required to render substantial future services as a condition of receiving the prize or award. However, if there is an employer-employee relationship existing between you and the person or organization making the gift, the tax-free nature of the gift may be difficult to successfully sustain.

Example Without her knowledge, Linda was nominated to receive an award by seniors and alumni for overall past service to the college which employs her. Linda need not include this award in her taxable income because the award was made in recognition of educational achievement, without any action on her part, and in recognition of past services. [Rev. Rul. 19, 1957-1 C.B.33.]

Union Strike Benefits

Chances are very good that any strike benefits paid to you by your union will be considered income. While an old U.S. Supreme Court case held, under an unusual set of facts, that strike benefits were a non-taxable gift, every subsequent court case has held strike benefits to be taxable income.

INTEREST

The amount of all interest received or credited to you during the year should be entered on line 8 of Form 1040, and dividend income is entered on line 9. If you received more than $400 in interest, you must also complete Part 1 of Schedule B.

Educators commonly receive interest from banks, credit unions, savings and loan associations, building and loan accounts, notes, loans and mortgages, tax refunds, bonds and debentures, U.S. Treasury Bills, and U.S. Savings Bonds. Remember, that interest may be credited to you without having actually been posted in your passbook.

Non-Taxable Interest Income

There are several situations where interest is either not currently includible or is completely tax-exempt. First, if you own U.S. savings bonds, you have two options with respect to reporting interest income attributable to these bonds. You can defer reporting any interest until the bonds mature or are cashed in. Alternatively, you may declare the yearly increase in the value of the bonds as income. If you purchase bonds for your children, you should use their social security numbers so that income earned is taxable to your children and not to you.

Example Bill owns several savings bonds and does not plan to cash them in for some time. Bill need not report the interest earned on the bonds each year. He can report the increase in the value of the bonds each year or he can wait until he cashes the bonds in and report the interest in that year.

Interest on U.S. Treasury Bills is taxable only in the year in which it matures and the interest is received. This can allow for a deferral of interest from one year to the next. Interest on obligations of state and local governments is generally completely exempt from federal taxation.

Original Issue Discount

If a corporation issues bonds or other obligations at a discount, they are offering them for sale at a price less than the face value or the redemption price at maturity. The original issue discount (OID) is the amount of the difference between the issue price and the redemption price. It is allocated on a daily basis over the life of the bond. If the bond was issued after July 1, 1982, the amount of the daily portion of original issue discount, determined for each day during the tax year the bond is held, is included in taxable income.

If the bond was issued before July 2, 1982, the includible amount of OID is determined according to the number of complete and partial months you held the bond, rather than on a daily basis. Although the process may appear complex, the Form 1099 that the corporate obligor sends you will instruct you as to the amount of OID includible on your 1984 tax return.

If you purchased a bond which had accrued interest, and you paid the amount of accrued interest as part of your purchase price, you should report as income only that amount of interest that you receive which exceeds the sum you paid.

Example Christine purchased some corporate bonds and her purchase price included the interest which had accrued since the last payment date. Chris need not report all of the interest paid on the next payment date since the amount of accrued interest is not income.

All-Savers Certificates

The law creating the "once-in-a-lifetime" benefit from All-Savers Certificates required that the certificates be issued before 1983. The term of these certificates was limited to one year. Therefore, for 1984, you should not have any interest income from All-Savers Certificates.

DIVIDENDS

Dividends are distributions of money, stock or other property from corporations in which you hold an interest. They are generally fully taxable, regardless of the form in which they are paid. However, you can exclude up to $100 ($200 for married couples filing jointly) of dividend income received from a U.S. corporation.

In most instances, the three types of corporation distributions with which you will become involved include ordinary dividends, capital gains distributions and non-taxable distributions. The first type includes dividends which are paid out of a corporation's current or accumulated earnings and profits. Capital gains distributions are dividends paid from capital gains earned by the corporation. While they do not qualify for the dividend exclusion, they do qualify for the more favorable long-term capital gains rate which allows you to deduct 60 percent of the amount of capital gain received. Thus, you are taxed only on the remaining 40 percent. Mutual funds, public utility companies and real estate investment trusts frequently make distributions of this type. The third category, non-taxable distributions, are distributions which are non-taxable because they represent a return of your cost or basis in the stock. Once you have recovered your cost or basis, subsequent distributions will be taxable at the capital gains rates.

Stock dividends are non-taxable, unless the corporation gave you the option to receive cash or other property instead of the stock dividend. Likewise, mutual insurance company dividends, which merely reduce the amount of premiums you pay, are also non-taxable.

Example Larry receives a dividend on his life insurance policy each year which reduces the amount of premium that he pays. The dividend is non-taxable.

If you own stock in a qualified public utility, you have an unique opportunity to exclude dividends. If the utility has a qualifying reinvestment plan, you can elect to receive your dividends in "qualified common stock" rather than in cash or other property. As mentioned above, this option would ordinarily make the dividend taxable in full. However, you can elect to exclude up to $750 ($1,500 on a joint return) of the qualified common stock dividend distributed to you this year as a result of this election. This exclusion is noted on Part II, line 8 of Schedule B.

Example Joanne is an owner of stock in a qualified public utility which has a dividend reinvestment plan. The utility paid a quarterly dividend and Joanne elected to receive common stock instead of cash. Although the option to receive money instead of stock would ordinarily make this dividend taxable, she can elect to exclude from her gross income $750 ($1500 on a joint return) of the stock dividend she received.

REPORTING DIVIDEND INCOME

If you received $400 or less in dividends (including capital gain and non-taxable distributions), include the amount of your ordinary dividends only on line 9a of Form 1040. At line 9b,

you may subtract up to $100 ($200 if you are filing a joint return) of your dividend income which qualifies for the exclusion. Note that the $200 exclusion on a joint return is available, regardless of which spouse earns the dividends. Generally, only dividends from U.S. corporations qualify, and your Form 1099 should specify which dividends qualify for the exclusion. Also note that dividends paid by your money market fund or by an S corporation (out of past S election earnings) usually will not qualify for the exclusion. The taxable portion of any such distribution from an S corporation is reported on Schedule E.

If you received over $400 in dividends, including capital gains and non-taxable distributions, you must complete Part II of Schedule B, "Interest and Dividend Income." On line 4 of Schedule B, you should list all of the dividends you received, including capital gains, non-taxable distributions and non-cash distributions, and identify the payer. If your securities are held in a brokerage account, the brokerage firm is the payer. The total amount of dividends is entered on line 5 of Schedule B.

On lines 6 to 8 of Schedule B, report capital gain, non-taxable and reinvested public utility dividends. These amounts will reduce the total dividends you report. If you have capital gain distributions and will be filing Schedule D, enter the amount of this type of distribution on line 6 of Schedule B and on line 15 of Schedule D. If you will not have to file Schedule D because you have no other capital gains to report, you should enter 40 percent of your capital gains distributions on Form 1040, line 14.

The next step is to add all of your non-taxable distributions together and enter the amount on line 9 of Schedule B. Note, however, that you must reduce your cost or other basis in the asset by the amount reported as a non-taxable distribution. Next, on Schedule B, line 10, do the necessary arithmetic and insert the total on line 9a of your Form 1040. And finally, complete Part III of Schedule B if you (1) had more than $400 of interest or dividends (2) had an account in a foreign country, or (3) were a grantor of, or a transferor to, a foreign trust.

STATE AND LOCAL INCOME TAX REFUNDS

State and local income tax refunds are taxable only if you took an itemized deduction for these taxes paid in an earlier year's return. Thus, if you merely used the standard deduction, do not report the refund as income. Remember also that you never have to report a federal income tax refund as income. Only the interest, if any, you earn on a federal refund is taxable.

The IRS provides a worksheet in your Form 1040 instruction booklet. This worksheet will assist you in determining what portion of your state income tax refund is taxable.

Worksheet (Keep for your records)

1. Enter the income tax refund from Forms 1099-G. . . . . **1.** _____
2. Enter the state and local income tax deduction from your 1983 Schedule A, line 11 . . . . . **2.** _____
3. Enter the amount from your 1983 Schedule A, line 30. . **3.** _____
4. Subtract line 3 from line 2 and enter the result. If the result is zero or less, enter zero (-0-). . . **4.** _____
5. Subtract line 4 from line 1 and enter the result here and on Form 1040, line 10. This is the taxable part of your refund **5.** _____

ALIMONY RECEIVED

As a general rule, if your former or estranged spouse deducts his or her payments to you from his or her gross income, you should include the payments in your gross income. In order for payments to be deductible from your ex-spouse's gross income, they must be made pursuant to (1) a written instrument incidental to your decree of divorce or separate maintenance, (2) a written separation agreement, or (3) a written decree of support.

Periodic Payment Requirement

Payments received through 1984 must qualify as periodic in order to be deductible. After 1984, different rules will apply. Periodic payments include (1) payments in a fixed amount which are payable for an indefinite period of time and (2) payments made in an indefinite amount for a fixed or indefinite period.

You should also note that certain types of payments are treated as being periodic even though they do not meet the preceding requirements. For example, a principal sum which is payable over more than ten years will qualify as a periodic payment. However, you are only required to include up to 10 percent of the principal sum in any one taxable year. Your spouse's deduction for alimony paid is similarly limited.

If you are to receive a fixed amount which will be payable in installments over less than a ten-year period, this is not a periodic payment, unless the payments are subject to change or discontinuance upon your death, remarriage, or change in the economic status of either spouse.

Example Sheryl's written separation agreement requires her to make monthly payments of $100 to her estranged husband until his death or remarriage. Since the payments are for a fixed amount and for an indefinite period of time, they are deductible by Sheryl and includible in her spouse's gross income.

Example Frank is required by a dissolution decree to pay his ex-spouse $15,000 over a five-year period. Since the amount is fixed and is payable over less than a ten year period, Frank cannot deduct the payments and his ex-spouse need not report the payments as income.

Example Ed and Judy's dissolution decree provided that Ed would pay the principal sum of $125,000 over an eleven year period at the rate of $15,000 per year for the first three years and $10,000 per year for the remaining eight years. Even though the payment is for a fixed amount, and over a fixed period, it will qualify as a periodic payment because it will be paid over a period in excess of ten years. Judy must therefore include in income up to 10 percent of the principal amount each year. For the first three years, Judy will include $12,500 in her income and for the remaining eight years she will have to include each $10,000 annual payment as income.

Child Support And Alimony Distinguished

Payments for the support of minor children are nontaxable to you and are not deductible by your spouse. As was explained earlier, however, child support payments do count as support provided by your ex-spouse when you are figuring out who is entitled to the dependency exemptions for the children. Where your payments specifically consist of both child support and alimony, and your spouse pays less than the amount owed for the period, you can presume that the child support is paid in full before any alimony. Any balance paid is then allocated to the alimony portion of the obligation and is includible in your income, if it is deductible by your ex-spouse.

B USINESS INCOME OR LOSS

If you operate a business as a sole proprietorship in addition to your regular teaching job, you may have self-employment income to report on Schedule C. Your "business" may be any one of a number of activities, including consulting, editing, tutoring and, of course, other business activities even less directly related to the educational profession.

If your outside business activity produces a loss, the deductibility of the loss depends on whether the activity was actually a business or whether it was a hobby. The test is whether you intend to make a profit. If you are an overly optimistic type and believe in your ability to make a profit, while others express doubt, don't despair, you may still be able to convince the IRS of your profit-making intent. Showing a profit for two out of five years will give rise to a presumption that you had a profit-seeking motive. This will put the ball in their court. And, even if your activity is determined to be a hobby, certain otherwise deductible expenses, e.g., interest and certain taxes, will still be deductible. [See Part IV, "Losing Business Ventures," for more information.]

COMPLETING SCHEDULE C

Schedule C is used to report business income rather than investment income. Although you may not always be able to determine whether an activity is a "trade or business" or an "investment activity," the answer is important. You can deduct business expenses, regardless of whether you have sufficient other deductions to itemize. Investment expenses, like other non-business expenses, on the other hand, are deductible on Schedule A only if you exceed the zero bracket amount.

side business will be determined to a certain extent by your accounting method. If you are on the cash basis, include all of the income you have actually received. If you are on the accrual method include all of the income you have earned. And if you are selling items on an installment basis, you should report only the portion of the profit received within your tax year.

Part III	Cost of Goods Sold and/or Operations (See Schedule C Instructions for Part III)		
1 Inventory at beginning of year (if different from last year's closing inventory, attach explanation)	1		
2 Purchases less cost of items withdrawn for personal use	2		
3 Cost of labor (do not include salary paid to yourself)	3		
4 Materials and supplies	4		
5 Other costs	5		
6 Add lines 1 through 5	6		
7 Less: Inventory at end of year	7		
8 **Cost of goods sold and/or operations.** Subtract line 7 from line 6. Enter here and in Part I, line 2, above. . .	8		

For Paperwork Reduction Act Notice, see Form 1040 Instructions.   Schedule C (Form 1040) 1984

Although you will find many of the key areas discussed on the following pages, you should be sure to consult the discussion of Schedule C in the Form 1040 instructions which are sent to you by the IRS.

The IRS requires you to file a separate Schedule C for each business that you conduct. However, if your single business is engaged in a variety of activities, only one schedule is necessary.

Inventory Valuation And Accounting Methods

Inventories can be valued at cost, lower of cost or market, or any other method approved by the IRS. The most common method is cost. Cost is the actual price that you paid to purchase the inventory. Market is the current cost if you were to replace your inventory. If you had no inventory at the end of the year, write "none" in this space.

A cash basis accounting method is one in which income is reported when actually or constructively received. Income is constructively received when you have the right to the funds without restriction. If you do not keep books of account, you must use the cash method. Expenses are generally deductible in the year paid.

An accrual method taxpayer reports income when the right to receive such income arises. Expenses are deductible when you become liable to pay them, regardless of whether you actually pay them. Generally, a taxpayer maintaining an inventory will be required to use the accrual method of accounting.

Calculating Your Business Income

The amount of income which you derive from your out-

The costs of goods sold on Schedule C is calculated through the determination of six major operating costs components. The first is the inventory at the beginning of the year. You should make sure that this is the same figure used on your 1983 tax return for the value of your inventory at the close of 1983.

The next group consists of purchases less cost of items withdrawn for personal use. This figure will include the items you paid for and, if you are an accrual basis taxpayer, those items for which you are obligated to pay. Subtract the cost of any items withdrawn from your merchandise for you and your family's personal use. The third group is comprised of labor costs incurred by the business. Enter labor costs included in the production of merchandise. However, you should not include other labor costs which will be deductible under Schedule C, Part II. And any "wages" you paid to yourself must also be excluded.

Materials and supplies comprise the fourth group. The figure entered here refers to materials and supplies necessary to produce or manufacture the merchandise. Materials and supplies used in running the trade or business are deductible under Part II. The fifth group consists of "other costs." These costs are generally applicable only if you are in the manufacturing business and would include miscellaneous items such as equipment depreciation and other direct overhead expenses. You must provide a list of these costs. Year-end inventory comprises the final cost category. These items will be valued in a manner to be selected by you and which you specified in item D of the introductory portion of Schedule C. You should include goods you are holding and raw materials.

The gross profit of your business is the difference between your gross receipts and the cost of goods sold. You must add to this any other income you had. Examples of other income would include sales of scrap, recovery of bad debts previously deducted, and interest on bank accounts.

Deduction Of Business Expenses

In order for you to take a deduction for any particular expense, you must show that it was "ordinary and necessary." This determination is a factual question and therefore requires some degree of judgment on your part. An expense is considered ordinary if it is a common and accepted practice in the particular trade or business. Such expenses need not be incurred on a regular basis. One-time expenses are deductible if otherwise applicable requirements are met. A necessary expense is one which is appropriate and helpful in the conduct of your business. There is no requirement that the expense be absolutely indispensable to qualify.

No deductions are allowable for personal living or family expenses. When assets or expenses relate to both business and personal purposes you will need evidence to support any business usage.

Now that you have passed the first hurdle and determined that an expense is deductible under the "ordinary and necessary" test, the next step is to determine whether the expense is a "current" one or one which must be "capitalized." A current expense is fully deductible in the year paid. An expense that is capitalized must be written off over a period of years. [See Part III for a complete discussion of Depreciation.]

As you can see, you will receive the largest current benefit by expensing items. However, any expense that creates an asset or improvement with a useful life of more than one year must be capitalized, unless you elect the Section 179 deduction. [See Part III for more information.] For example, expenditures for repairs and maintenance can be expensed but additions and improvements cannot. Sometimes this distinction is not clear and may require some judgment on your part.

As you can see from Schedule C, Part II, there are a large number of operating expenses that are deductible. There is no limit to the type of expenses that are deductible if they meet the ordinary and necessary test. If an expense is incurred partially for business and partially for personal purposes, it must be allocated between the two. [See Part III for details on "listed" property depreciation.]

The following is a listing of some of the important operating deductions that can benefit you.

Automobile Expenses

All of your expenses for the use of your car or truck in your business are deductible (based on the percentage used in the business), including depreciation, oil, gas, repairs, licenses and insurance. [See "listed" property limitations in Part III.]

Business Casualty Losses

If you suffer a "sudden or unexpected" loss from a fire, flood, hurricane, earthquake, vandalism, theft, embezzlement or other occurrence, you may be able to take a deduction for the amount of your loss, minus insurance payments or any salvage value. If your loss is significant, consult a tax adviser about the tax consequences and your ability to reinvest any insurance proceeds tax free.

Entertainment Expenses

Subject to the substantiation rules, any reasonable expense that is "associated" with your business can be deductible. This is true even without a showing that it produced income or provided a specific business benefit. A partial list of entertainment expenses includes business meals, tickets to plays or sporting events, dues paid to civic, social or professional organizations, and country club expenses.

Business Gifts

Up to an amount of $25 per person can be deducted, and employees can receive up to $400 each as "awards."

Home Office Expense

A pro rata share of the expenses of maintaining your residence can be deducted if you qualify.

Retirement Plan

A self-employed person can set up a Keogh plan or an Individual Retirement Account to reduce or eliminate any income from his or her business that would otherwise be taxable.

Travel Expenses

Expenses incurred "while you are away from home" on business are fully deductible. This includes meals, lodging, transportation and laundry.

Wages

You can pay reasonable salaries to family members who may be in lower tax brackets than yourself. Payments to your wife or your children can also reduce your self-employment taxes if you are below the base amount, since payments to them are not subject to social security.

1984 Tax Law Change

The 1984 Tax Reform Act imposes new record keeping requirements. Travel and entertainment expenses must be substantiated by "adequate contemporaneous records." Under the old law, you could support your deductions by offering corroborating evidence. From now on, a complete diary that is kept on a current basis will help you lock up those deductions. You should also retain all business related receipts.

Self-Employment Taxes

It is important to remember to file Schedule SE, Computation of Social Security Self-Employment Tax, with your return if any self-employment tax is due. You will not have to file Schedule SE if your net earnings from self-employment were less than $400 or you earned more than $37,800 from your teaching job or other employment from which social security taxes were withheld. No additional social security taxes are withheld on earnings which exceed $37,800.

CAPITAL GAINS AND LOSSES

You must file Schedule D when you have a capital gain or loss to report. Schedule D contains a summary of your sales or exchanges of capital assets during 1984. The net gain or loss obtained from Schedule D is entered on line 13 of Form 1040.

Generally, a capital asset is any property of value except (1) inventory, (2) accounts or notes receivable, (3) depreciable business property or business real property, or (4) copyright, literary, musical or artistic composition in the hands of the creator or acquired from him or her under special circumstances. A capital asset includes property you own and use for personal purposes. If you sold property used in your trade or business, you should include information relating to those transactions on Form 4797, rather than on Schedule D, and enter the amount on line 15 of Form 1040, Supplemental Gains or Losses.

A short term capital gain is taxed at the ordinary rate just like your salary or business income. A gain recognized upon the sale of a capital asset held for longer than one year (i.e., a long term capital gain), on the other hand, qualifies for an important tax break. You can deduct 60 percent of your gain from gross income. Only the remaining 40 percent is subject to taxation. You should also note that the Tax Reform Act of 1984 reduced the holding period for long term capital gains. If you acquired a capital asset after June 22, 1984, it will qualify for long term capital gains treatment after only six months. However, if your capital gain is large enough and your other income relatively small, there is a special Alternative Minimum Tax that may increase your tax liability. [See Part III.]

Combined Capital Gains And Losses

If you have both capital gains and losses this year, Schedule D requires you to obtain separate figures for your long-term and your short-term transactions. Thus, your first step is to separate your long-term transactions from your short-term transactions.

If you have more short-term gains than losses, you will have a net short-term gain. And if your short-term losses exceed your gains you will have a net short-term loss. You should make this same determination with respect to your long-term transactions. The tax treatment of your short and long-term transactions will usually correspond with one of the four situations which follow.

Long and Short-Term Gains

If you have a net long-term capital gain and a net short-term capital gain, each is treated separately. The full 100 percent of your net short-term gain is taxable at the ordinary rate, but 60 percent of your long-term gain is not subject to taxation. Only the remaining 40 percent is taxable.

Long and Short-Term Losses

Your net long-term loss and your net short-term loss are also treated separately. Both losses can be used to offset up to $3,000 of your 1984 ordinary income. Your short-term capital loss must be used first. These losses will reduce your income on a dollar for dollar basis up to $3,000. If this $3,000 limit is not consumed by your short-term losses, you can then use your long-term loss to offset income on a 2 for 1 basis, i.e., every dollar of a net long-term loss will offset 50 cents of ordinary income.

If you have a capital loss which exceeds $3,000, you should not ignore it. You can carry it forward until it is used up. Also, Part V of your 1983 federal tax return will contain the amount of capital loss which can be carried forward from last year and used in 1984 to offset your capital gains and, if any is left over, up to $3,000 of ordinary income.

Net Short-Term Loss and Long-Term Gain

Add your short-term loss and your long-term gain together. If your gain exceeds your loss, you may exclude 60 percent of your gain from taxation. The remaining 40 percent is taxable. If your loss is greater than your gain, your short-term loss can be used to offset up to $3,000 of your ordinary income on a dollar for dollar basis. As explained above, any excess loss can be carried forward until used up.

Net Short-Term Gain and Long-Term Loss

Just as you did in the previous situation, you combine these two amounts and obtain a single net gain or loss figure. If your long-term loss is greater than your short-term gain, your loss can offset up to $3,000 of ordinary income on a 2 for 1 basis, i.e., every dollar of a net long term loss can offset 50 cents of income. Any unused loss is then carried forward. To the extent that your short-term gain exceeds your long-term loss, this gain is fully includible in your income.

Example Jerry, a business professor, dabbles in the stock market. During 1984 he sold securities in his portfolio with the following results:

Long term capital loss.....($1,000)	Short term capital loss......($2,000)
Long term capital gain.......2,500	Short term capital gain........5,000
Net long term capital gain......$1,500	Net short term capital gain.......$3,000

Jerry should net his short-term gains and losses and then his long-term gains and losses. By doing so, he will arrive at a net long-term capital gain of $1,500 and a net short-term capital gain of $3,000. All of Jerry's short-term gain is taxable, while his $1,500 long-term gain is entitled to a deduction of 60 percent. This leaves Jerry a total taxable gain of $3,600 [$3,000 short-term gain, plus $600 long-term gain ($1,500 x 40 percent)].

Example Chris, also a dabbler in the stock market, had $28,000 of ordinary income in 1984. He also had a net short-term capital loss of $1,000 and a net long-term capital loss of $6,000.

Chris can use his net short-term loss to offset $1,000 or ordinary income and use $4,000 of his long-term capital loss to offset $2,000 of ordinary income. Chris can carry the remaining $2,000 of unused long-term capital loss over to his 1985 return. [I.R.C. §1202.]

SALE OF INHERITED PROPERTY

If you inherited property from a decedent, your basis in the property is the fair market value of the property on the decedent's date of death, or six months after death if the executor of the estate elected to value the property on the alternate valuation date. The executor of the decedent's estate will be able to tell you what your new basis in the property is. The benefit to you is that you receive a tax-free step-up in basis. If you decide to sell the property after you inherit it, you pay a tax only on the increase in value since the decedent's death. All of the pre-death gain escapes tax forever. As a result, if you sell the property shortly after the decedent's death for its date of death value, no gain is recognized.

Example Ken inherits an apartment house from his aunt. His aunt purchased the property in 1954 and her basis in the property was $10,000 on the date of her death. The fair market value of the realty upon her death was $200,000.

Ken's new basis in the property is $200,000. He has received a ''stepped-up'' basis in the property. Thus, if Ken immediately sells the property for $200,000, he will not recognize any gain for tax purposes.

INSTALLMENT SALES

If you sell property at a gain and the buyer will be paying at least a portion of the price next year, you are automatically allowed to report this gain over the period of time that the buyer will be making payments. For sales after June 6, 1984, however, recent legislation has created an exception for depreciation recapture, all of which must be recognized in the year of the sale. This applies even if little or no cash is received in the transaction. You should exercise extreme care here because the tax bite can be significant. If you want to report all of your gain this year, you must make an affirmative election to do so by checking the box in Part IV of Schedule D.

The IRS requires most sales involving deferred payments to carry interest. If related parties are involved, you must charge at least 11 percent simple interest or the IRS will ''impute'' interest of 12 percent compounded semi-annually. Where the parties are not related, the interest must be at least 9 percent simple interest or the IRS will impute 10 percent interest compounded semi-annually. Under this rule, the IRS will treat an additional amount of the contract payments as interest and a lesser amount as principal payments. As a result, the seller will have additional interest income and the buyer will have an additional interest deduction.

TAX LOSS FOR WORTHLESS SECURITIES

You may treat any security which became worthless during the year as a short or long-term capital loss. This security must be totally worthless. You cannot deduct a partially worthless security.

CAPITAL GAINS DISTRIBUTIONS

Capital gain distributions are normally paid by mutual funds, regulated investment companies, and real estate investment trusts. The payments take the form of cash or additional shares. If you receive a taxable capital gains distribution, and did not have to file Schedule D because you had no other capital gains, enter 40 percent of your taxable capital gains distribution on line 14, Form 1040.

SUPPLEMENTAL GAINS OR LOSSES

If you sold or exchanged assets used in a trade or business, you must fill out Form 4797, Supplemental Schedule of Gains and Losses, and report the amount obtained on this line. Depreciable property used in your trade or business and business real property are not capital assets but qualify for similar favorable tax treatment.

As with capital assets, holding periods may be either short or long-term. If the assets are sold and the gain is long-term, this gain may also be eligible for the 60 percent deduction from gross income available for capital gains. If you have a loss, the entire amount is deductible as an ordinary loss this year. This is, of course, even more favorable than the treatment of short and long term capital losses.

If you sold depreciable business property, you may have to report all or part of the gain as ordinary income, if the property is subject to the recapture provisions. The recapture provisions can come into play when property is sold for more than its adjusted basis, which is generally its cost less any depreciation taken. [Refer to Part III for a more detailed discussion of the recapture provisions.]

PENSIONS, IRA DISTRIBUTIONS AND ANNUITIES

Fully taxable IRA distributions, annuities, and pension benefits are reported on line 16 of Form 1040. Generally, if you did not pay taxes on the funds when they were originally deposited in your retirement plan, you are taxed on the funds when you receive distributions from the plan. Your employer will be able to provide you with complete information about the taxability of your retirement benefits.

If you contributed to your pension or retirement plan and your contributions have already been taxed, a portion of the distribution that you receive will be tax-free. The amounts that you contributed constitute your cost and will not be taxed again. And if you will be able to recover the entire cost of your retirement benefit within three years of the first payment, you can defer paying any taxes until your cost is completely recovered. After the cost is recovered, the benefit will be fully taxable. If you will not be able to recover your cost within that three-year period, you will begin to pay taxes, on the proportion attributable to contributions that have not yet been taxed, as soon as you start receiving the benefits. These partially taxable distributions should be reported on line 17 of Form 1040. Use the worksheet provided in the instruction booklet accompanying your 1040 form to determine your taxable amount from the distribution.

Example Philip retired in June, 1984 with a monthly pension of $500. Both he and his employer contributed to the plan. The employer's contributions have not been taxed. Philip's contribution of $15,000 has already been taxed and is the cost of the pension to him.

During the first three years he receives pension payments, Philip will recover his cost (36 months x $500 = $18,000). Therefore, during those years he should report the pension he receives on line 16 of his Form 1040, but he will not be receiving any taxable payments until January, 1987, at which time his $15,000 cost will have been fully recovered.

Lump Sum Distributions And Rollovers

The following two methods will enable you to reduce the amount of income immediately recognizable as a result of a lump sum distribution of benefits from your retirement plan. Under the special ten-year averaging method, you are taxed on receipt of a lump sum distribution from a qualified plan as though it were being paid in equal parts over a ten-year period. The amount received is taxed independently of any other income. In order to qualify for this favorable tax treatment, certain rules must be followed and you must file Form 4972 with your return. You should also note that this special ten-year averaging method is not available for distributions from Individual Retirement Accounts.

You may avoid any current tax on a lump sum distribution from a qualified plan by electing to roll over all or a part of the distribution into an Individual Retirement Account (IRA). These funds can remain in your IRA until retirement, at which time your income will probably be lower. Note, however, that you must begin to receive

the benefits before you reach age 70½. And the rollover must be completed within 60 days after the lump sum distribution is received by you. Tax-free rollovers to an IRA of distributions from a qualified pension plan are reported on line 17a. If the entire amount is being rolled over, however, these distributions are not included on line 17b.

If you are the beneficiary of a decedent and are receiving death benefits from that person's employer, you may exclude up to $5,000. This exclusion applies only to amounts paid by reason of the death of the employee. It does not apply if the employee had a nonforfeitable right to receive this amount during his or her lifetime.

Example Rhonda received a lump sum distribution from her school district's qualified pension plan when she retired at the age of 45 in 1984. She had worked for the district since 1970 and had been enrolled in the pension plan for the duration of her employment. She has several options to choose from in trying to determine what will save her the most money in taxes.

If she does not currently need the funds, Rhonda can elect to roll over all or a part of the money into an Individual Retirement Account. This election must be made within 60 days after the lump sum distribution is received. The funds can remain in the account until she reaches age 70½, allowing her to avoid any current tax on the distribution. If she elects to roll over only part of the funds, the amount she retains is completely taxable within the year of receipt. Note, however, that Rhonda cannot elect ten-year averaging or capital gains treatment on the amount rolled over into an IRA.

Since Rhonda's lump sum distribution is composed of both long term capital gain, attributable to her pre-1974 years of service and ordinary income, she can also elect the special ten-year averaging for the ordinary income portion of the distribution. The capital gain part of the distribution qualifies for the 60 percent capital gain deduction and is included on Schedule D.

The special ten-year averaging method election is made by filing Form 4972. Rhonda will be able to treat her distributions as having been received over a ten-year period for income tax purposes. She may also elect ten-year averaging for the capital gain portion of her distribution if she determines that her overall tax liability will be reduced by making the election.

RENTS, ROYALTIES, PARTNERSHIPS, ESTATES AND TRUSTS

If you own rental property, receive royalty income, or have income/loss from a partnership, estate or trust, you must provide the information requested on Schedule E, Supplemental Income Schedule, and then enter your totals on Form 1040, line 18. On Part I of Schedule E, you should record the gross amount of your rental receipts. Gross rental receipts can then be reduced by a variety of expenses which appear as items 4 through 15 of Schedule E.

You may deduct travel expenses incurred during a journey to inspect your rental property, or legal expenses incurred trying to evict an undesirable tenant. You may also deduct payments to family members for managing or maintaining the property and thereby shift income to lower bracket taxpayers. Also deductible are amounts expended for repairs necessary to keep the property in satisfactory operating condition.

Expenditures which improve your property's value or prolong its life are depreciated over a period of time. Remember that depreciation is a paper expenditure. Your actual cash receipts are not reduced by the amount of depreciation taken, but depreciation deductions will reduce the amount of your income subject to taxation. [Refer to Part III for a more complete discussion of expensing and depreciation.]

If you occupy one of your rental properties, only those expenses applicable to the rental portion are deductible. You may not deduct any of the expenses attributable to your occupancy. And if you own a vacation home which you occupy for part of the year and rent out for the remainder of the year, you should keep the following in mind. If you or a member of your family uses this vacation property for more than the greater of 14 days or 10 percent of the number of days the property was rented, you cannot deduct expenses which exceed your gross rental income. However, you can still deduct interest, taxes and casualty losses if you itemize your deductions.

If you reside in property and rent it out for less than 15 days during the year, you need not report any of the rental income. In addition, you can still deduct your interest, taxes and casualty losses on Schedule A.

Partnerships, estates, trusts and S corporations all serve as conduits for passing through income or losses to you. You will receive a K-1 statement from the general partner, executor or S corporation involved. This K-1 will inform you of your share of the income/loss. You should then include this information Part II of your Schedule E.

UNEMPLOYMENT COMPENSATION

Unemployment compensation may be taxable income if it exceeds a certain base amount. A portion of your unemployment compensation benefits will be taxable, if your adjusted gross income, government unemployment compensation, plus the two-earner married couple deduction exceeds (1) $18,000 for married persons filing jointly,(2) zero if you are married filing separately, or (3) $12,000 for all other taxpayers.

The instructions for Form 1040, line 20, provide a worksheet which allows you to determine the exact amount includible. In general, if your income exceeds the base amount, one-half of the excess is taxable up to the full amount of unemployment compensation received.

SOCIAL SECURITY BENEFITS

Prior to 1984, your social security benefits were not taxable. Beginning in 1984, however, your benefits are partially taxable if your modified adjusted gross income exceeds a specified base amount. The base amount for married persons filing jointly is $32,000, for a married person who lived with his/her spouse during part of 1984 and who elects not to file a joint return, the base amount is zero, and for anyone else, it is $25,000.

Your modified adjusted gross income is your adjusted gross income as entered on line 32, exclusive of social security benefits, the two-earner married couple deduction amount, any excluded foreign earned income, and tax-exempt income.

If your modified adjusted gross income exceeds the base amount limits, you are taxed on the lesser of 50 percent of the benefits you receive, or 50 percent of the amount by which your modified adjusted gross income, plus one-half of your 1984 social security benefits, exceeds your base amount.

Example John and Carla have an adjusted gross income of $25,000 and receive social security benefits of $5,000. Their benefits are not taxable because their modified adjusted gross income does not exceed $32,000.

Example Daniel and Jeanette have an adjusted gross income of $33,000 and social security benefits of $7,000. Their benefits are partially taxable. They should include $2,250 in their 1984 income. This figure is derived from the following calculation:

Modified Adjusted Gross Income	$33,000
plus	
1/2 of the benefits	3,500
	$36,500
Less: the base amount	(32,000)
	$ 4,500
	x 50%
	$ 2,250

ADDITIONAL SOURCES OF INCOME

All income is taxable unless specifically exempted by the Internal Revenue Code. For a sampling of what is and is not taxable, you should review the lists included in this section on page 9. You should add any taxable income not includible elsewhere on line 21 on your 1040 form. The IRS requires that you identify the nature and source of the income.

ADJUSTMENTS TO INCOME

				24			
Adjustments to Income	24	Moving expense *(attach Form 3903 or 3903F)*		24			
	25	Employee business expenses *(attach Form 2106)*		25			
	26a	IRA deduction, from the worksheet on page 12		26a			
(See Instructions on page 11.)	**b**	Enter here IRA payments you made in 1985 that are included in line 26a above ▶					
	27	Payments to a Keogh *(H.R. 10)* retirement plan		27			
	28	Penalty on early withdrawal of savings		28			
	29	Alimony paid		29			
	30	Deduction for a married couple when both work *(attach Schedule W)*		30			
	31	Add lines 24 through 30. These are your **total adjustments** . . . . ▶		31			
Adjusted Gross Income	32	Subtract line 31 from line 23. *This is your* **adjusted gross income.** *If this line is less than $10,000, see "Earned Income Credit" (line 59) on page 16 of Instructions. If you want IRS to figure your tax, see page 12 of Instructions.* . . . . ▶		32			

You can reduce the amount of your gross income by deducting available adjustments, including certain moving expenses, employee business expenses, IRA or Keogh payments, penalties on early savings withdrawals, alimony payments, and the deduction for married couples when both work.

MOVING EXPENSES

If you are moving to a new home due to a job change, you can deduct a portion of your moving expenses if certain requirements are met. First of all, the distance between your new job and your former residence must exceed the distance between your old job and your former residence by 35 miles. Secondly, you must remain employed in your new job for at least 39 weeks of the year following your move. This requirement is waived if (1) you die or become disabled, (2) you are involuntarily separated from your work through no misconduct on your part, or (3) you are transferred to another location by your employer.

The 39 weeks of employment need not be consecutive, nor do they have to be for the same employer. And if you expect to comply with the time requirement by the end of 1985, you need not wait until the end of the 39-week period to claim the deduction.

If you made the move in 1984, claim the expense adjustment on Form 3903, Moving Expense Adjustment, and attach it to your 1984 return. If you fail to fulfill the requirement, you can file an amended return, Form 1040X for 1984.

Expenses Deductible

The moving expenses which qualify for deduction include the actual costs of moving and insuring your furnishings and effects and the actual costs of transporting your family to the new residence. This includes a one way trip for each family member. You are not required to travel together. And there is also no dollar limitation. Actual costs include transportation, food, lodging and gasoline. You can use a standard mileage rate of 9 cents per mile to figure the expense of traveling by car in lieu of keeping track of actual operating expenses. Parking fees and tolls can be deducted in addition to the standard mileage rate.

You can also deduct the costs of house-hunting trips after you get the new job. The costs of meals and lodging in temporary quarters at the new location for a period of 30 days are deductible. And the costs of selling your former home and buying your new home or the costs of settling your old lease and obtaining a new lease are also deductible. Sales costs include sales commissions, advertising, title fees, attorney's fees and points. You should note, however, that if you used any of these costs to reduce your gain on selling your old residence, you cannot deduct them again.

While there is no limit on the amount you can deduct for moving your furnishings or transporting your family, the amounts that you can deduct for house-hunting trips, temporary quarters and sales costs are limited. You can deduct up to $3,000 ($1,500 if married filing separately) or $6,000 ($3,000 if filing separately) for an overseas move. And your total deduction for temporary quarters and house hunting trips cannot exceed $1,500.

If your new employer reimburses you for any expenses, any excess reimbursement over your costs is income, and must be reported on line 7 of Form 1040. The costs of moving your home office, figured as a pro rata share of your total moving costs, are deductible even if you do not meet the requirements for deducting your moving expenses.

Example Joan accepts a teaching position in Los Angeles and incurs the following expenses in her move from San Francisco:

Moving and Insurance Costs	$3,000
Airfare to Los Angeles	90
House-Hunting Trip	1,000
Temporary Quarters	500
Costs of Selling her Home	500
	$5090

All of these expenses are deductible. There is no limit on the cost of moving her household goods and transporting herself. Her house-hunting and temporary quarters costs did not exceed $1,500, and those expenses plus her selling expenses were under $3,000.

Example Bob is a high school teacher in Atlanta. He and his wife moved to Boston where Bob obtained employment in a similar capacity. Bob was laid off when a number of teaching positions were eliminated by the city school system, and he was unable to find a new job for over a year following the move. Bob and his wife can still deduct their moving expenses. Even though the 39-week employment requirement was not fulfilled, Bob was involuntarily separated from his job through no fault of his own.

EMPLOYEE BUSINESS EXPENSES

As a general rule, you can deduct travel and transportation expenses connected with your employment in the educational field as adjustments which reduce your taxable income. Job-related travel and transportation expenses are deductible even if you do not itemize your deductions on Schedule A. Expenses incurred for travel in connection with your self-employment activity are deductible on Schedule C, Profit or Loss From Business or Profession. Any other business expenses that you incur in connection with your teaching job are probably deductible as miscellaneous itemized deductions on Schedule A.

In addition to transportation expenses (e.g., airline tickets or car rental fees), travel expenses include living costs such as meals, lodging, baggage charges, cleaning and laundry expenses, business telephone calls and tips. Living costs, however, are deductible only if you are away from home overnight. If you are not away from home overnight, only your transportation expenses are deductible. For purposes of this test, "home" is the general area of your principal place of employment and is sometimes referred to as your tax home.

TRAVEL EXPENSES COMMONLY INCURRED BY EDUCATORS

Travel and transportation expenses relating to your duties as an educator and primarily for the purpose of maintaining or improving your skills are deductible. And the act of traveling itself can be a deductible expense if your trip is properly planned. Be prepared to show a direct relationship between your travel and skills required in your teaching position.

If you travel from one job location to another within the same day, you can deduct your transportation expenses incurred for travel between your two jobs. You may also deduct travel expenses to your temporary job away from home, if you can establish that the job will end within a reasonably short time, generally one year. All travel and living costs while attending conventions or seminars requiring you to remain away from home overnight and which are directly connected with your profession are deductible. You may also deduct travel expenses if your trip had as its primary focus seeking new employment in your current profession, even if you are not successful.

Unless you are able to establish a bona fide business purpose for their presence, travel expenses of family members accompanying you on business travel will not be deductible. However, the mere fact that family members accompany you does not require you to allocate expenses among all family members. You can deduct, in full, the amount it would have cost you to travel alone. Only the incremental amount attributable to the companionship of a family member is non-deductible.

Combined Business And Pleasure Trips

If you travel within the United States primarily for business reasons, travel expenses, other than those specifically connected with personal activities, are deductible. In determining whether business or pleasure was the primary purpose of the trip, courts tend to look at the length of time spent on each.

If you travel outside the United States for a week or less, or if you traveled for longer than one week, and spent less than 25 percent of the time on non-business activities, you may deduct all of your transportation costs and your travel expenses attributable to business activities. If your trip lasted more than one week and you spent more than 25 percent on personal activities, you may deduct only in proportion to the time spent on business.

In any case, it is important to retain receipts and maintain, on a current basis, a diary of travel related expenses that identifies the date, type of expense, amount and business purpose for the expense. The Tax Reform Act of 1984 imposes more stringent record keeping rules with respect to travel expenses. Under the old rules, you were required to keep adequate records to substantiate your travel deductions. If you did not have adequate records, you could offer other corroborating evidence. Beginning in 1985, the new law requires that your travel expense deductions be supported by "adequate contemporaneous records." [See "Records" discussion in Part I.]

The IRS provides you with the option of using a per diem deduction for the cost of meals consumed on business trips. You may use the per diem rate in lieu of keeping track of your actual expenses. However, you still have to keep track of time, place and business purpose of the travel. For travel during 1984, the per diem meal allowance for a stay of less than 30 days in one general locality is $14 per day. It is $9 per day for a stay requiring 30 days or more in one locality. It is clearly to your advantage to keep records of actual expenses because the per diem allowances are low.

You should report your travel and transportation expenses on Form 2106, Employee Business Expenses. Any reimbursements that you receive must also be reported. If your reimbursements exceed expenses, you report the amount of the excess on line 7 of Form 1040 as compensation. You do not have to file the Form 2106 if you account to your employer for your expenses by submitting receipts and a diary which is kept current. If you elect to rely on the account you furnish to your employer and do not file Form 2106, you cannot take any deduction if your expenses exceed your reimbursements. Therefore, if you think your expenses will exceed your reimbursement, you should keep adequate and contemporaneous records so that you can claim these expenses as deductions.

IRA DEDUCTIONS AND PAYMENTS TO KEOGH PLANS

Your Form 1040 instruction booklet provides a worksheet to assist you in determining how much of a deduction to claim on line 26a. On line 26b, enter the amount of the deduction you are claiming that is attributable to contributions made in 1985 which are to be treated as reducing your 1984 taxable income. Your IRA and Keogh plan contributions reduce the amount of your income subject to current taxation and, at the same time, allow you to invest for your retirement years. As a result of a 1984 tax law amendment, all IRA contributions must be made by April 15, 1985, regardless of whether or not you were granted an extension to file your 1984 Return.

PENALTIES ON EARLY WITHDRAWAL OF SAVINGS

If you withdrew money from a bank or savings and loan account before the maturity date and in so doing incurred a penalty, you can deduct this penalty from your gross income. You may deduct this penalty even if you do not elect to itemize your deductions.

ALIMONY PAID

If your alimony and separate maintenance payments were included in your spouse's gross income, be sure to deduct those payments here. They will reduce your taxable income even if you do not itemize.

DEDUCTION FOR A MARRIED COUPLE WHEN BOTH WORK

This benefit was enacted in 1981 to eliminate some of the inequities under prior tax law that occurred when educators and other taxpayers with relatively equal incomes married. Because of the progressive nature of our tax rate structure, the second earner's income is taxed at a higher marginal rate than if both had remained single. If both you and your spouse work, you will receive some tax relief by claiming the two earner deduction.

To claim this deduction, you must file a joint return, have qualified earned income (i.e., income earned from services with certain adjustments) and not exclude income from foreign sources or claim the foreign housing deduction. "Earned income" is income you receive for services you provide. It includes self-employment income, but does not include interest, dividends, pensions, annuities, IRA distributions, unemployment compensation or non-taxable income. Schedule W is used to figure the amount of your deduction. Remember, this deduction is available even if you do not itemize.

TAX COMPUTATION — ITEMIZED DEDUCTIONS

Where allowable Schedule A deductions total more than the zero bracket amount for your filing status, you can reduce your taxes by itemizing deductions. The zero bracket amount is, in essence, a minimum standard deduction which is allowed to all taxpayers. If your Schedule A deductions total more than this zero bracket amount, it will always be to your advantage to itemize deductions on Schedule A, since more deductions result in a lower tax liability.

The applicable zero bracket amounts are $3,400 for married taxpayers filing a joint return and for qualified widows and widowers, $2,300 for single taxpayers and those who are heads of households, and $1,700 for married taxpayers filing separate returns. You should note that, in the case of married taxpayers filing separate returns, where one spouse itemizes, the other spouse must also itemize his/her deductions.

You may deduct all allowable medical and dental expenses that exceed 5 percent of your adjusted gross income (as shown on line 33, Form 1040). When deducting medical expenses, you should include amounts you paid on behalf of yourself, your spouse, all dependents listed on your return, and all other individuals (e.g., a child or parent) for whom you furnished over one-half of their support, but cannot claim as a dependent since they had over $1,000 in income or filed a joint return.

You should also note that on your 1984 return, you can deduct any credit card charges incurred during 1984 for medical purposes. These deductions are available even though you did not pay the credit card company until 1985.

To the extent you were not reimbursed, you can deduct costs incurred for or payments to prescription medicines and drugs, hospital or health insurance, dentist, physicians, nurses, eyeglasses, braces and transportation expenses (at 9 cents per mile or your actual gas costs) to

MEDICAL AND DENTAL EXPENSES

					1			
Medical and Dental Expenses **(Do not include expenses reimbursed or paid by others.)** (See Instructions on page 19)	1		Prescription medicines and drugs; and insulin	**1**			
	2	a	Doctors, dentists, nurses, hospitals, insurance premiums you paid for medical and dental care, etc.	**2a**			
		b	Transportation and lodging	**2b**			
		c	Other (list—include hearing aids, dentures, eyeglasses, etc.) ▶	**2c**			
	3		Add lines 1 through 2c, and write the total here	**3**			
	4		Multiply the amount on Form 1040, line 33, by 5% (.05) . . .	**4**			
	5		Subtract line 4 from line 3. If zero or less, write -0-. **Total** medical and dental . ▶	**5**			

obtain medical and dental services.

Cosmetic surgery (including hair transplants and hair removal through electrolysis), an abortion or vasectomy, and equipment installed in your home for medical reasons (e.g., air conditioning, an elevator or special ramps) are also deductible medical expenses. You should note that where installed medical equipment increases the value of your property, your deduction will be reduced by this increase.

1984 Tax Law Changes

For medical treatment away from home, you can deduct transportation costs, meals and lodging. And upon your arrival, you can deduct lodging expenses of up to $50 per night for each individual. Beginning with the 1984 tax year, the former 1 percent limitation no longer applies to deductions for drugs and medicines. And payments for over-the-counter medications will no longer be deductible.

Example Ed and Mary incurred $1,470 in medical expenses in 1984. Their adjusted gross income is $21,045. Ed and Mary can deduct all medical expenses that exceed 5 percent of their adjusted gross income.

$1,470	(total medical expenses)
–1,052	($21,045 x 5%)
$ 418	(deductible medical expenses)

Example Donna paid $1,560 of medical expenses on behalf of her mother. If Donna provided over one-half of her mother's support, she can take a medical deduction. [Grow v. Commissioner, 42 T.C.M. 1395 (1981).]

Example Joe used his bank credit card on November 15, 1984 to pay his $510 hospital bill. Joe paid the credit card company in January, 1985. Joe can take a medical deduction in 1984 for the amount he paid in 1985. The use of a credit card to pay medical expenses qualifies as a payment in the year the credit card charge is made, regardless of when the bank is paid. [Rev. Rul. 39, 1978-1 C.B. 73.]

Example To obtain medical care during 1984, Matthew drove his car 514 miles. He also spent $11 for tolls and $31 for parking. On another occasion, he took a taxi and spent $19. Matthew can deduct $107, computed as follows:

$ 46	(514 miles x $.09)
11	(tolls)
31	(parking)
19	(taxi)
$107	

Example Marjorie suffers from allergies during the summer months. Her physician recommended that she use air conditioning to help maintain her good health. She spent $380 for an air conditioner. Since the purchase of the air conditioner was for medical purposes, Marjorie can deduct its cost. [Blackburn v. Commissioner, 44 T.C.M. 1121 (1982).]

Example William placed his 69-year-old father, Homer, in a nursing home. Homer required constant medical attention. William paid all expenses. William can take a medical deduction for the cost of maintaining Homer at the nursing home, including expenses for meals and lodging, since the principal reason for Homer's presence at the home was to receive medical care. [Counts v. Commissioner, 42 T.C. 755 (1964).]

DEDUCTIBLE AND NONDEDUCTIBLE TAXES

Although there are some taxes that are not deductible, the following taxes may be claimed as itemized deductions:
- ☐ Real estate taxes on property which you own.
- ☐ State and local income taxes.
- ☐ State and local sales and use taxes.
- ☐ State disability fund contributions.
- ☐ Personal property taxes.
- ☐ Foreign income taxes.

The following taxes are nondeductible on Schedule A:
- ☐ Federal income, gift or estate taxes.
- ☐ Federal or state excise taxes on gasoline, telephones, tobacco, or alcoholic beverages.
- ☐ Federal social security taxes.
- ☐ Federal self-employment taxes.
- ☐ State or local gasoline taxes.

Real Estate Taxes

You can deduct payments for real estate taxes on pro-

TAXES

		6			
6	State and local income taxes	6			
7	Real estate taxes	7			
8 a	General sales tax (see sales tax tables in instruction booklet)	8a			
b	General sales tax on motor vehicles	8b			
9	Other taxes (list—include personal property taxes) ▶	9			
10	Add the amounts on lines 6 through 9. Write the total here. **Total** taxes . ▶	10			

perty you own that was not used for business on Schedule A. (If the property was used for business, you could deduct tax payments on your Schedule C or E.) While a special assessment tax for sidewalks or sewers is not deductible, you are entitled to deduct the taxes paid by you on any real estate you sold during the year, apportioned to the time period you owned the property.

Example Bill paid real estate taxes of $600 for the tax period January 1, 1984 to June 30, 1984. Bill then sold his home on May 31, 1984. Bill can deduct $500 since he owned the property for 5 out of the 6 months in the tax period (5/6 x $600 = $500).

State And Local Income Taxes

Deductible state and local income taxes include amounts withheld from your school paycheck, any amounts paid between January 1, 1984 and December 31, 1984 for state estimated taxes, any balance due amounts on your 1983 state income tax return, which you paid April 15, 1984, and any prepayment of 1985 state income taxes made by December 31, 1984.

Example On January 15, 1984, Ann made a $150 state estimated income tax payment for tax year 1983. On April 15, 1984, Ann paid a $77 balance due for her 1983 state income tax return. During 1984, Ann had $975 of state income taxes withheld from her teacher's paycheck. She also had $24 withheld for state disability.

Ann can deduct $1,226, computed as follows:

$ 150 (even though the payment was for year 1983, it was paid in 1984)
   77 (balance due)
  975 (state withholdings)
   24 (state disability)
$ 1,226

General Sales Taxes

The IRS provides state sales tax tables which show how much you can deduct for your income and family size. Remember, the use of these tables is optional. If you kept records that show you paid more state sales tax than the tables list, deduct this larger amount. In addition to the above amounts, you can deduct any sales tax you paid for a car, motorcycle, motorhome or truck. And you can deduct the sales tax paid for a boat, plane, home or

materials you purchased to build a new home, if the tax rate was the same as the general tax rate and it was stated separately on your receipt.

Example Frank decides to use the optional IRS State Sales Tax Tables. In determining the income amount upon which his deductions should be based, Frank should begin with his adjusted gross income (line 33, Form 1040), then he should add to it such non-taxable items as (1) deduction for a married couple when both work (line 30, Form 1040), (2) untaxed portion of long-term capital gains, (3) worker's compensation benefits, (4) non-taxable portion of social security, (5) dividends exclusion (line 9b, Form 1040), (6) non-taxable portion of unemployment compensation, and (7) tax-exempt municipal bond interest.

State Disability Fund Contributions

California, New York, New Jersey, Washington and Rhode Island require mandatory employee contributions. Payments made in compliance with such requirements are deductible.

Personal Property Taxes

Unless you use your car for business, you generally cannot deduct your auto license and registration fees. However, if part of your registration fee is based on the value of the automobile, you can deduct that part as a personal property tax. Check with your state department of motor vehicles.

Example Ralph, a California high school teacher, paid $190 to register his new car which he did not use for business. Ralph can deduct $167 as a personal property tax deduction. California charges a standard registration fee of $23. While this is not deductible, the excess amount — determined by the car's value — is deductible. You should check with your state department of motor vehicles.

Foreign Income Taxes

You have the option of taking a Schedule A tax deduction or a foreign tax credit. Frequently, the credit will be more advantageous to you.

Example Frank received a $300 dividend from a Canadian corporation and $30 in Canadian taxes were withheld. Frank can take a $30 Schedule A deduction or he can take a foreign tax credit. Frequently, the credit will

INTEREST EXPENSE

Interest You Paid

(See Instructions on page 20)

11 a Home mortgage interest you paid to financial institutions . .

	11a		

b Home mortgage interest you paid to individuals (show that person's name and address) ▶..............................

	11b		

12 Total credit card and charge account interest you paid . . . .

	12		

13 Other interest you paid (list) ▶..............................

....

....

....

	13		

14 Add the amounts on lines 11a through 13. Write the total here. **Total** interest . ▶

	14		

---

be more advantageous. To claim the foreign tax credit, attach Form 1116 to your return.

INTEREST EXPENSE

If you paid interest on a personal debt or obligation, you can deduct it on Schedule A. Any interest expense connected with your business, rental property or farm would be deductible on Schedules C, E and F, respectively.

Typical Interest Deductions
☐ Home mortgage interest.
☐ Credit card interest.
☐ Interest on a personal loan from a bank, credit union or another person.
☐ Revolving charge account interest.
☐ Points (sometimes called a loan origination fee) paid by a borrower. If you paid points on a mortgage for the purchase or improvement of your principal residence, you can deduct the total amount this year. A deduction for interest paid on a mortgage to purchase a rental home or vacation home, however, must be spread over the life of the mortgage.
☐ Installment buying interest/finance charges. If you purchased a car, furniture, TV, clothing or any other personal property under an installment plan, don't forget to deduct the finance charges.

☐ Interest on life insurance loans.
☐ Broker's margin account interest.

There are two main limitations on interest deductions. You cannot deduct on your 1984 return any interest payments you made which apply to 1985, i.e., you cannot deduct prepaid interest. And if you paid interest during the year on money borrowed to buy or hold investment property, the amount of interest you can deduct will be limited to your net investment income plus $10,000. If your interest expense is limited for this reason, you are entitled to an unlimited carryover with this amount being available for deduction in future years, subject to the annual limit. Form 4952 is used to compute your investment interest expense deduction.

CONTRIBUTIONS

You can generally deduct your charitable contributions to qualified organizations. Up to 50 percent of your adjusted gross income can be deducted. You should contact the IRS if you are unsure whether the proposed recipient of your contribution is a qualified organization. Regardless of when it was pledged, your deduction is allowed only in the year you pay it. However, if you made a contribution using your credit card during the year, it is deductible even if you did not pay the credit card company until January of 1985.

CONTRIBUTIONS

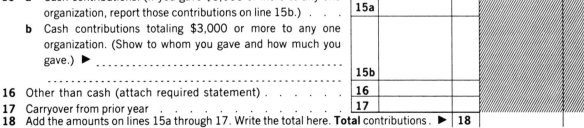

Contributions You Made

(See Instructions on page 20)

15 a Cash contributions. (If you gave $3,000 or more to any one organization, report those contributions on line 15b.) . . .

	15a		

b Cash contributions totaling $3,000 or more to any one organization. (Show to whom you gave and how much you gave.) ▶ ....

....

	15b		

16 Other than cash (attach required statement) . . . . . .

	16		

17 Carryover from prior year . . . .

	17		

18 Add the amounts on lines 15a through 17. Write the total here. **Total** contributions . ▶

	18		

Your political contributions are not deductible as a charitable contribution on Schedule A. However, you are allowed to take a political contribution credit — subject to certain limits.

While you are not permitted to deduct the estimated value of services volunteered to a charitable organization, you may deduct out-of-pocket costs for supplies, postage, uniforms and transportation at 9 cents per mile (12 cents per mile in 1985), plus parking and tolls. You can also deduct meals and lodging if you are away from home.

Contributions Of Property

The amount of your deduction for contributing property to charity depends upon whether the property decreased or increased in value during your ownership. For property which has decreased in value (e.g., clothing contributions to Goodwill), you can deduct the property's fair market value at the time of your donation. For property which has increased in value (e.g., real estate, stock or securities that have appreciated in value during your ownership), the rules are very complex. If you have contributed such property to charity, see Part III.

Deduction For Maintenance Of Non-Dependent Student

If you pay the expenses of a full-time student (in grades K-12) while he/she lives in your home, you can deduct up to $50 per month. Although the student may be a U.S. or foreign citizen, he/she cannot be a relative or dependent. The student must be a member of your household under a written agreement between you and a qualified organization.

All of your cash contributions totaling less than $3,000 should be entered on line 15a of Schedule A. If you contributed more than $3,000 to any one organization, you would enter the amount on line 15b. Property contributions would be entered on line 16. A statement is required for each gift of property for which you claim a deduction of more than $200.

Example In December, 1984, Sheryl pledged $500 to the American Heart Association. Sheryl paid the $500 by check in January of 1985. Sheryl can take her contribution deduction in 1985. If Sheryl used her credit card in December, 1984, she would be permitted to take a deduction on her 1984 return even if she didn't pay the credit card company until January, 1985. [Rev. Rul. 38, 1978-1 C.B. 67.]

Example Ralph is a Red Cross volunteer. In performing his volunteer work, he wears a uniform and uses his car. Ralph can deduct the cost and upkeep of his uniform, as well as 9 cents per mile for transportation, plus parking and tolls. He cannot deduct the estimated value of his services.

Example Linda contributed clothing and furniture to the Salvation Army. The property originally cost Linda $1,240. At the time of the donation it was worth $350. Linda can take a contribution deduction for $350 — the fair market value of the property at the time of her donation. And since the value of the property was over $200, Linda must attach a statement to her return.

Example Denise and her husband contributed $150 to the re-election campaign of the mayor. They cannot take a charitable deduction on Schedule A. However, They can take a partial credit for political contributions on line 44, Form 1040. The amount of the credit would be $75.

CASUALTY AND THEFT LOSSES

Definitions And Computation

A casualty is defined as the damage, destruction, or loss of property resulting from an identifiable event that is sudden, unexpected or unusual. Examples include earthquakes, hurricanes, tornadoes, floods, storms, fires, auto accidents and bursting of frozen water pipes. A theft is the unlawful taking of your property. In computing your loss due to casualty or theft, you take the lesser of (1) the difference between the value of the property immediately before and immediately after the casualty or theft or (2) your cost or adjusted basis of the property.

Timing Of Deduction

You can deduct a non-business casualty or theft loss if the total exceeds 10 percent of your adjusted gross income. However, the first $100 of each loss is nondeductible. And if you used the property for business, there is no $100 reduction, no 10 percent test and the loss is deductible from your gross income instead of as an itemized deduction. To take a deduction, you must prove that there was a casualty or theft, and you must also support the amount of the loss. In substantiating a theft loss, it is important that you file a police report.

For casualty losses occurring in 1984, you can take a deduction on your 1984 return, even if the damaged property is not repaired or replaced until next year. Deductions for theft losses should be taken in the year you discover that your property is missing.

If you suffered a casualty loss in a location declared a federal disaster area, you have two choices. You can deduct this loss on your current year's return, i.e., on your 1984 return for a loss suffered in 1984, or you may deduct the disaster loss on your tax return for the year immediately preceding the year in which the disaster occurred, i.e., on your 1983 return for a loss suffered in 1984. In determining the tax year in which to claim your loss, you should compute the amount of tax savings that will result from each choice, then select the more advantageous option. Finally, you should keep in mind that you can take a casualty or theft deduction even if you elect not to file an insurance claim. Two recent court decisions allowed taxpayers to deduct casualty losses even though no insurance claims were filed.

Example Karen purchased a ring for $2,000, which increased in value to $3,800 before it was stolen. Karen's adjusted gross income is $17,200. Karen's loss is $2,000, computed as follows:

	$3,800	(value before theft)
	– -0-	(value after theft)
Lesser of:	$3,800	or the cost of the ring, $2,000.

Karen's deduction is $180, computed as follows:

$2,000	(amount of loss)
– 100	(non-deductible)
$1,900	
– 1,720	($17,200 x 10% = $1,720)
$ 180	

Example In December, 1984, Steve's uninsured home was damaged by a tornado. Steve did not repair the house until January, 1985. Since the casualty took place in 1984, Steve can take a deduction on his 1984 return, even though he didn't repair his home until 1985.

Example Because of a major flood in August, 1984, Betty's property was damaged. The location was declared a federal disaster area by the President. Betty can choose to deduct her losses on her 1984 or 1983 returns. If Betty elects the 1983 return, she must file an amended 1983 return (Form 1040X) no later than April 15, 1985. [I.R.C. §165(i).]

Example Peter's home was burglarized on April 1. Some $2,140 worth of property was stolen. Peter elected not to file an insurance claim, even though the stolen property was covered by insurance. Peter is still entitled to take a casualty loss deduction. A recent court decision concluded that such losses are deductible since they are caused by the theft of the property, not by the owner's failure to file an insurance claim. [Hills v. Commissioner, 691 F.2d 997 (11 Cir. 1982); see also Miller v. Commissioner, 84-1 U.S.T.C. 8411 (6 Cir. 1984.)]

Education Expenses

All of your expenses for continuing education and professional training courses are deductible if the education maintains or improves skills required in performing your teaching assignments, or is required by your employer or by law for retaining your salary, status or job. On the other hand, your expenditures for education will not be deductible if the education is part of a program of study that will lead to qualifying you in a new trade or business, or is required in order to meet the ''minimum educational requirements'' to qualify you as a teacher at the time you were hired.

A final requirement for deducting your education expenses is that you must have a present teaching or school administration position. However, there is an exception to this ''present teaching position'' rule. If you take a ''temporary'' absence from teaching, take education courses and then return to teaching, you can still deduct your education expenses.

You can deduct expenditures for tuition, books, supplies, correspondence courses, lab fees and typing to prepare a paper. These expenses are deducted on line 22, Schedule A. You can also deduct certain travel and transportation costs related to education. You must also complete Part III of Form 2106 to explain to the IRS how your education expenses relate to your present teaching or school administration position.

15 Educator-Related Deductions

☐ Membership dues for educator organizations.
☐ Subscription fees for magazines and journals connected with teaching.
☐ Expenditures for books specifically used in connection with your teaching.
☐ Renewal fees for teaching license.
☐ Cost of supplies and small tools.
☐ Uniforms and special clothing required for your

EDUCATOR-RELATED DEDUCTIONS

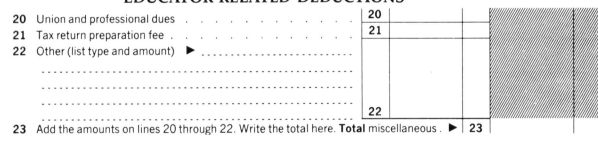

Miscellaneous Deductions (See Instructions on page 21)				
	20	Union and professional dues	20	
	21	Tax return preparation fee	21	
	22	Other (list type and amount) ▶		
		....		
		....		
		....	22	
	23	Add the amounts on lines 20 through 22. Write the total here. **Total** miscellaneous . ▶	23	

For most taxpayers, this part of Schedule A is of minor importance. However, if you are an educator, pay special attention. The miscellaneous deductions portion of Schedule A is where you deduct your (1) education expenses, (2) educator-related expenses, and (3) general miscellaneous expenses.

teaching position.
☐ Legal fees related to doing your job or keeping your job.
☐ Expenses incurred in looking for a new teaching job (except for expenses incurred in seeking your first teaching job).

- ☐ Telephone expenses incurred for teaching-related purposes.
- ☐ Payments to substitute teachers.

- ☐ Gambling losses, but not in an amount greater than the gambling winnings reported on line 22, Form 1040.

SUMMARY OF ITEMIZED DEDUCTIONS

Summary of Itemized Deductions

(See Instructions on page 22)

24 Add the amounts on lines 5, 10, 14, 18, 19, and 23. Write your answer here.	**24**		
25 If you checked Form 1040 { Filing Status box 2 or 5, write $3,400 } { Filing Status box 1 or 4, write $2,300 } { Filing Status box 3, write $1,700 }	**25**		
26 Subtract line 25 from line 24. Write your answer here and on Form 1040, line 34a. (If line 25 is more than line 24, see the Instructions for line 26 on page 22.) . . . . ▶	**26**		

- ☐ Entertainment expenses incurred as a representative of your school or directly related to your teaching position.
- ☐ Performance bond fees.
- ☐ Research expenses of college professors.
- ☐ Home office deduction, if you meet certain tests. [See Part IV for more details.]
- ☐ Teaching equipment used to assist you in carrying out your teaching assignments. [The Tax Reform Act of 1984 imposed new rules applicable to deducting Teaching equipment.]

1984 Tax Law Change

The Tax Reform Act of 1984 has imposed new depreciation and investment tax credit eligibility rules. These rules apply to "listed" property, including: (1) automobiles, (2) home computers and related equipment, and (3) any property of a type generally used for purposes of entertainment, recreation or amusement. (This would seem to include camera equipment, audio-visual equipment, tape recorders and musical instruments.) The new law considers whether the "listed" property is used more than 50 percent for business purposes and whether such use is for the convenience of the employer and required as a condition of employment. [See Part III for additional information.]

Miscellaneous Deductions
- ☐ Tax counsel and assistance fees.
- ☐ IRA fees charged to you by banks or financial institutions.
- ☐ Investment counseling fees charged to you, as well as your expenditures for financial investing books and publications.
- ☐ Safe deposit box rental fees charged to you if you keep stocks, bonds or other investment-related papers and documents in them.
- ☐ Up to $1,500 of qualified adoption expenses if you legally adopt a child with "special needs" as described in the Social Security Act Adoption Assistance Program and as determined by your state.
- ☐ Any expenses you paid to produce or collect taxable income.

In computing your Schedule A deductions, you should initially total your itemized deductions and place this number on Schedule A, line 24. Depending on your filing status, you must now subtract the applicable zero bracket amount on Schedule A, line 25. (You actually do receive the full benefit of your itemized deductions because the zero bracket amount which you have just subtracted has already been built into the IRS tax tables and rate schedules.) You should now insert the remaining balance on Schedule A, line 26 and on Form 1040, line 34a. If you do not itemize your deductions on Schedule A, then you must place a 0 on Form 1040, line 34a.

NON-SCHEDULE A CHARITABLE CONTRIBUTIONS

For 1984, the maximum deduction allowed has been increased to $75 ($37.50 if married filing separately).

If you do not itemize your deductions on Schedule A, you are permitted to deduct 25 percent of your first $300 ($150 if married filing separately) of contributions to qualified organizations.

The IRS has provided the following worksheet:

Charitable Contributions Worksheet
1. Cash contributions (including checks, money orders, receipts, or other written evidence) .... _____
2. Other contributions .... _____
3. Total. Add lines 1 and 2 .... _____
4. Multiply the amount on line 3 by 25% (.25) .... _____
5. Enter here and on Form 1040, line 34b, but do not enter more than $75 ($37.50 if married filing separately) .... _____

Example During 1984, Ed and Connie contributed $200 to their church and $200 to the American Heart Association. They did not itemize their deductions on Schedule A. They can deduct $75 on line 34b for charitable contributions, computed as follows:

Total contribution	$400
x	25%
=	$100

Maximum deduction allowed — $75

TAX COMPUTATION METHODS

You can compute your tax liability by income averaging (Schedule G) or using the tax table, or Tax Rate Schedule X, Y or Z.

Although the Tax Reform Act of 1984 made significant changes to the income averaging rules, which have reduced the tax benefits available from income averaging, you can still save money by using this option. If your taxable income is significantly higher this year than it was for the past three years, you may qualify to use income averaging. Several requirements must be met for you to qualify for this tax saving option. During the current 1984 tax year, as well as 1983, 1982 and 1981, you must have been a citizen or resident of the U.S., and you must have provided at least 50 percent of your own support. If married, you and your spouse must have provided at least 50 percent of your combined support.

In addition, your taxable income for this 1984 tax year must exceed 140 percent of your average taxable income for 1983, 1982 and 1981 by more than $3,000. To see if you meet this second test, turn to Part III and review IRS form Schedule G.

If you do not qualify for income averaging, then look

simply being taxed at ordinary income rates. Should you qualify, you should use the 10-year averaging method because it will save you tax dollars. You should note that pre-1974 participation is taxed at capital gain rates or, if the tax works out lower, you can include the capital gains portion in with your ordinary income portion and use income averaging for both amounts.

To qualify for the special 10-year averaging method, there must be an entire distribution which you received within one tax year from a qualified retirement plan (other than an IRA) in which you were a participant for five or more years. The distribution must be triggered by your decision, after reaching at least age 59½, to withdraw the money or your death, retirement, voluntary or involuntary termination or being laid off from your job.

If you receive a lump-sum distribution, a second alternative is to transfer it tax-free into an Individual Retirement Account if you effect the transfer within 60 days of the distribution from the qualified plan. This alternative enables you to defer paying tax on the distribution until you withdraw the money. However, you can no longer use the very favorable 10-year averaging method when it is withdrawn from your IRA. The distribution is taxed at ordinary income rates.

CREDITS

Credits

(See Instructions on page 14.)

41	Credit for child and dependent care expenses *(attach Form 2441)*	41		
42	Credit for the elderly and the permanently and totally disabled *(attach Schedule R)*	42		
43	Residential energy credit *(attach Form 5695)*	43		
44	Partial credit for political contributions for which you have receipts	44		
45	Add lines 41 through 44. These are your total personal credits			45
46	Subtract line 45 from 40. Enter the result (but not less than zero) . .			46
47	Foreign tax credit *(attach Form 1116)*	47		
48	General business credit. Check if from ☐ Form 3800, ☐ Form 3468, ☐ Form 5884, ☐ Form 6478	48		
49	Add lines 47 and 48. These are your total business and other credits			49
50	Subtract line 49 from 46. Enter the result (but not less than zero). . . . . ▶			50

at the amount of your taxable income on line 37. If it is below $50,000, use the Tax Tables. If it is $50,000 or more, use the Tax Rate Schedule applicable for your filing status.

ADDITIONAL TAXES

Of the three additional taxes listed on line 39, only one is generally applicable to you as an educator. It is the Special 10-Year Averaging Method (Form 4972).

Special 10-Year Averaging Method

If you received a ''lump-sum distribution'' from a qualified retirement plan, all of your participation from 1974 to the present participation may be eligible for very favorable 10-year averaging treatment, as opposed to

It is important for you to understand the difference between a tax credit and a tax deduction. A tax credit reduces your tax dollar for dollar. Every dollar of tax credit is another dollar in your pocket. A tax deduction, on the other hand, reduces your taxable income. Every dollar of tax deduction will save you between 11 cents and 50 cents, depending upon your tax bracket. Both are good, but a tax credit is better.

CREDIT FOR CHILD AND DEPENDENT CARE EXPENSES

If you pay someone to care for your child or disabled dependent, you may be able to claim a tax credit of between 20 percent and 30 percent of the amount you pay. Indeed, some educators qualify for a $1,440 per year tax credit. To qualify for the credit, you must meet the requirements set forth in Part III.

CREDIT FOR THE ELDERLY AND DISABLED

Starting in 1984, you, as an educator under age 65, will be eligible for this credit only if you retired with a permanent and total disability and have income from a public or private employer because of that disability. Educators age 65 and older need not be permanently and totally disabled to qualify for the credit.

Credit For The Elderly

If you were single and age 65 or older by the end of 1984, or married and your spouse is age 65 or older, you may be eligible for a 15 percent tax credit. Your eligibility depends upon your adjusted gross income, the amount of any non-taxable social security benefits you received and the amount of any non-taxable pension or annuity benefits you received. If you meet the age requirements stated above, review Schedule R in Part III to see if you qualify for the credit.

Credit For The Permanently And Totally Disabled

This part of the credit replaces the disability income exclusion, which was available in prior years. If, by the end of 1984, you or your spouse retired on permanent and total disability and he/she received taxable disability benefits, then that spouse may be eligible for a 15 percent tax credit. Your eligibility depends upon your adjusted gross income and the amount of disability income you receive.

The IRS considers a person permanently and totally disabled when he or she cannot engage in any substantial gainful activity because of a physical or mental condition, and a physician determines that the disability has lasted or can be expected to last continuously for at least a year or can be expected to lead to death. To claim this credit, a physician must sign your Schedule R. If you meet the disability test stated above, you should review Schedule R in Part III to see if you qualify for the credit. You may also be eligible for the credit for dependent care expenses.

RESIDENTIAL ENERGY CREDIT

There are two different types of residential energy credits and you may be eligible for both. The first is for installation of prescribed energy conservation property and the second applies to installation of renewable source property.

Energy Conservation Credit

A tax credit of 15 percent is allowed on the first $2,000 you spend on "qualified" items to save energy in your home. The list of qualified items includes:
- ☐ Insulation.
- ☐ Storm windows or doors.
- ☐ Caulking or weatherstripping of exterior doors or windows.
- ☐ Fuel saving furnace replacement burner.
- ☐ Device modifying flue openings to make a heating system more efficient.
- ☐ Automatic energy-saving setback thermostat.
- ☐ Furnace ignition system which replaced gas pilot light.
- ☐ Meter which displays cost of energy usage.

In order to be eligible for the credit, one of these energy-saving devices must be installed in your principal residence which was substantially completed by April 20, 1977. The item must have been new when you purchased it and expected to last at least three years. The credit is available to renters as well as owners.

Renewable Energy Source Credit

A tax credit of 40 percent is allowed on the first $10,000 you spend for solar, wind and geothermal energy items that heat or cool your principal residence or provide hot water or electricity for it. The item must be new and expected to last at least five years.

In connection with this credit, you should note that a new $2,000 limit for energy conservation and a new $10,000 limit for renewable energy source applies if you move to another home which becomes your new principal residence.

Example During 1984, Sheryl had the attic in her home fully insulated. She had been living in this home since 1976. Sheryl also installed storm windows and doors. She purchased these windows and doors new. They are expected to last seven to ten years. All of these items cost Sheryl $1,200. Sheryl can claim a 1984 tax credit of $180 ($1,200 x 15% = $180).

PARTIAL CREDIT FOR POLITICAL CONTRIBUTIONS

You may claim a tax credit for one-half of any money donated to a political campaign. The maximum credit is $50 for a single person and $100 on a joint return. You must have a written receipt to prove your contributions.

Example Tom and his wife, Cathy, contributed $400 to the re-election campaign of their town's mayor. They can claim a total credit of $100, the maximum allowed on a joint return.

FOREIGN TAX CREDIT

You may take an itemized deduction on Schedule A or a limited foreign tax credit for any foreign income taxes you paid to a foreign country. Generally, you will benefit more by taking the credit. Use Form 1116 to compute the credit.

GENERAL BUSINESS CREDIT

Out of the four general business credits listed on line 48, only the investment credit (Form 3468) is generally applicable to you as an educator. You may be eligible to claim an investment tax credit if, during 1984, you purchased new or used tangible personal property which you used in a trade or business. This includes equipment which you use in your teaching position or a car which you use professionally. [See Part III for additional details.]

EARNED INCOME CREDIT

If you have earned income, your adjusted gross income is less than $10,000, and you have a dependent child living with you, you may be eligible for the earned income credit. The maximum credit is $500. If you qualify for this credit, you can obtain a refund, even if you had no tax withheld from your pay. Consult the Earned Income Credit Worksheet and the 1984 Earned Income Credit Table in your IRS — Form 1040 instruction booklet.

EXCESS SOCIAL SECURITY TAX WITHHELD

If you worked for two or more employers in 1984 and your combined salary from them was over $37,800, check the amount of FICA (social security) tax that was withheld from your pay. If it was more than $2,532.60, you can claim the excess as a tax payment on line 61. But if you worked for only one employer who withheld more than $2,532.60 in FICA tax from your pay, you cannot take a credit. In this case you should ask the employer to refund the difference to you.

Of the five other taxes included in this section, only

in addition to your regular tax. Secondly, if both you and your spouse are subject to the tax, then both must file separate Schedule SE forms, even if you and your spouse are filing a joint return. Third, if you operate more than one business, for self-employment tax purposes, you must combine the net income/loss.

In computing your self-employment tax, you are given credit for any wages you earned which were subject to social security (FICA) tax. And finally, you generally should complete Parts I and III of Schedule SE. Part II is an optional method which gives you credit toward your social security coverage even though you had very low self-employment earnings or incurred a loss. Using this optional method will require you to pay additional self-employment tax.

ALTERNATIVE MINIMUM TAX

The alternative minimum tax is a flat 20 percent tax on an amount called "alternative minimum taxable income." You are required to pay this tax only if it exceeds your regular income tax. Since being in an alternative minimum tax situation has several disadvantages for educators, you should attempt to avoid this circumstance. [See Part III for additional details.]

TAX FROM RECAPTURE OF INVESTMENT CREDIT

If, during the current tax year, you sold or otherwise

OTHER TAXES

Other Taxes (Including Advance EIC Payments)			
	51	Self-employment tax (attach Schedule SE)	51
	52	Alternative minimum tax (attach Form 6251)	52
	53	Tax from recapture of investment credit (attach Form 4255)	53
	54	Social security tax on tip income not reported to employer (attach Form 4137)	54
	55	Tax on an IRA (attach Form 5329)	55
■	56	Add lines 50 through 55. This is your **total tax** . . . . ▶	56

---

three are generally applicable to you as an educator. They are the self-employment tax, the alternative minimum tax and the tax from recapture of investment credit.

SELF-EMPLOYMENT TAX

For 1984, the self-employment tax is effectively 11.3 percent, 14 percent minus a tax credit of 2.7 percent. You are required to pay self-employment tax (Schedule SE) for 1984 if you were self-employed during the year, your annual net earnings from self-employment were $400 or more, and your salary subject to social security (FICA) tax was less than $37,800.

With regard to self-employment tax, it is important to remember five factors. First, the self-employment tax is

ceased using for business an asset for which you previously claimed an investment credit, you may be required to now pay the credit back. To determine whether you are subject to this tax, the following steps should be taken. First, determine how long you actually used the property for business. Then you must compare this to the minimum required period, i.e., three years for an auto and five years for teaching equipment. If you actually used the property less than the minimum required period, you must now pay back part or all of the investment credit. [See Part III and IRS Form 4255 for more details.]

EXTENSION OF FILING DEADLINE

The IRS will grant you an automatic four-month extension of time to file your 1984 Federal income tax return. To be eligible for this extension, you must file Form 4868 no later than midnight on April 15, 1985 and pay the estimated amount of tax you owe on your 1984 return. This payment must accompany your Form 4868.

If your payment falls short, the IRS will charge you interest. Their interest meter starts running from April 16, 1985, and it stops the day the IRS receives your check.

If your payment is short by more than 10 percent of your total tax, i.e., you did not pay in 90 percent of your total tax by April 15, 1985, the IRS may hit you with a late payment penalty of one-half of 1 percent of the unpaid tax per month. If the IRS hits you with this penalty, remember that it can be waived if you had "reasonable cause" for paying late. The question of whether a taxpayer had reasonable cause depends upon the facts of each case. Even if you are granted an extension to file your 1984 return, you must still pay the first installment of your 1985 estimated tax payment on April 15, 1985, provided you are required to make estimated payments.

If you are going to request an extension of time to file your 1984 tax return, and are required to pay estimated taxes for 1985, here is a four-step tax planning strategy to help you avoid this IRS penalty.

Step 1. Take the amount you estimate you owe on your 1984 return and add to it the amount you plan to pay on the first installment of your 1985 taxes.

Step 2. Submit this combined amount as your 1984 Form 4868 extension payment.

Step 3. Do not submit any payment for your first installment of 1985 taxes.

Step 4. When you file your 1984 return, apply this overpayment to your 1985 estimated taxes. This is done by inserting the overpayment amount on line 67, Form 1040.

By following these steps you will avoid an IRS penalty for underestimating your 1984 tax liability.

Example It is April 13, 1985, and John has decided to request an extension to file his 1984 income tax return. He estimates that his 1984 balance due will be $600. John also estimates the first installment of his 1985 taxes to be $700. John should combine the $600 with the $700 and submit a check for $1,300 with his Form 4868. On May 15, 1985, John completes his 1984 tax return and his actual 1984 liability turns out to be $1,100 instead of $600. John has effectively avoided the IRS penalty. He can now increase his federal payroll tax withholdings to cover the $500 ($700 − $200) shortfall of his 1985 first installment.

If you (and/or your spouse) are outside the U.S. on April 15, 1985, you are given special privileges by the Internal Revenue Code. You are automatically allowed until June 15, 1985 to file your 1984 income tax return. If you do not pay your balance due, you cannot be charged a penalty, provided your payment is made by June 15, 1985. However, the IRS will charge you interest.

FINAL REMINDERS

☐ Use the pre-printed IRS label. This will help speed up the processing of your return. Double-check to make sure that the information on your label is correct. If it is not, make the necessary corrections directly on it.

☐ Make sure your social security number appears on every form and schedule. Also check to see that you have used your correct social security number.

☐ Verify that you have included all required information and that it is readable.

☐ Re-check your addition and subtraction.

☐ Figure your tax a second time.

☐ Attach Copy "B" of all W-2 forms to your return. You should staple them to the middle of the front page of your 1040, on the left side. If you are unable to include a W-2 form, be sure to attach a statement explaining why.

☐ Make sure you sign and date page 2 of your Form 1040. If you are filing jointly, both you and your spouse must sign.

☐ If your return shows a refund, complete line 66 if you want this amount refunded to you, or line 67 if you want it applied to your 1985 estimated tax.

☐ If your return shows a balance due, be sure to enclose a check payable to the Internal Revenue Service. On your check, write "1984 Form 1040," and your social security number. Staple your check to the front page of Form 1040.

☐ Retain a photocopy of your completed return. This copy will be useful for preparing your 1985 return, income averaging in future years, a possible IRS audit, and applying for bank loans.

☐ Use the pre-addressed IRS envelope enclosed with your forms.

☐ Have your return postmarked by midnight on April 15, 1985. After April 10, 1985, do not use a metered mail machine. Instead, use a stamp so that the post office will postmark it.

☐ Remember, the first installment of your 1985 estimated tax payment is also due on April 15, 1985. Attach a separate check payable to the Internal Revenue Service. On your check write "1985 Form 1040ES," and your social security number.

☐ Don't forget to also mail your 1984 state income tax return.

3

SPECIFIC TAX LAWS AFFECTING EDUCATORS

This section of the handbook is designed to serve as a reference source. It provides extensive explanations of a number of Internal Revenue Code provisions which affect taxpaying educators. Here you will find in-depth treatment of such sticky areas as credits for child care expenses, the Accelerated Cost Recovery System (ACRS) and related depreciation rules, special rules for "listed" property, and the investment tax credit.

The inclusion of detailed explanations of sophisticated tax topics makes the handbook more self-contained. This should minimize the need for you to consult additional reference books when completing your tax return or mapping your tax planning strategies.

ALTERNATIVE MINIMUM TAX

Since there is an exclusion of $40,000 on a joint return and a $30,000 exclusion for returns filed by single taxpayers or heads of households, the items listed below must include large dollar amounts to trigger the imposition of the alternative minimum tax. [For more information, consult Form 6251.]

Items That Can Trigger The Imposition Of Alternative Minimum Tax
- ☐ Long-term capital gains, excluding the 60 percent capital gain deduction portion from the sale of your personal residence.
- ☐ Accelerated depreciation from your real estate investments.
- ☐ Depletion and oil/gas intangible drilling costs from any oil and gas investments.
- ☐ Tax credits (e.g., investment credit).
- ☐ Tax and miscellaneous deductions from Schedule A.

Three Main Disadvantages Of Being In An Alternative Minimum Tax Situation
- ☐ Except for the credit for foreign tax payments, you do not get the current benefit of your tax credits. This includes no current tax benefit for any investment credit or any child care credit you may have.

- ☐ You receive no tax benefit from certain itemized deductions, e.g., taxes and miscellaneous deductions. For teachers, this is an important deduction the loss of which could make your tax liability substantially higher.
- ☐ You pay a 20 percent tax on certain "preference" items which otherwise are never included in your regular tax computations.

CONTRIBUTIONS OF APPRECIATED PROPERTY

This section sets forth additional information relating to charitable contributions of real estate holdings, stocks, securities or other similar items which increased in value during the time you owned them. The 1984 Tax Reform Act changed the requirements for long-term capital gain treatment, and these changes affect the amount of your contribution deduction. The amount of your deduction is now based on when you acquired the property and the length of time you held it before you made your donation.

Property Acquired Before June 23, 1984

If you acquired property before June 23, 1984, and donated it to charity within 12 months thereafter, your deduction is limited to your cost rather than the appreciated value at the time of your donation. If you acquired the property prior to this date and donated it to charity more than 12 months thereafter, your deduction is the full appreciated value at the time of your donation.

Example On October 13, 1984, Ed and Connie contributed 100 shares of ABC stock to the American Heart Association. The stock was acquired originally in 1980 at a total cost of $800. At the time of their donation the stock was worth $12,000. Ed and Connie are entitled to a charitable contribution deduction of $12,000. The stock was acquired before June 23, 1983. The couple owned the stock over 12 months before they donated it. Their deduction is the full appreciated value — $12,000. Also note that they are not taxed on the appreciation. Thus, this type of contribution provides a double benefit.

Property Acquired After June 22, 1984

If you acquired property after June 22, 1984, and donated it to charity within six months thereafter, your deduction is limited to your cost. If, on the other hand, you acquired property after June 22, 1984 and donated it to charity after six months (i.e., between December 22 and December 31, 1984), your deduction is the full appreciated value at the time of your donation.

Special Limitation On Certain Appreciated Property

Although the general rule allows the full fair market value of appreciated property to be taken into account for charitable contribution purposes, certain exceptions apply. The more important of those exceptions are:

☐ **Ordinary income property such as inventory, or assets subject to depreciation recapture.** With respect to such property, the amount of the contribution is reduced by the amount of ordinary income that would be recognized on a sale of the property.

☐ **Tangible personal property donated to a donee (recipient) whose use of the property is unrelated to its charitable purpose.** In this case, the amount of the contribution is reduced by 40 percent of the long term gain that would be recognized on a sale of the property.

CREDIT FOR CHILD AND DEPENDENT CARE EXPENSES

The seven requirements discussed below must be met for you to qualify for the 20 percent to 30 percent credit for child and dependent care expenses.

Qualifying Individual Requirement

The individual for whom expenses were incurred must be (1) a dependent under age 15 for whom you may claim an exemption, (2) your spouse who is physically or mentally unable to care for himself or herself, or (3) any physically or mentally disabled dependent of any age, whether or not he or she can be claimed as your dependent, but who could have been claimed as your dependent under the support test.

If you are legally separated or divorced, you may claim the credit for dependent care expense if you had custody of the qualifying individual during the greater part of the tax year. You may claim the credit for such an individual's care even if you are not entitled to the dependency exemption. The following examples will help to clarify these concepts.

Example To enable both of them to work, Ed and Mary place their 2-year-old son, Matthew, in a day care center. They can claim a credit for child care expenses since Matthew is their dependent and he is under age 15.

Example Bill is a high school teacher. His wife has

Parkinson's disease and is physically unable to care for herself. Bill hires a nurse to care for her while he is at work. Bill can claim a credit for dependent care expenses. A spouse who is physically unable to care for herself is considered a "qualifying" person for the purpose of the credit. [I.R.C. §44A(c)(1).]

Example Ann lives with her mother who has arthritis and is physically unable to care for herself. To enable her to work, Ann hires a nurse to provide care for her mother while she is at work. Ann can claim a credit for dependent care expenses, provided Ann claims her mother as a dependent or provides over 50 percent of her support. [I.R.C. §44A(c)(1).]

Residence Requirement

One or more of the "qualifying" persons must have actually lived in your home during 1984.

Support Requirement

You must have paid over 50 percent of the cost of maintaining your home. This includes property taxes, mortgage interest, rent, utilities, home repairs, insurance and food. However, it does not include clothing, education, medical costs, mortgage principal and vacations.

Qualifying Expenses

Among the expenses which qualify for this credit are the cost of babysitters, nurses, housekeepers, maids and cooks, if they performed ordinary household services that were partly for the well-being and protection of the "qualifying" person. However, all of your expenses for housework are deductible, even if only part of them are for a "qualifying" person.

Example Phil and Arlene pay a housekeeper to care for their 10 and 16-year-old daughters so they both can work. The housekeeper spends most of the time doing the regular household work of cooking and cleaning. Phil and Arlene can claim a credit for child care expenses. The 10-year-old child is considered a "qualifying" person since she is under age fifteen. The other child, age 16, is not. Even though one child is not a "qualifying" person, Phil and Arlene do not have to deduct any amount for the care of the 16-year-old child, because the household expense is partly for the well-being and protection of the "qualifying" 10-year-old.

Expenses incurred for care provided outside your home will qualify for the credit if the care was for your dependent under age 15 or for any other qualifying person who regularly spends at least eight hours each day in your home. Such expenses would include day care centers, summer camp and nursery/pre-school. However, you cannot include the cost of school for a child in the first grade or above.

Example Susan, a single parent, places her 9-year-old child in a boarding school so that she can work full time. Only part of the boarding school expense qualifies for the credit. Susan's expenses which are for the care of the child qualify for the credit. Since her child is above the kindergarten level (i.e., first grade or above), Susan cannot use any of the cost which represents tuition for education as qualifying for the credit. [Treas. Reg. 1.44A-1(c)(7).]

Work Requirement

Expenses for which the credit is claimed must have been incurred to allow you to work or seek employment. Unless one spouse was a full-time student or was physically or mentally unable to care for him/herself, both spouses must be employed or seeking employment. Volunteer work does not qualify. However, one spouse may be employed on a part-time basis.

Example Bill is a high school teacher and his wife, Rose, is currently unemployed. They hired a babysitter to care for their 3-year-old child during the times Rose went on job interviews. They can claim a credit for child care expenses since these costs were incurred to allow Bill to work and to allow Rose to look for work. [Treas. Reg. 1.44A-1(c).]

Example Tom is a full time graduate student and his wife, Carol, is a teacher. During the times Tom is at school and Carol is working, they pay a babysitter to care for their 2-year-old son. They can claim a credit for child care expenses since these costs were incurred to allow Tom to attend school and to allow Carol to work. Since Tom was a full time student during at least five months of 1984, and Carol was employed full time, they are eligible for the credit.

Example Ralph is a high school principal and his wife, Cathy, does full time volunteer work at the local blood bank. They place their 3-year-old daughter in a day care center. They cannot claim a credit for child care expenses. With respect to this credit, volunteer work does not constitute gainful employment. [Treas. Reg. 1.44A-1(c).]

Example Mark and his wife, Susan, are both high school math teachers. Every Friday night they hire a babysitter to watch their 6-year-old son so they can go the the theater. They cannot claim a credit for child care expenses since these expenses were not incurred to allow them to be gainfully employed. [Treas. Reg. 1.44A-1(c).]

Third Party Payment Requirement

The person to whom you paid these expenses must not be your spouse or a person you could claim as a dependent. Thus, you can pay your parents, grandparents, any other relative, or even one of your other children who is at least 19 years old to care for your child or other qualifying individual. Thus, any relative is a qualifying recipient so long as he or she is not your dependent. You should note that if the total wages you pay exceed $50 per calendar quarter, you may be subject to social security taxes as an employer.

Example Martha, a single parent, hires her mother to care for her 2-year-old while she works. Martha can claim a credit for child care expenses, provided that her mother is not her dependent for tax purposes.

Joint Return Requirement

If married, you must file a joint tax return, unless your spouse did not live in your home during the last six months of the year.

DETERMINING YOUR CREDIT

The credit ranges between 20 percent and 30 percent of the amount you paid depending upon your adjusted gross income.

If Adjusted Gross Income Is:		Percentage Is:
Over—	But not Over—	
0 - $10,000		30% (.30)
$10,000 -	12,000	29% (.29)
12,000 -	14,000	28% (.28)
14,000 -	16,000	27% (.27)
16,000 -	18,000	26% (.26)
18,000 -	20,000	25% (.25)
20,000 -	22,000	24% (.24)
22,000 -	24,000	23% (.23)
24,000 -	26,000	22% (.22)
26,000 -	28,000	21% (.21)
28,000		20% (.20)

The maximum amount of "qualified" expenses eligible for the credit is $2,400 for one dependent and $4,800 for two or more dependents. The amount of "qualified" expenses eligible for the credit cannot exceed your earned income for the year or, if married, the lesser of either spouse's earned income. If, for any month, one spouse is either a full-time student or is not able to care for him/herself, that spouse will be considered to have earned $200 per month, if there is one qualifying person, and $400 if two or more.

Example Jack earned $44,000 in 1984. His wife, Catherine, earned $3,600. They incurred $4,700 in qualified child care expenses during 1984 for their three kids. Since the amount of qualified expenses eligible for the credit cannot exceed the lesser of either spouse's earned income, $3,600 of the couple's income is eligible for the credit.

Example Paul and Susan are both teachers. Their 1984 adjusted gross income is $41,050. To enable them to work, they incurred the following expenses for child care for their three children:

$4,600	(day care center)
1,300	(paid to Susan's mother for babysitting while Paul and Susan were at work)
475	(paid to a babysitter to enable Paul and Susan to attend movies and the theater
$6,375	during 1984)

Paul and Susan's 1984 credit for child care expenses is $960 ($4,800 x 20%). The $475 in expenses were not incurred to allow Paul and Susan to be gainfully employed. Thus, this amount is not eligible for the credit. The maximum amount of qualified expenses eligible for the credit, for two or more dependents, is $4,800. The $1,300 in expenses is eligible for the credit, even though it was paid to Susan's mother. Since their adjusted gross income is over $28,000, Paul and Susan's credit is at the 20 percent level.

DEPRECIATION AND THE SECTION 179 DEDUCTION

The information provided in the following sections can help you save tax dollars if, during 1984, you placed in service an asset which you used in a business, in your teaching job, or to earn rent or royalty income. The asset must have a useful life of more than one year and its cost must have exceeded $100.

There are two basic methods through which you can deduct the cost of an asset. The first is called depreciation and the second is called the Section 179 deduction. If you use a depreciable asset a certain percentage of the time for personal use, then you must reduce your deduction by that percentage.

APPLICABLE DEFINITIONS

Depreciation is the recovery of an asset's cost over a designated period of time. Thus, it will take you at least several years to fully deduct the cost of an asset you purchased in 1984. The Section 179 deduction is a relatively new option. By electing it, you may be able to immediately deduct up to $5,000 of qualifying property acquired during 1984. This amount is treated as a current expense. You are not required to depreciate the cost over a number of years. However, if you elect to expense property pursuant to Section 179, you lose any investment tax credit attributable to it. [See Investment Tax Credit discussion in Part III.] If you placed in service "listed" property after June 18, 1984, you may not be eligible to use the Section 179 deduction or the amount of your Section 179 deduction may be limited.

Depreciation and the Section 179 deduction may appear in several areas as you prepare your tax return. It may be found in Schedule C where you report your business income or loss or in connection with rental income or loss and royalty income on Schedule E. If you purchased equipment which you use in your teaching position, the miscellaneous deduction portion of Schedule A may be applicable. Finally, these items may appear on Form 2106 with regard to automobile expenses.

DEPRECIATION RULES

The rules for depreciation vary depending on when you placed the asset in service, i.e., began using it for business/teaching purposes. If you purchased an asset in 1981, but did not begin

using it for business/teaching until 1984, then, for depreciation purposes, you placed it in service in 1984.

If you placed the asset in service before 1981, you are not eligible for the Accelerated Cost Recovery System (ACRS) method. Under the prior "regular" depreciation rules you could elect to use the straight line method or one of several accelerated methods. If you are using an accelerated method, you have the option of switching to straight line at any point for the asset's remaining useful life.

If you placed the asset in service between January 1, 1981 and June 18, 1984, you are generally required to use the ACRS method of depreciation. Under this system, you have two methods to choose from. One is the accelerated method, the other is the straight line method.

Accelerated (ACRS) Method

The accelerated method requires that the cost of most tangible depreciable property be recovered over certain specified periods, ranging from 3 to 18 years. The applicable period will depend on the type of property involved. The accelerated method allows you to depreciate your property faster than the straight line method. Thus, if you want larger depreciation deductions initially, you should choose the accelerated rather than straight line method. Depreciation schedules for 3, 5 and 15/18 year property are set forth below.

☐ Depreciation schedule for 3-year property [autos and light trucks].

1st year	25%
2nd year	38%
3rd year	37%
4th year	N/A
5th year	N/A
	100%

☐ Depreciation schedule for 5-year property. [All other depreciable business personal property, including teaching equipment.]

1st year	15%
2nd year	22%
3rd year	21%
4th year	21%
5th year	21%
	100%

☐ Depreciation schedule for 15/18-year property. This category includes houses, apartments and other buildings. The land on which a building stands is not depreciable; thus, you must allocate the cost of the property between the land and the building. You should use the 15-year tables for qualifying property placed in service before March 15, 1984. For property placed in service after March 15, 1984, but before June 23, 1984, use 18-year table "A." For property placed in service after June 22, 1984, use 18-year table "B."

Accelerated Recovery Schedule For 15-Year Real Property

If the Recovery Year Is:	The applicable percentage is (use the column representing the month in the first year the property is placed in service):											
	(Month)											
	1	2	3	4	5	6	7	8	9	10	11	12
	(Percentage Rate)											
1	12%	11%	10%	9%	8%	7%	6%	5%	4%	3%	2%	1%
2	10%	10%	11%	11%	11%	11%	11%	11%	11%	11%	11%	12%
3	9%	9%	9%	9%	10%	10%	10%	10%	10%	10%	10%	10%
4	8%	8%	8%	8%	8%	8%	9%	9%	9%	9%	9%	9%
5	7%	7%	7%	7%	7%	7%	8%	8%	8%	8%	8%	8%
6	6%	6%	6%	6%	7%	7%	7%	7%	7%	7%	7%	7%
7	6%	6%	6%	6%	6%	6%	6%	6%	6%	6%	6%	6%
8	6%	6%	6%	6%	6%	6%	5%	6%	6%	6%	6%	6%
9	6%	6%	6%	6%	5%	6%	5%	5%	5%	6%	6%	6%
10	5%	6%	5%	6%	5%	5%	5%	5%	5%	5%	6%	5%
11	5%	5%	5%	5%	5%	5%	5%	5%	5%	5%	5%	5%
12	5%	5%	5%	5%	5%	5%	5%	5%	5%	5%	5%	5%
13	5%	5%	5%	5%	5%	5%	5%	5%	5%	5%	5%	5%
14	5%	5%	5%	5%	5%	5%	5%	5%	5%	5%	5%	5%
15	5%	5%	5%	5%	5%	5%	5%	5%	5%	5%	5%	5%
16	…	…	1%	1%	2%	2%	3%	3%	4%	4%	4%	5%

18-year — Table "A"
Use the column for the month of taxable year placed in service

Year	1	2	3	4	5	6	7	8	9	10	11	12
1st	10%	9%	8%	7%	6%	6%	5%	4%	3%	2%	2%	1%
2nd	9%	9%	9%	9%	9%	9%	9%	9%	9%	10%	10%	10%
3rd	8%	8%	8%	8%	8%	8%	8%	8%	9%	9%	9%	9%

18-year — Table "B"
Use the column for the month of taxable year placed in service

Year	1	2	3	4	5	6	7	8	9	10	11	12
1st	9%	9%	8%	7%	6%	5%	4%	4%	3%	2%	1%	0.4%
2nd	9%	9%	9%	9%	9%	9%	9%	9%	9%	10%	10%	10%
3rd	8%	8%	8%	8%	8%	8%	8%	8%	9%	9%	9%	9%

COMPUTING YOUR DEPRECIATION DEDUCTION

To compute your deduction, determine the applicable ACRS percentage to be applied. This percentage is based upon the nature of the property, i.e., whether it is 3, 5, 15 or 18-year property. Now, multiply this percentage by your unadjusted basis in the property. The unadjusted basis is generally your cost, less (1) any amount you elected to expense pursuant to the Section 179 option and (2) one-half of any investment tax credit taken on property placed in service after December 31, 1982. The entire net result is your ac-celerated (ACRS) depreciation deduction for 1984. If, in the initial year, you did not place the asset in service until September or October, your deduction is still the entire net result you just computed. In other words, you do not have to prorate it according to months.

Straight Line (Alternate) Method

Under the straight line method, your depreciation deduction is uniform during the useful life of the property, except for the first year. To determine your deduction, simply divide your cost by the number of years in the asset's recovery period. You can choose from among four different alternate recovery periods for each class of property. The choices are:

3-year property . . . . 3, 5 or 12 years
5-year property . . . . 5, 12 or 25 years
15-year real property . . . . 15, 35 or 45 years
18-year real property . . . . 18 or 40 years

For the initial year of depreciating these item, your deduction is one-half of the amount you just computed, regardless of which month you placed the asset in service. Thereafter, it is the full amount until you have recovered your cost. This differs from the rules for the accelerated (ACRS) method. There your initial year's deduction is not reduced to one-half of the amount.

RULES GOVERNING
SECTION 179 DEDUCTION

You can deduct the full cost of qualifying assets purchased between January 1, 1984, and June 18, 1984, without having to depreciate the cost over a number of years. The limit for the entire 1984 tax year is $5,000. Although the item(s) may be new or used, you are not allowed an investment tax credit for any portion of the cost expensed in this manner. You should determine whether electing an immediate Section 179 deduction outweighs the value of the investment tax credit which will be lost. Most educators will benefit greater by claiming the investment tax credit and not electing the Section 179 deduction.

Special Rules For 'Listed' Property

The Tax Reform Act of 1984 made significant depreciation and investment credit rule changes. These changes apply to "listed" property placed in service after June 18, 1984. The tax law now considers whether the "listed" property is used more than 50 percent for business purposes and whether such use is for the convenience of the employer and required as a condition of employment. Beginning with your 1985 tax year, the Internal Revenue Code requires that "adequate contemporaneous records" be kept to support your deductions for "listed" property. Thus, for 1985, you should begin to keep a diary.

For purposes of these amendments, "listed" property includes:

☐ Passenger automobiles and any other property used as a means of transportation.
☐ Home computers and related equipment.
☐ Any property of a type generally used for purposes of entertainment, recreation or amusement. This would seem to include camera equipment, audio-visual equipment, tape recorders and musical instruments.
☐ Any other property specified in the Income Tax Regulations.

If you purchased an asset which is not "listed" property, then the rules previously stated above still apply. On the other hand, your eligibility for depreciation and investment credit for "listed" property placed in service after June 18, 1984, depends upon several factors. First, the "listed" property must be required (1) for the convenience of your employer and (2) as a condition of your employment. If so, you may be entitled to take an investment credit, use the Section 179 deduction, or take depreciation. Unless these two conditions are met, however, you are not eligible for any depreciation nor are you eligible for investment credit.

Whether the asset was required for the "convenience of your employer" presents a question of fact. In order to satisfy the "condition of employment" requirement, the property must be required in order for you, the educator, to properly perform the duties of your professional employment. This requirement is not satisfied merely by an employer's statement that the property is required as a condition of employment. If you are required to use "listed" property as a condition of your employment, try to have this condition stated in an employment contract. Secondly, the asset must be used for business (or teaching) more than 50 percent of the time on an annual basis. In such case, you are eligible for investment credit. You are also eligible for ACRS accelerated depreciation or the Section 179 deduction.

If the 50 percent requirement is not met, you are not allowed any investment credit, the Section 179 deduction is not available, and you must figure depreciation on the straight line method over a period of years longer than the minimum period otherwise provided for under ACRS. For three-year property the minimum recovery period will be five years. For five-year property, the minimum recovery period will be 12 years. And for real estate, the applicable period is 35 and 40 years.

ADDITIONAL RULES FOR AUTOMOBILES

The Tax Reform Act of 1984 placed ad ditional limitations on investment tax credit and depreciation for "luxury" automobiles placed in service after June 18, 1984. Even if you use your auto for business more than 50 percent of the time and you, as an employee, also meet the "convenience/condition" test, the maximum investment tax credit available is $1,000 per car. And your depreciation deduction is limited to $4,000 in the first year and $6,000 in each succeeding year.

If you elect the Section 179 deduction, the first year write-off amount attributable to the auto cannot exceed $4,000. These maximum limits are reduced proportionately for any personal use.

Example On July 1, 1984, Sheryl purchases a Porsche automobile for $35,000 and places it into service. This automobile is used exclusively in Sheryl's business. The amount of Sheryl's 1984 investment tax credit is limited to $1,000. Her depreciation deduction for 1984 is limited to $4,000. For 1985, it increases to $6,000.

Example On September 24, 1984, Richard purchases and places into service an automobile costing $14,000.

Richard uses this car 40 percent of the time for business purposes. Because Richard does not use his car more than 50 percent in his business, he may not claim an investment tax credit. Also, Richard must depreciate his car using the straight line method over a five-year period.

RECAPTURE OF DEPRECIATION

If, during the current tax year, you sold or otherwise disposed of an asset for which you previously claimed a depreciation deduction, you may be required to recognize ordinary income.

Real Property

If you placed real estate in service before 1981, ordinary income is recognized to the extent of the excess of depreciation actually claimed over what depreciation would have been claimed if the straight line method was used. If the straight line depreciation method was used, there is no recapture for depreciation taken on real property placed in service since 1981.

If ACRS was used for nonresidential real property, ordinary income is recognized to the extent of all ACRS deductions taken. If ACRS was used for 15-year residential real property, ordinary income is recognized to the extent of the excess of ACRS depreciation actually claimed over what depreciation would have been claimed if 15-year straight line was used.

Tangible Depreciable Property

If the asset was depreciable property (other than real property) and you used the accelerated method for depreciation, ordinary income is generally recognized for all ACRS deductions claimed on the asset. [See Form 4797.]

Recapture Of Section 179 Deduction

You must include in ordinary income the benefit you received from any Section 179 deduction for qualifying property that is not used predominantly in a trade or business within prescribed time periods. Generally, recapture will be required if the property was not so used before the close of the second tax year following the year in which you placed the property in service.

INVESTMENT TAX CREDIT

The Tax Reform Act of 1984 significantly altered the rules governing investment tax credit eligibility. These changes apply to "listed" property placed in service after June 18, 1984. The tax law now considers whether the "listed" property is used more than 50 percent for business purposes and whether such use is for the convenience of the employer and required as a condition of employment. [See preceding discussion of Listed Property.]

An investment tax credit, ranging between 4 percent and 10 percent, may be claimed in the year certain qualified property is placed into service. However, you are not allowed an investment tax credit for the portion of an asset expensed under Section 179.

In connection with this credit, qualified property includes:

☐ Automobiles used in a trade or business
☐ Equipment which you use in your teaching position
☐ Most other five year category property used in a trade or business

Property used to furnish a home which you rent out, however, does not qualify for this credit.

Because of 1984 tax law changes, different investment credit eligibility rules apply to property placed in service between January 1, 1984, and June 18, 1984, and property placed in service after June 18, 1984. There are also special rules with respect to automobiles placed in service after that date. [See preceding discussion in Part III.]

If you are eligible for investment credit, you have two options. You can take a 6 percent credit for autos and/or a 10 percent credit for your teaching equipment and other five-year depreciable property. The credit is 10 percent of the cost of the property multiplied by the percentage of time you use the property for teaching purposes. If you select this option, you must reduce the cost of the property by one-half of the investment credit when computing your depreciation and gain/loss on a subsequent sale. Most taxpayers benefit more by selecting this option.

The second option allows you to take a 4 percent and/or 8 percent investment credit and not reduce the cost of the property for depreciation and gain/loss purposes.

Recapture Of Investment Credit

If, during the current tax year, you sold or otherwise ceased using for business an asset on which you previously claimed an investment credit, you may now be required to repay the credit.

In determining whether investment tax credit recapture applies, your first step is to determine how long you actually used the property for business. Then you must compare this to the minimum required period, i.e., three years for automobiles and five years for teaching equipment. If you actually used the property less than the minimum required period, you must now repay part or all of the investment credit. [See IRS Form 4255.]

LIST OF FREQUENTLY USED IRS FORMS

2119 Sale or Exchange of a Principal Residence
3903 Moving Expense Adjustment
4797 Supplemental Schedule of Gains and Losses
4868 Application for Automatic Extension of Time to File
4972 Special 10 Year Averaging Method
Schedule G Income Averaging
Schedule R Credit For the Elderly and the Permanently and Totally Disabled

4 TAX PLANNING FOR EDUCATORS

This part of the handbook focuses upon basic tax planning techniques which you, as an educator, can use to reduce your tax liability. Tax planning is not difficult, and contrary to popular belief, its advantages are not restricted to wealthy taxpayers. The basic principle of tax planning is to control the timing of taxable income and deductible expenses. By doing so, you can minimize the tax consequences of significant fluctuations in your taxable income.

The sections which follow provide straightforward explanations of five tax planning devices which are available to most educators. They are:

- ☐ Shifting income to family members in lower tax brackets
- ☐ Shifting income to a corporation
- ☐ Deferring the payment of taxes
- ☐ Tax shelters
- ☐ Deducting expenses incurred for travel, education and charitable deductions

SHIFTING INCOME TO OTHER INDIVIDUALS

Because of the graduated rate system, it is generally beneficial to shift income away from taxpayers in the higher tax brackets to taxpayers in lower brackets. This is especially true with your children, since they may have little or no other income and may escape taxes altogether. Besides your children, you may support other people (e.g., parents, live-in friends) with after-tax dollars. In many instances you can shift a portion of your income to them and let them support themselves.

Hire A Relative In Your Outside Business

This type of planning is not practical if your income consisting solely of earned wages. If you have an outside business, however, you may be able to hire your children, mother or other relatives to assist you. Most businesses have several routine tasks that can easily be shifted. Children can generally answer telephones, clean, sort mail, run errands, or do light clerical work.

Any wages that you pay to them will be deductible by you and taxable to them. In order for the shift of income to be upheld, these individuals must actually work in the business and be paid only an amount that would be reasonable. The shift will not be successful if it is only on paper. A child must earn in excess of $3,300 ($1,000 exemption plus $2,300 standard deduction) before he or she will owe any income tax. Even if your shifting creates income in excess of that amount, each additional dollar a child earns starts out being taxed at only an 11 percent rate.

Reduce Your Employment Taxes

Besides shifting income tax consequences, payments to spouses and children from proprietorships are also exempt from social security, unemployment and disability insurance. In cases where the owner-spouse is not contributing the maximum amount, this alone can result in a substantial savings, regardless of the income tax consequence.

Example Robert teaches law part time at the local law school, earning $10,000 per year. He also has a private practice that earns $20,000 of net income each year. His wife, Ellen, works part time as his secretary and does the bookkeeping for his office. If she does not get paid for her work, Robert will be subject to a self-employment tax of $2,260 (11.3% x $20,000). However, if the reasonable value of Ellen's services is $10,000, then Robert would only be subject to a self-employment tax of $1,130 (11.3% x $10,000). This yields a savings of $1,130. If Robert's daughter, Karen, can help with the filing and run errands (e.g., deliver documents or purchase supplies) and the value of her services is $2,000 per year, Robert will save another $226 in self-employment taxes. And since Robert is in the 25 percent tax bracket, he will save $500 in federal income taxes.

IRA Deduction

As an added benefit, income shifted to your spouse is eligible to be placed into an IRA. Thus, if your spouse does not have other earned income, this income splitting will allow up to $2,000 each year to be invested in an IRA, further reducing your current income tax liability.

Qualifying Individuals

Income tax benefits can also be gained by shifting income to relatives or live-in friends you are otherwise supporting. Remember, if you are not supporting them, your payments to them will reduce the cash you have available for your benefit. If you do support them, then you are only shifting money to them you would otherwise spend. Although payments to them will be subject to employment taxes, they will generally be in lower income tax brackets than yourself. Thus, you can be supporting them with after-tax dollars taxed at their rates rather than yours. Often little or no income tax will have to be paid by them.

Shifting Income Where No Services Performed

The basis of the previous income shifting techniques has been the performance of services equal to the wages paid by the supported individual. In appropriate circumstances, you can set up a limited partnership, a co-ownership arrangement (for real property), or an S corporation and shift income to people you would otherwise support. In such case, there is no requirement for them to perform any services. However, this income shifting procedure requires you to relinquish ownership of a percentage of the asset or business, since the income recipients must have an equity or ownership interest in the venture.

The required ownership interest can normally be given to the supported party. As a result of the 1981 increase in the annual gift tax exclusion, you can give $10,000 each year to as many individuals as you wish free of any gift tax liability. Your spouse has the same right. Accordingly, the two of you, as a unit, can give $20,000 to each person. Thus, if you have three children, you can transfer $60,000 of income-producing assets to them each year.

Example You and your wife own a duplex that is valued at $90,000. The current annual rental income of $10,000 is offset by annual expenses totaling $3,000, leaving the two of you with a net income of $7,000. You and your wife transfer a 20 percent interest in the property to each of your three children. The value of the gift to each child is $18,000 ($9,000 from each of you). From that point, each child would be reporting $1,400 (20 percent) of income which would be free of income tax.

The same concept allows you to place business interests into an S corporation or a partnership and thereafter make gifts of the stock or partnership interests. Because the income of an S corporation or a partnership is reported by the shareholders or partners in proportion to their individual ownership interest, business earnings can be shifted to your children. But keep in mind that a reasonable salary must be paid to you for any services you perform.

C LIFFORD TRUSTS

A Clifford Trust is a living trust created by you and funded with income producing property. It is irrevocable for a term of at least 10 years or the life of the beneficiary. When the trust's term is up, property in the trust will revert back to you. During the period of the trust's existence, income earned by the trust is taxed either to the trust or the trust's beneficiary, usually a child or other relative, and not to you. When the term of the trust has expired, the proper-

ty placed in the trust is returned to you. In effect, you have transferred the income tax liability on the trust's assets for a period of years without relinquishing the assets forever. Since the rules for establishing a Clifford Trust are complex, you should consult an attorney who specializes in estate planning matters if you elect to use this device.

Using Trusts To Maximize Tax Benefits

If you are supporting an elderly parent or other relative or are concerned about providing for your children's college education, a Clifford Trust may be useful to you. This device is also useful if your financial situation prevents you from making permanent gifts. In general, the trust should not be established to pay expenses which are part of a parent's legal obligation of support.

You should fund the trust with income-producing property. Corporate bonds, cash and certain income-producing securities are generally the best funding choices. It is best to stay away from property which you intend to sell during the period of the trust's existence because capital gain on the sale will be taxed to you, not the trust or beneficiary. To lessen trustee costs, it is best to transfer property which requires little or no management. For example, rental property is more expensive to take care of than cash or securities. Also, by transferring rental property you may be losing tax benefits from depreciation deductions available to owners of rental property.

Income Tax Consequences

The trust income is taxed to the beneficiary (i.e., your child or parent) if the trust instrument requires the income to be currently paid out or credited to this beneficiary's account. If the trust income is to be accumulated in the trust in order to be distributed to the beneficiary at a later date, the trust will pay the income taxes. Since the trust and/or the beneficiary are in lower income tax brackets than you, the creator/grantor of the trust, creation of a Clifford Trust can result in substantial tax savings.

Gift Tax Consequences

A transfer of property to a Clifford Trust is a gift of a right to receive income for the period of the trust's existence. Since the principal reverts back to you, the grantor, upon the expiration of the trust's term, you are not making a gift of trust principal. A gift occurs even if the trustee has the power to accumulate income so long as the income is accumulated for eventual distribution to the beneficiary. A gift of the use of an income from property for a period of ten years is 61.45 percent of the value of the property. Thus, putting $10,000 in a Clifford Trust in order to shift the income to someone else for ten years results in a gift of $6,145.

A gift to a Clifford Trust will qualify for the annual $10,000 (per donee) exclusion if the trust instrument requires that all trust income be distributed at least annually. If the trustee has the power to accumulate income in the trust, the annual exclusion is usually not available. In the case of a minor beneficiary, however, the annual exclusion is available if all of the accumulated income must be distributed to the minor upon his or her 21st birthday.

Valuing A Gift To A Clifford Trust

The IRS provides valuation tables in the regulations accompanying the gift and estate tax sections. (See Treas. Regs. §§ 20.2031-7(f) and 25.2512-5(f).) These tables assume that the assets in the trust will earn 10 percent per year. You can place assets worth $16,274 in trust for each donee (recipient of your gift) and the value of the gift will be slightly less than the $10,000 exclusion. If you and your spouse both make gifts, $32,548 worth of assets can be transferred each year into a 10-year Clifford Trust free of any gift tax.

As a practical matter, you can use the unified credit to offset any gift tax currently due up to the sum of $325,000 as of 1984. In that event, however, the amount of credit available to you, if you make subsequent gifts or upon your death, will be reduced by the amount of gift tax offset. You should also be cognizant of state gift tax consequences since many states do not have exclusions as generous as the $10,000 federal tax exclusion.

Example Fred and Wanda, both university employees, have substantial joint incomes and have enjoyed success in the stock market. They have one child and are supporting Wanda's aged mother. Fred and Wanda are prime candidates for establishing a Clifford Trust. They can transfer securities worth up to $32,549 to separate 10-year Clifford Trusts for the benefit of their child and Wanda's mother without incurring any federal gift taxes.

THE UNIFORM GIFTS TO MINORS ACT

The Uniform Gifts to Minors Act (UGMA) allows you to transfer property to a minor quickly, simply and inexpensively. This can usually be accomplished by simply registering it upon delivery to a custodian of your choosing.

If you are prepared to make an irrevocable gift and do not have any reservations about the donee (recipient) receiving the gift upon reaching the age of majority, you may want to consider the UGMA over a more expensive alternative such as a trust. During the custodial term, the custodian has discretionary authority to use trust assets for the minor's maintenance, support, education and benefit. The property and any appreciation is out of your estate. You no longer pay any income taxes on it and, if the gift was less than $10,000, you never pay any federal gift tax.

Each state's rules as to the type of property that can be the subject of a custodial gift may vary. Generally, all states allow gifts of money, securities, endowment insurance policies and annuity contracts. You should note, however, that, if you transfer an insurance policy on your life and

die within three years of the gift, the policy proceeds will be taxed in your estate.

Choosing A Custodian

Consult your particular state act to find out who can serve as custodian and the documentary requirements for the creation of a custodial arrangement. If you are the donor and die while serving as custodian, the value of the custodial account will be includible in your estate. This generally should not create a problem for federal tax purposes if your estate is currently less than $325,000 ($650,000 if your estate plan has taken advantage of the unified credit) or less than $600,000 (or $1,200,000 if your estate plan takes advantage of the unified credit) after 1987. Again, remember to check your state death tax rules.

Example Betty has ten shares of General Motors stock that she would like to give to her 5-year-old nephew. UGMA is tailor-made for this situation. It is inexpensive and easy to accomplish. Betty can register the stock in her nephew's name and appoint her sister or brother-in-law as custodian. The gift is complete upon the registration. The value of the stock will likely appreciate over time. Any dividends received can be used for her nephew's benefit and will be taxable to him.

INTEREST-FREE LOANS

For the past 25 years, there has been an ongoing battle between the IRS and taxpayers regarding the tax treatment of interest-free loans. The Tax Reform Act of 1984 finally settled this dispute by setting forth a set of very specific rules. While many observers consider the effect of these rules to be a victory for the IRS, interest-free loans today can, under certain circumstances, still be a useful planning tool for you.

Pre-1984 Act Treatment Of Interest-Free Loans

During the aforementioned 25-year period, the IRS asserted that interest-free loans resulted in income and/or gift tax consequences. However, most courts did not agree with this interpretation. In a noted court case dealing with this issue, a corporation controlled by Mr. and Mrs. Dean made interest-free loans to the two of them. In 1961, the IRS asserted that Mr. and Mrs. Dean should have recognized interest income, and incurred income tax liability, based on the value of the no-interest feature of the notes. The U.S. Tax Court disagreed. It ruled that Mr. and Mrs. Dean realized no taxable income attributable to the free use of borrowed money.

The IRS continued to vigorously litigate the issue of whether interest-free loans resulted in income tax consequences. Every subsequent case, with one exception, both in the U.S. Tax Court and the U.S. Court of Appeals, agreed with the decision in Dean favoring the taxpayer.

In 1977, Lester Crown made interest-free loans to 24 trusts for the benefit of his relatives using demand notes could be called for payment at any time. The IRS asserted that this gave rise to taxable gifts from Mr. Crown to these trusts. The U.S. Tax Court disagreed. It ruled that Mr. Crown was not subject to gift tax because the making of non-interest-bearing loans, under these circumstances, was not a taxable event, since the donor could bring back the money at any instant by calling the demand note.

Because of the decisions in Dean and Crown, many taxpayers began making interest-free demand loans. The goal of these loans was to shift taxable income, i.e., the future income which will be realized on the loan principal, from the person making the loan to the person receiving the loan.

Example Mom and Dad, who are in the 50 percent income tax bracket, lend their 19-year-old daughter $20,000 in the form of a demand loan. Daughter, who is in a very low tax bracket, invests the $20,000 into a money market account paying 10 percent. Daughter then uses the $2,000 annual interest to help pay her college expenses. The $20,000 principal remains intact. By using this technique, Mom and Dad have effectively shifted taxable income away from their 50 percent tax bracket into their daughter's very low tax bracket. The net result is that there will be more after-tax funds available to assist daughter with her college expenses.

In February, 1984, there was a major new development in this area. Mr. and Mrs. Dickman loaned large amounts of money, interest-free, to their son and a closely-held corporation in the form of a demand loan. The IRS asserted that gift tax consequences arose. The U.S. Supreme Court agreed. It ruled that these loans were subject to the gift tax, even though demand notes were used. The Court concluded that the taxable gift was measured as the reasonable value of the use of the money lent without charge.

While the U.S. Supreme Court in Dickman held that interest-free loans are subject to the gift tax, the Court did not completely eliminate the use of these loans as an income-splitting device. The Court did not address the income tax consequences of such loans. The effect of the Court's decision was simply to put a dollar limit cap on the size of loans available for tax-free use. This limit is the useful annual gift tax exclusion of $10,000 per donee/$20,000 for husband and wife.

Changes Effected By The Tax Reform Act Of 1984

The Tax Reform Act of 1984 sets forth very specific rules regarding the income tax and gift tax consequences of loans with "below-market" interest rates. Generally, these rules apply to specified demand loans as well as term loans made after June 6, 1984. A demand loan is any loan which is payable in full at any time on the demand of the lender. With respect to demand loans outstanding on June 6, 1984, these new provisions do not apply if the demand loans were repaid within 60 days of July 18, 1984. A term loan is any loan other than a demand loan. Note that any renegotiation, extension or revision after June 6, 1984, will be treated as a new loan.

The new law recharacterizes a demand loan with below-market interest rates as an arm's length transaction. In essence, the lender is considered to have made a loan to the borrower at the current applicable federal rate. [For 1984, the rate is 10 percent.] The lender is also considered to have provided the borrower with additional funds equal to the excess of the amount of interest due, less the interest due on the note as issued. Since these additional funds are treated as a gift from the lender to the borrower, the gift tax applies.

The borrower is treated as though he or she used the additional funds to pay the lender the interest due. Thus, the lender is treated as having interest income and the borrower is treated as having an interest expense deduction. Thus, under the new Act, both the gift tax and the income tax apply to loans with below-market interest.

Exceptions To The New Rules

There are three important exceptions to the new rules provided by the Tax Reform Act of 1984. First of all, there is no gift tax and no income tax consequences if the aggregate outstanding amount of loans between this borrower and this lender does not exceed $10,000. This exception does not apply if the funds were used to purchase or carry income-producing assets.

Secondly, there is no imputed interest income and no imputed interest expense if (1) the aggregate outstanding amount of loans between the borrower and the lender does not exceed $100,000 on any given date, and (2) the net investment income for the borrower does not exceed $1,000. This exception does not apply if one of the principal purposes for the loan is tax avoidance. And finally, if the borrower's net investment income does exceed $1,000 under the second exception, the amount treated as retransferred by the borrower to the lender is limited to the borrower's net investment income for the year.

Tax Planning Opportunities Still Available

The enactment of the preceding rules leaves you with two options. You can structure your loan to fit within one of the three above exceptions. A loan can be made to help fund a child's education expense, to help a child fund a down payment for a home or any other purpose that does not produce income. The second option is to use a Clifford Trust. [The advantages of using a Clifford Trust are discussed in preceding sections of Part IV].

INCORPORATION

The decision regarding whether or not to incorporate a small business is not an easy one. Although there are several tax benefits that may be available, you should review them carefully to determine whether they will be worth the cost of incorporating, and the additional formalities that are required, e.g., holding meetings and filing tax returns. In general, there are several possible reasons to incorporate. One important non-tax reason is the concept of limited liability. If you properly form your corporation and observe all of the corporate formalities, then you will not incur any personal liability to creditors of the corporation for corporate obligations, unless you personally guarantee a corporate debt. To some extent, liability insurance can be used as an alternative for a sole proprietor. In such case, incorporation may not be required to provide reasonable liability coverage.

If you incorporate for liability protection reasons, there is a way to use losses incurred by the corporation to offset your other income. To do so, you must make a timely "S" election for the corporation. This election allows your corporation to be treated very much like a partnership for tax purposes with a "flow through" of the income or losses of the corporation to you, the shareholder. In other words, you report individually on your Form 1040 the results of the corporate business. This is done by the corporation giving you, the shareholder, a Schedule K-1 which summarizes what you must include on your return. Unfortunately, you will not be able to take advantage of most corporate fringe benefits once the "S" election is made. However, this election can always be terminated. If it is, the corporation will then be treated as a "regular" corporation for tax purposes.

It is important to make the election or revocation of election in a timely fashion. They must be filed at any time during the entire year preceding the election or revocation year, or on or before the 15th day of the third month of the election or revocation year or March 15 for calendar year corporations. For new corporations, the election rule is the same. You can make the election to become an S corporation on Form 2553. You must complete all of the requested information and all shareholders must consent in writing to the election.

Example If a business is incorporated and begins its first taxable year on January 1, 1985, an election will be effective beginning with the corporation's first taxable year, provided the election is made within the period beginning January 1, 1985, and ending before March 15, 1985.

Example If a calendar year corporation which currently operates under an S election wants to terminate that election for 1985, it must file its notice of termination at anytime during 1984 or before March 15, 1985.

DISADVANTAGES OF INCORPORATION

Among the disadvantages of incorporating are additional record keeping and reporting requirements, professional fees and employment taxes. A corporation must file its own tax return, shareholders must hold regular corporate meetings and certain additional state and federal forms may be required. There will be attorney's fees to incorporate and accounting fees to do annual tax returns and keep corporate books. In addition, your tax situation will become more complicated and may require additional professional advice. While you may be able to purchase a "do-it-yourself" incorporation kit or do your own tax returns, this approach may wind up costing a lot more than you will save. The help of qualified professionals will pay off in the long run by maximizing your tax planning and avoiding those costly errors that result from inexperience.

An additional negative factor has been the increased amount of employment taxes that you would have had to pay. However, this difference is being phased out, and by 1990, the self-employment tax rate will be the same as the social security taxes required to be paid by the corporation and the employee. For 1984, the self-employment rate is 11.3 percent, while the combined corporation/employee rate is 14.0 percent. If your venture is not making at least a minimum amount of money, e.g., $5,000, the costs and extra work will probably not warrant incorporating for the tax benefits alone.

ADVANTAGES OF INCORPORATION

The principal tax benefits from incorporating include (1) splitting income between the corporation and the owner/employees and taking advantage of the corporation's low rates for the first $25,000 or $50,000 of income, (2) receiving certain fringe benefits on a tax-free basis, (3) taking advantage of the 85 percent dividends-received credit, (4) deferring the recognition of income, and (5) converting ordinary income to capital gain.

Income Splitting

Your ability to split income stems from the fact that a corporation is a separate taxpaying entity which, like an individual, has a graduated rate structure. The first $25,000 of a corporation's income is taxed at a 15 percent rate, the next $25,000 is taxed at 18 percent, the next $25,000 is taxed at 30 percent, the next $25,000 is taxed at 40 percent, and all remaining income is taxed at a 46 percent rate.

Although this graduated system creates a corporate income tax of $25,750 on the first $100,000 of income for an effective rate of just over 25 percent, it is the first $25,000 bracket that may be the most important for you. This is so because a 15 percent corporate tax is often significantly lower than the current tax you may be paying individually on that income. Keep in mind that shifting income to the corporation removes income that would otherwise be taxed at your higher rate.

For example, if you have $30,000 of taxable income, you would pay $4,818 in federal taxes for an effective rate of 16.06 percent. However, your last dollars of income are being taxed at the 28 percent rate so that for each $1 of income that you shift to the corporation, you are saving $.28 of individual tax liability. Based on the corporation being taxed at a 15 percent rate, you would be currently saving $.13 out of every dollar by shifting income to the corporation.

The following table shows the significant amount of

money that can be saved by using this technique:

Business Operated As Proprietorship		Business Incorporated			Savings
Taxable Income	Tax	Taxable Income			
		Individual	Corporation	Combined Tax	
$20,000 ..	$ 2,461	$15,000	$ 5,000...	$2,331	$ 130
30,000 ..	4,818	20,000	10,000...	3,961	857
40,000 ..	7,858	25,000	15,000...	5,815	2,043
50,000 ..	11,368	30,000	20,000...	7,818	3,550
60,000 ..	15,168	35,000	25,000...	9,968	5,200

The benefits increase greatly as a person's taxable income increases and more income is shifted to the corporation.

Fringe Benefits

There are a host of fringe benefits that a corporation can offer its employees. These benefits, which are not available to sole proprietorships, allow you to use pre-tax dollars to cover expenses that you would normally have to use after-tax dollars to pay. The income and employment tax benefits can be quite significant.

Among the fringe benefits available to corporate employees are:
□ Tax-free medical benefits under a proper medical reimbursement plan.
□ Tax-free disability insurance.
□ Tax-free life-insurance coverage.
□ Tax-free death benefit.
□ Cafeteria Plans allow you to use pre-tax dollars to pick among several useful benefits including medical and dental expenses.
□ Qualified Retirement Plans.

The Dividends Received Credit

One additional benefit that is present when corporate money is invested in the stock market is the dividends-received exclusion. This provision allows 85 percent of all dividends to be excluded from the corporation's income. This allows the corporation to invest its earnings without significant additional taxes. An individual taxpayer, on the other hand, is allowed only a $200 ($400 if married) dividend exclusion. Since a mere 15 percent of the corporation's dividends are being taxed at the corporation's 15 percent tax rate, the effective rate of tax upon those dividends is only 2.25 percent.

In view of this significant tax benefit, the 1984 Tax Act eliminated a corporation's ability, in certain circumstances, to borrow money for the purpose of investing in the stock market. Although the benefit remains available for corporations investing on an all cash basis, the dividend income must be only incidental to regular business income. An additional tax will be due and any advantage will be lost if this rule is violated.

Deferring Income

By making creative use of the corporation's fiscal year end, you can defer a portion of your income by simply not paying it out to yourself until after December 31 of any year. This is generally done by having a salary contract which provides for the corporation to pay some or all of your salary to you in January of the following year.

To make this work in the most favorable way for you, the corporation's fiscal year end should be January 31. You can elect a January 31 year end for your corporation by filing a timely first return which so indicates. In addition, the corporation must be on the cash method of accounting since the 1984 Tax Act eliminated this technique for accrual method corporations. A corporation can elect the cash method of accounting unless it is required to keep an inventory as a major part of the business of the corporation.

Example Douglas, who teaches elementary school, has also written several children's books as a separate business which he incorporated in February of 1984. The corporation is on a cash method of accounting, has a January 31 fiscal year end and has earned $25,000 in royalties from its books. It has been paying Douglas a salary of $500 per month since March of 1984, so that Douglas has received $5,000 as of December 31, 1984. Based on his salary contract, Douglas receives $10,000 on January 1, 1985.

On this basis, he will only have to report $5,000 of income for 1984 personally and the corporation will only have to report $10,000 of income, since it will get a deduction for the full $15,000 of payments to Douglas which were made prior to January 31, 1985. The corporation will pay $1,500 of tax on its $10,000 of income. Assuming Douglas' other taxable income (i.e., other than his writing activities) is $25,000, he would end up with $4,818 of federal tax on $30,000 of taxable income for 1984. Adding the corporation's tax of $1,500, Douglas (and the corporation) would be paying $6,318 in federal income taxes. Had Douglas not incorporated, he would have had $50,000 of taxable income and $11,368 in taxes to pay. His current net tax savings by using this deferral and income splitting technique is more than $5,000.

This deferral technique is a one-time benefit since you must report a the bonus as income in the following year. You should also document bonuses carefully so that they will not be treated as nondeductible dividends.

Convert Ordinary Income Into Capital Gains

Under normal corporate income tax rules, each shareholder will have capital gain, equal to the excess of the fair market value of the assets that he receives over his income tax basis in his stock, when a corporation liquidates. The basis a shareholder has in his stock is generally his cost or his adjusted basis in the assets he contributed in exchange for stock.

This rule allows all of the income that has been retained by the corporation to be distributed to the shareholder at capital gains rates. If a shareholder received the retained income of the corporation as a dividend or salary it would be ordinary income to him. Thus, the corporate form has enabled a shareholder to convert ordinary income to capital gain. Since the maximum rate for capital gain is at only 20 percent while the ordinary income rates can be as high as 50 percent, this benefit can be substantial.

Example Wayne, who teaches kindergarten, has operated a mail order business as a corporation over the last ten years. During that time, he has left $10,000 of income in the corporation each year to be taxed at the corporation's 15 percent rate. The money has been invested in a money market account which has earned a 10 percent return after taxes. At the end of the 10-year period, the corporation has accumulated $145,000 in its money market account which it then distributes out to Wayne as part of the liquidation. If Wayne's basis in his stock is $15,000, he will have a long term capital gain of $130,000 which will result in $52,000 ($130,000 x 40%) being included in his income. Even if Wayne was in the 50 percent tax bracket, his tax on those proceeds would only be $26,000. As a result, Wayne would end up with $119,000 of his original $145,000. If he had taken the extra $10,000 of earnings out as salary he would have ended up with only $5,000 after taxes which, if invested at 10 percent, before taxes, would have grown to $65,000. In effect, Wayne has saved $54,000.

TAX DEFERRAL

Tax deferral simply means that you are allowed to postpone paying tax until some future date. It enables you to currently have the use and/or benefit of funds which ordinarily would not be available.

RETIREMENT PLANS TAX-SHELTERED ANNUITIES

As an educator, you are in a very select group of taxpayers who are eligible for a special tax shelter, the Tax-Sheltered Annuity plan. Tax-Sheltered Annuities (TSA) are special retirement plans for employees of public school systems and tax-exempt educational organizations. Frequently, these plans are used by educators to supplement their regular retirement plan.

To be eligible for this tax saving device, you must be an employee of a public or tax-exempt educational institution. To satisfy this requirement, you need not be a full-time employee. If you are self-employed in the educational field, however, you are not eligible. As an employee, you must be performing services, either directly or indirectly, for this educational institution. Thus teachers, principals and librarians are eligible for a TSA plan. Also, in 1973 the IRS ruled that general clerical, janitorial and custodial employees are indirectly performing services for educational institutions and are also eligible for a TSA plan.

Tax Advantages Of A TSA Plan

There are three main tax advantages of a TSA plan. First, you do not pay any current income tax on the amount of your salary that you invest yearly with the plan. Secondly, the interest/dividends earned within the plan also escapes current taxation. Finally, since you control the withdrawal of these funds, you decide the date upon which the funds will be subjected to taxation.

A TSA plan simply postpones the taxation on the amount you invest. At some point, you will be required to pay tax on these funds. However, after you retire your income may be lower. In such case, you will pay less tax because you will be in a lower tax bracket.

How TSAs Operate

A TSA plan can be funded only by contributions paid by a qualified employer. While some educational institutions provide contributions for their employees, many do not. The IRS allows employees to, in a sense, fund the annuity themselves by executing an appropriate "salary reduction agreement." In this case, you authorize your employer to withhold a portion of your salary, up to a specific amount, and that amount is contributed by your employer to the annuity plan.

Example Betty is a high school librarian. Her annual salary is $19,000. If she decides to fund a TSA plan with $1,000, she will execute an appropriate "salary reduction agreement" with her employer. Her salary will then be lowered to $18,000. Her employer will then contribute $1,000 to a TSA plan on her behalf.

You should note that a salary payment which you already received cannot be used for your employer contribution. You cannot defer the tax by returning it to your employer for contribution toward your TSA plan. Thus, it is very important that you execute an appropriate "salary reduction agreement" beforehand.

Types Of Plans

"Fixed" and "variable" are the two major types of TSA plans. Under a fixed plan, a set dollar amount will be paid to you each month or in a lump sum when you ultimately begin to withdraw funds from your TSA account. Under a variable plan, a variable amount, based on underlying investment performances, will be paid to you. There are many variations of these two general plans. You should carefully review these options to select the plan that best fits your needs.

Investment Limitations

Although you can invest your entire salary in a TSA plan, there is a limit on how much you can exclude from your gross income. Generally, it will not be advisable to contribute more than you can exclude from your income since you will be responsible for paying income taxes on those contributions.

Subject to certain exceptions, you may invest up to 20

percent of your original salary (before entering into a salary reduction agreement) in a TSA plan. You can then exclude this entire amount from your gross income. After entering into a 20 percent reduction in your current salary, your employer will be contributing up to 25 percent of your "reduced" salary.

Example Suppose your original 1984 salary was $23,000. The maximum contribution permitted under the general rule set out above is $4,600. This is computed as follows:

$$\$23,000 \times .20 = \$4,600$$

Although the general 20 percent rule should be helpful in determining the amount you can contribute to a TSA plan, the technical rule provides that you may exclude from your gross income only an amount equal to the lesser of (1) the exclusion allowance for your tax year or (2) the annual employer contribution limitation.

Exclusion Allowance

One of the exceptions to the 20 percent rule set out above is the exclusion allowance. This rule takes into account contributions into a TSA plan during previous years. If your past contributions have been low, you may be able to exceed the 20 percent general rule. And if your past contributions have been high, you may not be able to contribute the full 20 percent. If you currently work for more than one qualified educational organization, you are entitled to a separate exclusion allowance for each.

The exclusion allowance for your tax year is determined yearly on December 31. The IRS has provided the following worksheet to assist you in computing it:

Exclusion Allowance Worksheet

1. 20% 20%
2. Includible compensation
   (i.e., your reduced salary) .... $_____
3. Years of service (with this employer) .. _____
4. (1) X (2) X (3) .... $_____
5. Less: TSA plan amounts previously excluded from your gross income .... _____
6. Exclusion allowance (before reduction for any excess contributions) ..... $_____

Example At the end of 1984, Jack, a high school English teacher, had completed three years of service with his employer, the San Diego School District. Although his salary for 1984 was originally $24,800, after executing a salary reduction agreement for $4,800 Jack received $20,000. In the previous two years, Jack's prior salary reductions totaled $7,200. Jack's exclusion allowance for 1984 is $4,800. It is determined as follows:

1. 20% 20%
2. Includible compensation (i.e., reduced
   salary) $20,000
3. Years of service 3
4. (1) X (2) X (3) $12,000

5. Less: Amounts previously excludable .. (7,200)
6. Exclusion allowance (before reduction for any excess contributions) ..... $ 4,800

Annual Employer Contribution Limitation

Under this rule, your employer's annual contribution on your behalf may not exceed the lesser of (1) $30,000, or (2) 25 percent of your yearly compensation, i.e., 25 percent of your reduced salary.

Example Let's now continue the example started under exclusion allowance. As you will recall, Jack's 1984 exclusion allowance is $4,800. The annual employer contribution on Jack's behalf is limited to $5,000. This is the lesser of (1) $30,000 or (2) 25 percent of Jack's reduced salary (25% x $20,000) which is equal to $5,000. The maximum amount that Jack is permitted to exclude from his 1984 gross income is $4,800. This amount is the lesser of (1) $4,800 (his 1984 exclusion allowance), or (2) $5,000 (the annual employer contribution limitation).

The general rule would have allowed a contribution of $4,960 ($24,800 x .20). The general rule does not apply in this case, however, because of the amount of Jack's past contributions.

Alternative Limitations

You can also elect one of three alternative annual employer contribution limitations. These are ways in which you may be able to increase your contributions to a TSA plan despite the limitations discussed above. The three available alternatives are the year of separation from service limitation, the any year limitation, and an overall limitation.

Under the year of separation from service limitation, you may be able to exclude over one-half of your salary from gross income, up to a maximum of $30,000. This election can only be made in the year in which you left your job. The IRS has provided the following worksheet:

Year Of Separation From Service Limitation Worksheet

1. Maximum $30,000
2. Exclusion allowance (modified)
   a. 20% 20%
   b. Includible compensation
      (i.e., your reduced salary) ...$_____
   c. Years of service with this
      employer (limited to 10
      years) .... _____
   d. (a) X (b) X (c) ....$_____
   e. Less: Amounts previously
      excluded from your gross
      income during those 10 years _____
   f. Exclusion allowance
      (modified) ....$_____
3. Limitation on employer contributions
   [lesser of (1) or (2)(f)] .... $_____

47

Example William, a college professor, plans to retire on December 31, 1985, after 20 years of teaching at State U. His 1985 salary, before reduction, will be $50,000. During the previous ten years, William's TSA plan contributions totaled $22,000. For 1985, William wants to execute a salary reduction agreement for the maximum TSA amount permitted under law to be excluded from his gross income.

If William elects the year of separation from service option, $26,000 can be excluded from his gross income. This is computed as follows:

a. Maximum $30,000

b. Exclusion allowance (modified)
   (i)   20% 20%
   (ii) Includible compensation
       ($50,000 — $26,000) $24,000
   (iii) Years of service with this
       employer (limited to 10
       years) 10
   (iv) (i) X (ii) X (iii) $48,000
   (v) Less: Amounts previously
       excludable during 10 year
       period .... (22,000)
   (vi) Exclusion allowance
       (modified) $26,000

c. Limitation [lesser of (a) or (b)(vi)] $26,000

William can exclude 52 percent of his 1985 salary from gross income. Had he not elected the year of separation from service limitation, the annual employer contribution limitation would be $10,000 ($50,000 x 20% = $10,000).

Any Year Limitation

Under the any year limitation, you can raise the annual employer contribution limitation (i.e., 25 percent of your reduced salary) by $4,000; provided it does not result in your contribution exceeding your exclusion allowance or the amount of $15,000. This election may be made for any tax year. Also, it allows you to put an extra $4,000 in your TSA plan each year. However, if this is done on a consistent basis you will find that the exclusion allowance will eliminate your ability to use it.

The IRS has provided the following worksheet:

Any Year Limitation Worksheet

1. $4,000 plus [25% x Includible
   compensation (i.e., your reduced
   salary)] .... $ _____
2. Exclusion allowance
   a. 20% 20%
   b. Includible compensation .. $ _____
   c. Years of service (with this
      employer) _____
   d) (a) X (b) X (c) .... $ _____

   e. Less: Amounts previously
      excluded from your gross
      income .... _____
   f. Exclusion allowance ...... $ _____
3. Maximum $15,000
4. Limitation on employer contributions
   [least of (1), (2)(f) or (3)] .... $ _____

Example Betty is a high school principal with the Erie County school system. In 1985, her 16th year of service, Betty's salary will be $29,000 before reduction. During the prior 15 years, $32,500 was contributed to a TSA plan on her behalf. Under the any year option, Betty can execute a 1985 salary reduction agreement for $9,000, computed as follows:

Step 1 — Exclusion Allowance
1. 20% 20%
2. Includible compensation ($29,000 -
   $9,000) $20,000
3. Years of service 16
4. Multiply (1) X (2) X (3) $64,000
5. Less: Amounts previously excludable . (32,500)
6. Exclusion allowance $31,500

Step 2 — Any Year Limitation
7. a. $4,000 plus 25% of includible
      compensation
      $4,000 + (25% x $20,000) . $ 9,000
   b. Exclusion allowance (from
      line (6)) $31,500
   c. $15,000 .... $15,000
   d. Least of (a), (b) or (c) .... $ 9,000

If it were not for this option, $5,800 ($29,000 x 20%) would be the maximum 1985 TSA plan amount under the general rule.

Overall Limitation

The final alternative, the overall limitation, allows you to contribute an amount equal to the lesser of $30,000 or 25 percent of compensation, i.e., your reduced salary. This option does not consider your previous TSA plan contributions and thus allows you to consistently contribute the maximum amount. This option is most appropriate if you desire to make consistently large TSA plan contributions during your employment with an educational organization. The IRS has provided the following worksheet:

Overall Limitation Worksheet

1. Maximum $30,000
2. 25% X includible compensation (i.e.,
   your reduced salary) .... $ _____
3. Limitation on employer contributions
   [lesser of (1) or (2)]................. $ _____

Example Wilma has been a nurse in the local high school for the past ten years. For 1985, her pre-reduction salary will be $25,000. During the previous ten years, Wilma's TSA plan contributions totalled $38,000. If Wilma elects the overall limitation option, $5,000 can be contributed to a TSA plan on her behalf. This is computed as follows:

1. Maximum limitation on employer
   contributions $30,000

2. 25% of compensation
   ($25,000 x 20% = $5,000)
   ($25,000 — $5,000 = $20,000 x 25%) ... $ 5,000

3. Limitation on employer contributions
   and exclusion allowance — (lesser of
   (1) or (2)) .... $ 5,000

If it were not for this option, the maximum TSA plan contribution allowed would be $4,000 because of the exclusion allowance limitation. This is computed as follows:

Exclusion Allowance Limitation

1. 20% 20%

2. Includible compensation (i.e., reduced
   salary) ($25,000 — $4,000) $21,000

3. Years of service 10

4. (1) X (2) X (3) $42,000

5. Less: Amounts previously excludible ... (38,000)

6. Exclusion allowance .... $ 4,000

Effect Upon Participation In Other Retirement Plans

Your participation in a TSA plan does not affect your eligibility in the educational institution's own pension plan. Moreover, you are still permitted to open up your own Individual Retirement Account. You should note, however, that special rules apply in determining your TSA plan contribution limitations if you are also covered by a qualified pension plan.

Contributions to one TSA plan can be transferred, tax-free, to another TSA plan. This tax-free transfer must be made pursuant to a binding agreement, and you must immediately surrender the proceeds to your employer for reinvestment in another TSA plan for you. You can also elect to roll over your TSA account tax-free into an Individual Retirement Account. However, only certain distributions qualify for this treatment.

Taxation Upon Withdrawal

As a general rule, TSA plan payments received by or made available to you are fully taxable as ordinary income. However, if you have a cost basis in your TSA plan, you can recover this basis amount tax-free. Usually, you will not have a cost basis in your TSA plan. A cost basis would arise if your salary reduction TSA plan contributions exceeded the maximum amount excludable from your gross income, i.e., your salary reduction amount was more than permitted by the tax laws and thus only a portion of it was actually excluded from your gross income that year.

Cost Basis Taxation

If you have a cost basis, the way you will be taxed depends upon the manner in which you receive your payments. If you receive your payments in the form of an annuity, one of two tax rules will apply. If you can recover your cost basis during the first three years, all funds received until you recover your cost is non-taxable. Thereafter, all of your payments are taxable as ordinary income.

Example On June 10, 1984, Kirk retired from his junior high teaching position. Under the terms of his TSA plan, Kirk began receiving $250 per month for life. He received his first payment on July 1. Kirk has a cost basis in his TSA plan of $6,700. This resulted during two years in which his salary reduction TSA plan contribution amount exceeded the maximum amount excludable by law.

None of Kirk's 1984 payments are taxable. In the first three years of his annuity, Kirk will receive $9,000 ($250 x 36 months). Thus, he will be able to recover his $6,700 cost basis. Because of this, all funds received by Kirk until he recovers the $6,700 are tax-free. In 1984, Kirk received $1,500 ($250 x 6 months). Thus, the entire $1,500 is tax-free.

Under the second annuity tax rule, you may exclude a certain portion of each payment as a return of your cost if you cannot recover your basis within three years. You should use the worksheet provided in your Form 1040 instruction booklet, under annuities, to determine your taxable amount.

If you receive your money in a lump-sum payment, you include in income only the portion of this payment that is in excess of your cost basis in the TSA plan. This excess amount is taxable as ordinary income.

CONTRIBUTIONS TO IRAs

Individual Retirement Accounts (IRAs) are now available to all individuals under age 70½ who have earned income, regardless of whether or not you participate in any other plan. You can prepare for your retirement and reduce taxes by contributing up to $2,000 per year of your compensation. The limit can be as high as $4,000 if your spouse has sufficient earned income. The amount you contribute to an IRA plan reduces the amount of your current taxable income. Even if your spouse does not have any earned income, an additional contribution of $250 is still permitted. Thus, the combined total for both of you can now be $2,250. In all cases, however, the maximum contribution for any one person is $2,000.

Once your money is in an IRA it can earn income on a tax-free basis. This allows your money to multiply at a much faster rate than income upon which you must currently pay taxes. Of course, the funds built up in the IRA are ultimately taxed as ordinary income upon withdrawal at retirement. And although there is a 10 percent penalty for early withdrawals, the deferral of the tax clearly can work to your benefit.

For example, someone who contributes $2,000 per year for 10 years in an IRA and invests that money at a 10 percent return will have $35,062 in that account at the end of ten years. An individual in the 50 percent tax bracket would only be able to accumulate $13,207 over this same 10 year period.

As a result of the 1984 Tax Reform Act, IRA contributions for 1984 must be made by April 15, 1985. Under prior law, if you were granted an extension of time to file your return, you were then allowed to make your IRA contribution before that extended date. This is no longer the rule.

CHOOSING BETWEEN A TSA AND AN IRA

As previously stated, educators are eligible for both an IRA and a TSA plan. The following comparison may help you decide which option is best for you.

☐ **Yearly Income Exclusion** Generally, the tax laws allow you to contribute a larger amount to a TSA plan than an IRA. The more you are permitted to contribute, the greater your income exclusion can be. If you can afford to use both, you will be in the best position.

☐ **Early Withdrawal Penalties** If you withdraw IRA funds before reaching age 59½, you are subject to an IRS 10 percent penalty tax on the funds withdrawn. While the IRS imposes no penalty tax for an early withdrawal of TSA funds, many TSA plans have a redemption charge.

☐ **Investment Options** An IRA allows you much more freedom with respect to investment options. For example, an IRA allows you to invest in mutual funds, certificates of deposit and securities.

KEOGH PAYMENTS BY SELF-EMPLOYED EDUCATORS

A Keogh plan is a tax sheltered retirement plan that can be used to shelter self-employment income from tax. The income must have been earned as a result of work actually performed by you. For example, tutoring fees or income from writing will qualify as earned income, but interest earned on your business savings account will not.

Similar to IRA payments, the amount that you contribute reduces your current taxable income. For 1984, you may contribute 25 percent of your earned self-employment income up to a maximum contribution of $30,000. The contribution must be made before the date your return is due, including all available extensions.

An alternate plan to which you can contribute is a defined benefit Keogh plan. With a defined benefit plan, the maximum annual contribution is determined by the amount of funds necessary to pay an annual benefit of a specific amount at the time you retire. The amount of your annual contribution is determined by actuarial computations and depends on your age and current income. Currently, the annual benefit you can receive upon retirement is $90,000. This high benefit amount allows you to put away a lot more than 20 percent of your salary, especially if you are over 40. If you currently have significant self-employment income you would like to put into a Keogh plan, you should contact an attorney who specializes in the employee benefits area.

Example Dave, a part time psychologist employed by a city school district, also conducts a private practice. In 1984, he earned $30,000 from his private practice. Dave can put $7,500 ($30,000 x .25) into a Keogh Plan in 1984. Dave can also place up to $2,000 in an Individual Retirement Account (IRA). In addition, he can even have money diverted from his part-time work for the school district to a TSA.

CORPORATE RETIREMENT PLANS

If you have incorporated a part-time business which you operate, you are eligible to establish a corporate retirement plan. The advantages of establishing a corporate retirement plan include:

☐ The corporation is allowed a current tax deduction for its contributions to the plan.

☐ You, as the employee of the corporation and a participant in the plan, are not required to pay current tax on this contribution.

☐ The income earned by the funds in this plan are also not taxed currently.

☐ You, as the plan committee person for the plan and trust, within the limits of certain rules, can control the fund distribution date and, thus, the time at which the funds may be subject to tax.

☐ As a plan participant in the corporate plan, you will be able to borrow against the plan funds up to a limit of $50,000.

There are many variations of retirement plans which you can establish. It is important that you select and structure a plan which fits your specific needs. If you think a qualified pension plan is for you, you should consult an attorney who specializes in employee benefits.

DEFERRING GAINS BY USING THE INSTALLMENT METHOD

If you are about to sell real or personal property, you may want to structure the sale so that you receive payments over several years. By spreading out your payments over more than one tax year, the Internal Revenue Code allows you to report your gain under the installment method. By doing so, you can defer part of your gain into future tax years.

The installment method is available if you sell any real property, make a casual sale of non-inventory personal property, or sell personal property regularly. You must receive payments in at least one tax year after the year of sale and the sale must result in a taxable gain to you. (The installment method cannot be used to report a sale resulting in a loss.) Unless you can establish that tax avoidance was not a principal purpose for the disposition, your sale cannot be made to your spouse, child, parent or other relative. If you qualify for reporting your gain under the installment method, you must use it, unless you irrevocably elect not to.

Amount Of Annual Gain To Report

The amount you report as income each year under the installment method is determined by multiplying the payment you receive by your gross profit ratio. Your gross profit ratio is your gross profit divided by the selling price and your gross profit is your selling price, less your basis in the asset, i.e., that is, generally, cost less depreciation.

Example In September 1984, Bill sold a parcel of land to Fred for $37,000. The contract called for payments of $17,000 in 1984, $10,000 in 1985 and $10,000 in 1986. Bill originally purchased the land in 1979 for $17,000. Bill must report $9,180 as income from the sale in 1984. This total is computed as follows.

Selling Price	$ 37,000	
Basis	- 17,000	
Gross Profit	= $ 20,000	
Gross Profit	$ 20,000	= 54% gross profit ratio
Selling Price	$ 37,000	
1984	$ 17,000	received
	x 54%	gross profit ratio
	$ 9,180	taxable in 1984

By using the installment method of reporting your gain, you do not affect its characterization as a capital gain or ordinary income.

In deciding whether or not to use the installment method, you must compare the tax bracket you are currently in against the expected tax brackets you will be in when you receive future payments. If you have sold the asset and are receiving the payments on an installment basis, an election not to use the installment method of reporting the gain will require you to pay the tax before you receive all of the money from the sale. Keep this in mind and be sure that you have enough cash to pay the tax. You may need to demand a larger down payment. It is generally worthwhile if you have made an installment sale to report the gain on the installment method, since this defers a portion of the tax and spreads it out to prevent a "bunching" of income.

An important non-tax reason for determining whether you should make a sale on the installment basis (i.e., take back a promissory note) deals with the credit worthiness of the buyer. In certain circumstances, you may be better off making a sale for all cash and paying your tax up front. If you do sell on an installment basis, you always assume the risk of buyer default. In any sale, you should be certain that you have adequate security for the amount you are owed.

Finally, gains under the installment method are reported on Form 6252. An irrevocable election not to use the installment method is made on Schedule D or Form 4797.

The Problem Of Imputed Interest

If your sale results in a long-term capital gain, the IRS may treat part of it as interest. This problem usually arises where the sale contract specifies zero or an unreasonably low rate of interest. If you use a market rate of interest, then your tax will be based on that rate, and no interest will be imputed to you.

For sales during 1984 to unrelated parties, you must charge at least 10 percent interest compounded semi-annually. For 1985 and later years, the rate will be increased based on the current market rate of interest.

Recapture Depreciation

When you sell personal or real property for which you previously claimed (1) a depreciation deduction, (2) a Section 179 expense deduction or (3) an investment credit, a portion of the gain you recognize may be characterized as ordinary gain rather than capital gain. This treatment results from application of depreciation recapture provisions. [See Part III.]

The Tax Reform Act of 1984 provides that all depreciation recapture is taxable to the seller in the year of sale, regardless of whether cash is received. This rule applies to installment sales after June 6, 1984. The remaining gain is still reported proportionally, as payments are received. For all future installment sales, you, the seller, should structure the sale so that you receive sufficient cash to pay any tax attributable to depreciation recapture. If you sell property on the installment basis after June 6, 1984, you must recognize all of your depreciation recapture in the year of sale, even if you do not receive any payments in that year because of the way the sale was structured.

Example Carl sells a computer on an installment basis in September, 1984 for $10,000. He will receive $5,000 in 1985 and the same amount the following year. The computer's original cost was $8,000 and he had claimed depreciation of $2,000. The amount of capital gain and recapture of depreciation deductions are computed as follows:

Sales price	$ 10,000
Less: Original cost ($8,000) less depreciation deduction claimed ($2,000)	6,000
	$ 4,000

Of the total amount of gain, $2,000 (the amount of

depreciation taken) is ordinary income and the remaining $2,000 is capital gain. Even though Carl will not receive any payments in 1984, under the new law he must recognize $2,000 of ordinary income in 1944.

NON-TAXABLE LIKE-KIND EXCHANGES

Under the Internal Revenue Code, a "like-kind" exchange of property is generally non-taxable. This means that any gain from the exchange is not currently subject to tax. You carry over the basis you have in your old property to the new property. Also, any loss from the exchange cannot be deducted. Thus, if you are about to sell property that will result in a large gain, you may want to structure the transaction so that, rather than selling the property, you exchange it for "like-kind" property.

In order for a transaction to qualify for this tax break, there must be an exchange of "like-kind" property. Examples of "like-kind" property include a pick-up truck for a delivery van, i.e., personal property for personal property, or an apartment house exchanged for a store-front building, i.e., real property for real property. The property you traded must have been used by you for business or investment purposes, and the property you received must be used by you for business or investment purposes. Both the property you traded and the property you received must be tangible, i.e., no stocks, bonds, mortgages, notes or partnership interests. And neither the property you exchanged nor the property you received can be inventory, i.e. something you sell to customers.

If you also receive "unlike" property or money, in addition to "like-kind" property, you may have current taxable income. However, even if you do, your current taxable income is only based on the part of the gain that is attributable to the "unlike" property or money. In other words, the part of the gain that is attributable to the "like-kind" property is still non-taxable.

You should beware of exchanges of encumbered property. If the property you sell is subject to an encumbrance (e.g., a mortgage), the property you receive must have an encumbrance greater than or equal to yours or you may end up with gain being recognized.

Example John transfers tangible personal property used in his business which has a fair market value of $300 and is subject to a $200 liability. He also transfers $50 in cash and securities worth $50. In return he receives like-kind property with a fair market value of $250 which is subject to a liability of $50. John must recognize $50 in taxable income, computed as follows:

$200	(relief of indebtedness)
− 50	(indebtedness assumed)
−100	(cash and securities given)
$ 50	(Amount of income recognized)

SALE OF PRINCIPAL RESIDENCE

There are two tax advantages available if you sell your principal residence. The first includes the rollover of the proceeds from the sale of your residence and is available regardless of your age. The second benefit is available only if you have reached age 55. That relates to the exclusion of any gain which you realize upon the sale of your principal residence.

Rollover Provision

If you purchase or build a home which is more expensive than the home you sold and you use that home as your principal residence within two years of the sale of your old home, you will not have to currently recognize any gain on the sale of your old home. If your new home is not more expensive, the gain you will report will be equal to the difference between the adjusted sales price of your old home and your new home. The adjusted sales price is the sales price reduced by expenses of sale (e.g., broker's commissions) and any expenses incurred for fixing up the house to make it more marketable. The expenses must be incurred within 90 days of the sale and paid within 30 days after the sale of the house. If you must sell your replacement home within two years of a prior sale, you may have to report a gain on that sale, unless you show that the sale was necessary because of a job change to a location which is more than 35 miles from your residence.

The tax is deferred rather than completely eliminated. The basis you have in your new home is equal to the purchase price of your new home reduced by the capital gain not recognized on the sale. When you sell your final home, you will recognize a capital gain, unless you are eligible for the tax benefit provided to taxpayers 55 or over.

Exclusion Of Gain

If you are 55 or over, you can exclude, once in your lifetime, all or a portion of your gain on the sale of your residence, even if you do not purchase a new home. If you are 55 or over and do plan to purchase a new home, you should attempt to comply with the requirements and save your once-in-a-lifetime benefit for a later date.

The once-in-a-lifetime benefit allows you to exclude $125,000 of gain on the sale of a principal residence if you lived there for at least three out of five years prior to the sale. This benefit is available only once and married couples get one election per couple. If you and your wife make the election, divorce and remarry, you do not get another election even if your new spouse has never made the election.

Both of the foregoing tax benefits can be claimed by using Form 2119, Sale or Exchange of a Principal Residence, and entering the amounts on Schedule D. You should note that, generally, losses on the sale of a residence are not deductible.

SHIFTING INCOME AND DEDUCTIONS BETWEEN DIFFERENT YEARS

Year-end tax planning begins with a careful review of your present and future financial circumstances. Thus, as soon as possible during the year you should sit down and project your income, deductions and credits for the current as well as the following year. The more accurate these projections are, the more you will be able to maximize the savings attributable to your planning.

One of the more common year-end strategies deals with the shifting of income and deductions between different years. A simple example of this benefit would be a situation where two taxpayers each have $500 of income that they could defer until next year and $500 of deductions they could accelerate into this year. Assuming both are in the 40 percent tax bracket, if only the first taxpayer undertakes the requisite planning, i.e., defers the income and accelerates the deductions, that individual will save $400 in taxes over the second taxpayer ($1,000 x .40 = $400).

One potential benefit of shifting income can be attributed to the graduated rate system in effect today. Although there is much talk of replacing our current system with a flat rate of tax, this change does not appear likely in view of all the special interest groups that would be negatively affected.

The graduated rate system provides progressively higher rates of tax as taxable income increases. Thus, a married couple with $60,000 of taxable income will pay more than three times the amount of tax as a married couple with $30,000 of taxable income.

Equalize Income From Year To Year

Under this type of graduated system, it is generally beneficial for you to attempt to equalize your income from year to year. To some extent, income averaging can offset a portion of the "bunching" effect which occurs when you receive a large amount of income in one year.

Lower Tax Bracket

If you expect to be in a lower tax bracket next year, you should consider paying as many deductible expenditures as possible before the end of the year. In other words, you should make charitable contributions, prepay local property and/or state income taxes and purchase needed business or employee-related items such as computers, typewriters, cars and calculators. Next, you should shift your receipt of any income. Potential tactics would be to defer your billing if you have an outside business, delay efforts to collect rents from delinquent tenants and hold off on any sales of assets.

Same Tax Bracket

If you expect to be in the same tax bracket next year, then it pays to defer 1984 income into 1985. The benefit of deferring your tax liability into the next or future years is very much like getting an interest free loan from the government. By doing so, you can hold onto your money, invest as you wish, and keep the earnings.

Example Mary, who is dean of the local law school, normally makes a charitable contribution to the school in January of each year and that contribution results in a tax saving to her of $1,000.00. As part of implementing her deferral plan, she decides to make that contribution over the next 10 years on December 31 of each year. By so doing, she will have deferred the payment of that $1,000 in tax to the government for 10 years. If, during that 10-year period, she invested that $1,000 at 10 percent after-tax interest, her bank account would have grown to $2,707.04 at the end of the 10-year period. Thus, even after paying over $1,000 in taxes in year 10, she still would save $1,707.04 if she delays her contribution until January 1.

Another benefit of tax deferral stems from the effects of inflation, one of which is reduced "buying power" of money. Therefore, deferring a payment to the future will result in decreasing the effective cost of that payment. The value of a payment made in the future can be determined from a "present value" analysis. Using an interest factor of 10 percent, $1,000 today would be worth only $369.41 ten years from now.

If there is no change in our current laws, the inflationary benefit of deferring income may be eliminated. Legislation passed in 1981 gave a real benefit to taxpayers by requiring the tax rates (as well as exemptions and the zero bracket amount) to be indexed for inflation starting in 1985. The purpose of indexing is to eliminate "bracket creep," which arises when salary increases tied to inflation shift taxpayers into higher tax brackets. As a result of bracket creep many taxpayers have experienced a decrease in their "buying power" despite salary increases.

Higher Tax Bracket

If you expect to be in a higher tax bracket next year, you may want to accelerate income and defer deductions. Careful planning is important here since you must weigh the other advantages from the deferral of taxes very carefully to make sure the benefit of equalizing brackets will pay off.

Example Matthew is currently in the 25 percent tax bracket. Because his wife will also be working in the following year, the couple will be in the 38 percent tax bracket. If Matthew has a $1,000 deduction that can easily be shifted to 1985, he will increase his benefit from that deduction from $250 ($1,000 x .25 = $250) to $380 ($1,000 x .38 = $380). Delaying the deduction corresponds to a 52 percent return on the $250 in this particular case.

Accelerate Deductions

Itemized deductions provide a tax benefit only if you exceed the zero bracket amount, i.e., $3,400 for married couples, $2,300 for singles. If your itemized deductions in the current year will not exceed the zero bracket amount, but they will next year, then deferral is most appropriate.

In order to take any deduction, it must be considered paid on or before December 31 of that year. You can do this by paying cash, mailing a check before the end of the year, or even by using third party credit cards such as VISA, Master Card, or American Express. However, if you use a company charge card (e.g., Sears, J.C. Penney or Mobil Oil), the expense is not deductible until the bill is paid. So, even if you don't have the money currently to pay off the expense, charge it on a bank card.

Medical Expenses

Since medicine and drug expenses must exceed 5 percent of adjusted gross income to be deductible, planning is important. If your current year's medical expenses have exceeded the 5 percent floor, then any additional expense paid before the end of the year will be fully deductible. To accelerate your deductions, you should (1) pay off any existing medical or dental bills, (2) pay any medical insurance premiums that may be due, (3) stock up on any prescriptions drugs you regularly take, (4) purchase any special medical aids or supplies, and (5) consider undergoing any elective medical or dental work that you may have been postponing.

Interest Payments

The tax law provides that prepaid interest is not deductible. However, you should make sure that you do pay any interest that you do already owe, on or before the end of the year. This includes mortgage payments, credit cards, student loans, or any other interest-bearing obligation you have. Remember, interest on funds borrowed to carry tax-exempt securities, or to purchase certain life insurance contracts is not deductible. The limit on deductible investment interest in excess of investment income is $10,000.

Example Joe and Rita's house payment, consisting of principal and interest accrued during the prior month, is ordinarily due on the first of the month. They will benefit by making their January 1, 1985, house payment on December 31, 1984 since they will obtain a deduction for their December interest payments on their 1984 return.

Charitable Contributions

Contributions are easily shifted since you control the payment. All you need to do is prepay next year's contributions this year. You can deduct most contributions, so long as your deductions in any one year do not exceed 50 percent of your adjusted gross income.

Contributions can consist of property as well as cash. If the property has appreciated in value and would otherwise generate long-term capital gain if sold (e.g., appreciated stock), you will be entitled to a deduction based on the full fair market value of the property without having to recognize any of that built in gain.

Professional Expenses And Property Purchases

The miscellaneous professional expenses listed on Schedule A under "Miscellaneous Deductions" provide excellent shifting items. To the extent you purchase professional books, magazines, journals or teaching supplies, or pay membership dues in professional organizations, they are all deductible when paid. For teaching equipment purchases there may be an available investment tax credit or ACRS depreciation deduction. However, new 1984 tax rules for "listed" property make it much more difficult to qualify for these benefits. [See Part III.]

If you can qualify to take a deduction, you will receive a full ACRS deduction, even if the asset is acquired at the end of the year. In addition, you will get the full investment credit, 6 percent or 10 percent of the purchase price, no matter how late in the year the asset was purchased. The sole requirement is that the item be "placed in service" before the end of the year. Both of these benefits can be substantial and should not be overlooked.

You should also consider the Section 179 expensing rules. These rules allow you to take a deduction in 1984 for up to $5,000 of equipment purchases, even though the equipment must normally be written off over 5 or more years. While you lose the benefit of the investment credit by expensing, it can provide you with a "shot in the arm" at year's end that could aid your last minute tax planning. This can occur even after the year has passed, since this election only needs to be made with the filing of your return. Like the depreciation and the investment credit, the expensing option may not be available for "listed" property.

Taxes

Since state and local income taxes, real property taxes and sales taxes are all deductible items, you should consider prepaying these before the end of the year. If you are considering the purchase of a car, boat, motorcycle or airplane, you can add the amount of sales tax paid on these purchases to the general sales tax table amount you are allowed. Closing a sale before the end of the year may provide important benefits.

Defer Income

Although it may be beneficial to shift income into later years, most educators will find this goal difficult to achieve since they have no control over the timing of their salaries. However, if you engage in separate business activities (e.g., consulting, rental properties, writing or product sales), you may be able to defer your billings for services performed or products sold. In the real property rental area, you can set up your rental agreements to provide for the timing of rental payments.

In connection with income deferral, you must be careful with the "constructive receipt" doctrine. This doctrine will consider you as having received income, and therefore being taxable on it, when you have the ability to take control over it. Thus, if a tenant or your employer hands you a check and you refuse to accept it until

January 1, the IRS will consider it received by you when offered.

Interest income can also be pushed into the next year if invested in the right investments. Timing is important here since you will only be able to start deferring your interest income on the date it is invested. Early planning is essential. The most common interest deferral investment is in U.S. Treasury Bills. Treasury Bills are issued at a discount and are payable at their face amount without interest at maturity. You are taxed on the original discount, as interest income, only when the Treasury Bill matures.

NEGATIVE INCOME

While it is not worthwhile to intentionally lose money simply to get a tax deduction, there are certain "tax shelter" arrangements that can give you tax losses that exceed your cash investment. Thus, your paper loss is then more than your hard cash investment. Although your write-off may be as much as three or four times your investment, a great degree of care must be exercised in this area.

TAX SHELTERS

You have made an estimate of your current income and deductions and, despite all your aggressive tax planning efforts, you still find your tax bill higher than you would like. Are tax shelters the answer? If you are in a relatively low tax bracket (e.g., 30 percent) the benefits that you will receive from a tax sheltered arrangement are greatly reduced from the benefits received by a person in the 50 percent bracket. In other words, you will end up with more dollars at risk in such arrangements because you can't use the tax losses as efficiently. Before making a decision to get involved in a tax shelter, it would be worthwhile to consider the benefits afforded by retirement plans. For most educators, Tax Sheltered Annuities or IRAs will be preferable investments because of their safety and certain tax incentives that are built into the law. [See previous discussion in Part IV.]

Although so-called "tax shelters" can be a very effective way to reduce or eliminate your year-end tax liability, the results can be disastrous if the IRS disapproves of the investment. In such case, you will be responsible for back taxes, interest and, possibly, penalties. The IRS has been very aggressive in its pursuit of abusive tax shelters in recent years and has allocated a great deal of time and energy toward eliminating them. Major legislation passed in 1981, 1982 and 1984 all contained substantial provisions, including heavy penalties, to curtail the use of abusive tax shelters.

Although there is no easy definition of the term "abusive" in a tax shelter setting, the IRS will very likely review any investment where the losses that are generated are more than two times the amount of cash

invested. This trend of "hot pursuit" by the government is not likely to change. So, if you do plan on investing in a tax-sheltered investment, you must recognize that your chance of being audited is substantially increased. And in the event you do get audited for a tax shelter item, your chances of having the rest of your return reviewed also increase.

Weighing The Risks And The Profit Potential

Apart from the risk of IRS attack is the economics of the investment. If the investment turns out to be financially unsound, you may find yourself in the position where you would have been much better off if you had paid your taxes. Remember, with the maximum tax rate at 50 percent the most you can lose to the Federal Government in taxes is one-half of your money. A worthless investment could cost you l00 percent of your investment, and if you are required to pay interest and penalties, or if you signed a promissory note that subjects you to personal liability, you could pay even more. Thus, the bottom line in any investment is to make sure that it is economically sound, regardless of any tax consequences.

Cash flow is an important economic consideration. Although it may not occur in the early years, at some point you should receive a distribution of cash from a tax shelter. In some circumstances, shelters can be set up so that future appreciation and tax benefits are the only source of cash flow. Such arrangements, however, are much riskier. In any shelter, and especially large offerings, you should review sales commissions, promoter shares, management expenses and related party fees that may substantially deplete or eliminate any cash flow to you. You should beware of cash flow projections which are unrealistic or based on faulty assumptions or unreliable estimates.

Phantom Income

Another problem with many tax shelters is "phantom income." Phantom income is the situation in which taxable income is created without the receipt of any cash to pay the tax. Phantom income is normally the result of your ACRS depreciation deductions exceeding the principal payments made on any loan. In most tax shelters, income is recognized upon a sale of the shelter's assets. However, the cash that is received at this time may be used to pay off a bank loan. It would be best for you if the shelter partnership is structured in a way that allows the distribution of sufficient cash to cover any tax that is due.

Example You buy into an equipment leasing tax shelter that purchases computer equipment that is leased to IBM. Your share of the purchase price, $20,000, is payable with $5,000 down and a $15,000 note. The note is an interest only loan for five years with the principal due in a balloon payment in year five. The lease provides for the lessee to be responsible for all expenses with the lease payments being equal to the interest due on the note. Thus, there is no cash flow during the five-year lease.

During the five-year period, you write off the cost of the equipment and receive ACRS deductions equal to $20,000. (No investment credit is available because of certain technical requirements in the Code which do not allow investment credit for triple net lease arrangements.) If, at the end of the lease, the equipment is worth $15,000, you end up with $15,000 of phantom income ($15,000 selling price less adjusted basis in property of zero) which you must report on your income tax return. You receive no cash since your proceeds must be used to pay off the bank loan.

This arrangement would have been structured much more favorably if the lease payments had reduced the principal on the loan over the five-year lease period. In this way, you would end up with the same $15,000 of taxable income. However, you would now have cash available to pay all or a portion of the tax. The exact amount of cash depends on the loan balance at the time of the sale.

Appreciation Potential

A third important aspect of the economics of tax shelters is appreciation potential. In other words, is there going to be any increase in value to the asset or rights that are purchased? One way to look at this might be to review the past history of similar assets and hope the future will yield similar results. If there is no history for similar investments, then a degree of risk is added. Therefore, the projected return on your investment should be increased.

Many long-term shelters make economic sense primarily due to the appreciation aspect. Real estate generally fits into this category. This benefit is greatly increased in the real estate area where you can take deductions against your ordinary income. The property can then be sold and taxes paid in accordance with any appreciation, and all or a portion of those ordinary write-offs can be taxed at capital gain rates.

Investment Tax Credit

Another tax-oriented benefit that can add to the economics of the transaction is investment tax credit. In general, most of the benefits of tax shelters are only a matter of deferral. In other words, you get to take a loss today if the venture is successful, but at some point you will probably end up recognizing an equal amount of gain. Although all or a portion of that gain may be capital gain, equal gain will nevertheless be recognized.

Investment credit, on the other hand, can be an absolute tax benefit. In other words, assuming you hold the property for the proper length of time, you don't have to return it later. It is entirely yours and the amount of this credit can be as much as 6 percent for three-year ACRS property or 10 percent for five year ACRS property, of the cost of the property.

Alternative Minimum Tax

Careful planning is required when you are in a situation where the alternative minimum tax will apply. Based on the manner in which the alternative minimum tax is computed, it cannot be offset by losses in other areas of your return. In other words, if you are in an alternative minimum tax situation, no amount of tax shelter losses can reduce that tax.

As a general rule, alternative minimum tax is a flat 20 percent tax on an amount called alternative minimum taxable income, i.e., taxable income plus capital gain deduction, excess accelerated depreciation and disallowed deductions. One general circumstance where this tax applies relates to the taxpayer who has substantial capital gains. For example, if you sold a piece of investment real property at a capital gain of $1,000,000, you will end up paying a tax of approximately $200,000 (20 percent rate) on this gain, regardless of your tax bracket or how many tax shelters you invest in.

Types Of Tax Shelters Available

There are several general categories of tax sheltered investments that are available to you. These include real estate syndications, oil and gas investments, equipment leasing, farming, research and development, motion picture syndications and cable television.

Because of the unique characteristics of each investment, a careful review of the specifics of the offering must be made to determine whether it represents a good investment for you. Any investment, no matter how sound it might otherwise be, can prove very disappointing if you overpay for the asset, the general partner overpays himself or the IRS determines you have underpaid your tax liability.

Probably the key aspect of reviewing any of these investments is to review the credentials of the general partner or promoter. Does he have a track record and is it a good one? Does he have the proper expertise to make the venture successful? Is he charging reasonable amounts for that expertise?

Always attempt to determine all of the ways the promoters/general partners or their affiliated parties are getting paid. If you think their compensation is exorbitant or you want a second opinion, ask a competent investment adviser. Remember, every dollar the promoter takes is coming out of your pocket.

A final point to consider is the reasonableness of the investment. If the investment seems a little far-fetched, chances are you will lose your money. It is generally believed by many competent investment advisers that most good economic tax shelters are sold in the earlier part of the year.

If you are willing to assume the risks, tax shelters may be for you. In any event, you should consult with a qualified investment adviser or a tax specialist before investing. There are a lot of very poor investments being sold under the guise of tax shelters.

IMPORTANT POINTS TO CONSIDER BEFORE INVESTING

☐ Does your tax bracket warrant such an investment?
☐ Is the IRS likely to scrutinize this investment?
☐ Where's the cash?
☐ What are your chances of making money when the asset is ultimately sold?
☐ Is there any investment tax credit?
☐ What are the risks of incurring Alternative Minimum Tax?
☐ Who are the promoters and what benefits are they receiving?
☐ Does this investment seem a little farfetched?
☐ Have you reviewed this with a competent investment and/or tax adviser?

INVESTING IN REAL ESTATE

An ideal investment is one which outpaces inflation, is safe, and is eligible for special tax treatment. Some real estate investments accomplish all three of these goals, while other real estate investments do not.

If the value of your property rises rapidly, you can outpace inflation. And any increase in your investment is actually multiplied up to four or five times because of leveraging. If you made a 20 percent down payment, you have leveraged your investment five times. Thus, your investment rate of return can be very high.

Except for land, the tax laws allow you to depreciate the cost of your real estate investment over a 15 to 18 year period. Depreciating your investment for tax purposes does not cost you any current cash. Instead, it actually saves you current tax dollars. And each month, as you make your mortgage payments, you are increasing your equity in your real estate investment.

Tax Benefits

The three main tax benefits which you can obtain are current deductions, deferral and capital gains rates. Current deductions derive from taking depreciation deductions. As your real estate investment increases in value, you defer paying any tax on this appreciation until some future date. You also have the option of exchanging the property, tax-free, in a "like-kind" exchange. When you do sell your property, a portion of the gain may qualify for very favorable capital gain rates. You may also be eligible to defer part of this gain over several tax years.

Example Barry and Eileen purchased a condominium in January, 1984, for $45,000. They paid $9,000 down and obtained a $36,000 mortgage. On February 1, they rented it to Susan for $450 per month. Here is a list of their income and expenses:

Rent ($450 x 11) .... $ 4,950
Expenses
   Mortgage Interest $4,019

   Real Estate Taxes 890
   Insurance 140
   General Repairs 179   5,228
Balance ....($ 278)
Less Depreciation
   Condominium ($45,000 x 11%) ....(4,950)
Tax Loss ....($ 5,228)

Barry and Eileen were able to depreciate the condominium over a 15-year period using ACRS depreciation. If they had purchased the unit after March 15, 1984, then the depreciation period would have been 18 years.

Barry and Eileen's out-of-pocket cash loss is the $278, plus the portion of the mortgage payments that reduced their principal balance. While the $4,950 is a tax deduction, it did not cost Barry and Eileen any cash funds. Thus, assuming they are in the 35 percent tax bracket and the mortgage principal payments for the year are $200, the $5,228 loss will save them $1,830 and create a positive cash flow of $1,352.

LOSING BUSINESS VENTURES

There are certain rules which determine whether an activity which you engage in can be considered a trade or business for purposes of deducting losses that are incurred. You may have separate small business interests which you pursue during evening and weekend hours. If these activities have characteristics of recreation or pleasure, the IRS will be particularly interested. Their goal is to make sure you are not getting deductions for losses that stem from a personal hobby where no profit motive exists.

HOBBIES

Under the hobby classification, you are taxed on any profit that you make, but cannot report any loss if you lose money. Generally, the hobby rules were meant to apply to activities that could be fun in addition to profitable. Activities that may be challenged by the IRS under the hobby classification include art, photography, music, writing, sports and farming. The list can be much longer than this and includes some undertakings that may not be pleasurable. The real test of whether an activity is a business is whether it was entered into for profit, apart from anticipated tax benefits. This rule can include certain tax shelter arrangements where the economics of the transaction may be missing but certain substantial tax benefits are present.

If you enter into an activity and it does not result in a profit in at least two out of the first five years, there is a very good chance the IRS will want to know more about it. Although start-up businesses often lose money initially, the IRS does not feel comfortable if these losses continue indefinitely.

In determining whether you have a losing business acivity or a hobby, all of the facts and circumstances are to be taken into account to determine if your "profit" motive is present. The nine factors considered most important by the IRS include:

- ☐ The manner in which the taxpayer conducts the activities.
- ☐ The expertise of the taxpayer or his advisers.
- ☐ The time and effort the taxpayer spends in the activities.
- ☐ The expectation that assets used in the activities may appreciate in value.
- ☐ The taxpayer's success in similar activities.
- ☐ The taxpayer's history of income or losses with respect to the activities.
- ☐ The amount of profits which are earned.
- ☐ The taxpayer's finances.
- ☐ The presence of personal motives of pleasure or recreation in carrying on an activity.

THE LEGAL PRESUMPTION

Even if you find that satisfying the above factors may be difficult, there is a presumption that you are engaged in a business if the business has produced a profit in any two of the last five years. By satisfying this presumption, you will be in a better position to convince the IRS that you are not pursuing a hobby. However, a presumption does not prevent the IRS from attacking these losses. It merely shifts the burden of proving the profit motive from you to them. If there are other circumstances, you may still find the IRS after you despite some profitable years.

Your failure to meet this presumption will make your task more difficult since you must prove to the IRS that you have a profit motive. The nine factors listed above will give you an idea of what chance you have of succeeding. Keep in mind, the IRS will be tough to convince if you have substantial losses.

SIX PREPLANNING SUGGESTIONS Preplanning can be very important here. You must consider the above nine factors as you pursue the activity. That extra time, and perhaps expense, can pay off when your day of reckoning with the IRS arrives. Among other things, you should conduct the business in a businesslike manner. This includes keeping detailed records of the income, expenses, assets and liabilities of the venture. Try to separate your business from your personal activities by setting up separate bank accounts, telephone numbers, or renting office space. Make projections showing how you can make a profit, even if it will take years. You should also document your expertise. Talk to experts in the field and/or read extensively if your educational or working background does not support your expertise.

Keep track of the time you devote to both learning about and managing the business. You do not need to put in 40 hour weeks, but 10 to 15 hours of time each week will show you are reasonably pursuing a profit. A diary may be helpful to document this. Indicate any past successes in related or unrelated activities. Having a sound prior track record in business activities shows you can succeed. Your projections of profit and track record of succeeding can increase these odds. Remember, you don't actually have to make a profit if you can show you thought you could make a profit. In all cases, you should make every effort to have some profitable years. This may take some tax planning, e.g., shifting income and deductions, but it will be very helpful, especially if you can meet the two out of five year presumption.

Finally, you must limit or downplay any elements of recreation or pleasure. If there are any non-business aspects related to the activity, they should be kept separate. For example, if your business is buying and selling works of art, you should not be decorating your house with your art inventory.

If you fail, all is not lost. Regardless of whether you make any money, amounts allowable as itemized deductions (e.g., interest and taxes) are deductible in full. In addition, you will be allowed to use your business expenses — regardless of whether you are engaging in a hobby — to offset any income that may be generated by your hobby. Thus, even though you may lose some of your deductions, you should keep good records so that you can substantiate the deductions that are available.

DEDUCTIONS

By using all of your allowable deductions, you can substantially reduce your taxes. The basic rule regarding employment-related deductions is that the expense must be both ordinary and necessary in carrying on your teaching assignments. An ordinary expense is one that is normal, usual or customary in your particular job. It need not be habitual. A necessary expense is one that is appropriate and helpful in developing or conducting your job.

Qualifying Educator Expenses

Educator-related expenses that are considered ordinary and necessary include:
- ☐ Expenses incurred to attend an educator's convention.
- ☐ Membership dues in educational organizations.
- ☐ Subscription fees for journals related to the teaching profession or your specific discipline.
- ☐ The cost of certain teaching supplies which you purchased because they were not supplied by the school and which were needed to carry on your teaching assignment.

Expenses Which Don't Qualify

Educator-related expenses not considered ordinary and

necessary include gifts to students and non-related publications. In one case, Sam Patterson, an elementary school teacher, purchased small birthday and Christmas gifts for students in his class. The Tax Court denied Mr. Patterson's tax deduction, holding that these gifts were not ordinary and necessary in carrying out his teaching assignment. [Patterson v. Commissioner, 37 T.C.M. (P-H) 710 (1968).] Likewise, the purchase of publications not connected with the teaching profession or your specific discipline (e.g., a high school math teacher purchasing People magazine) do not qualify.

1984 Tax Law Change

The Tax Reform Act of 1984 has imposed additional requirements with respect to deductions of "listed" property used by employees in connection with their employment. These new requirements apply only to "listed" property which was placed in service after June 18, 1984. "Listed" property includes automobiles, home computers and related equipment, and any property of a type generally used for purposes of entertainment, recreation or amusement.

You are still eligible to deduct "listed" property placed in service after June 18, 1984, provided that the property was required for the convenience of your employer and as a condition of your employment. Whether the "listed" property was required for the "convenience of your employer" presents a question of fact. In order to satisfy the second part, the "condition of employment" requirement, the property must be required in order for you, the employee, to properly perform the duties of your employment. This requirement is not satisfied merely by an employer's statement that the property is required as a condition of your employment.

If you are required to use "listed" property as a condition of your employment, try to have this condition stated in an employment contract. Inclusion in an employment contract can also help substantiate deductions with respect to the "ordinary and necessary" test stated above.

EDUCATION EXPENSES

Unlike many other taxpayers, educators frequently take continuing education and professional training courses. All of your expenses for these courses are deductible if the education either maintains or improves skills required in performing your teaching assignments or is required by your employer or by law for retaining your salary, status or job.

Example Frank, a high school science teacher, takes a "current developments in science" course. Frank can deduct his expenses since the class will improve Frank's skills and knowledge. This will help Frank perform his current teaching assignments. [Treas. Reg. 1.162-5(a)(1).]

Example Susan is an elementary school teacher. Her school district requires all teachers to earn a master's degree within five years of obtaining their license in order to keep position. Susan enrolls in a master's degree program at State U. Susan can deduct her expenses. The additional education was required by Susan's employer. She was required to incur these education expenses in order to retain her job. [Treas. Reg. 1.162-5(a)(2).]

Example Rita, a junior high school teacher, is required by her school district to take an annual college course to keep her teaching job. Rita takes the course, paying for it herself. Rita can deduct her expenses. She was required to take the course to retain her job. Rita can deduct these expenses even if, as a result of the education, she eventually receives a master's degree and an increase in salary. [Treas. Reg. 1.162-5(a)(2).]

Your expenditures for education will not be deductible if the education is related to a new trade or required to meet minimum education requirements. In the first category, the educational expenses are not deductible, even if you do not intend to enter that new trade or business, and your motive for taking these courses was solely to improve your teaching skills.

New Trade Or Business

A change of duties is not considered a new trade or business if the duties involve the same general work you presently do. Under the tax law, all teaching and related duties are considered the same general work. Thus, an educator can deduct education expenses incurred to prepare for duties which have changed in the following ways:

☐ Elementary to secondary school classroom teacher, or vice versa.

☐ Classroom teacher of one subject, such as history, to classroom teacher of another subject, such as english.

☐ Classroom teacher to guidance counselor.

☐ Classroom teacher to school administrator.

Example Jack, a high school English teacher, will be teaching history classes next fall. To prepare for it, he enrolls in two history "refresher" courses. Jack can deduct his expenses. Even though he changed from teaching English to history, for tax purposes, he is still considered to be performing the same general work. Since he is not in a new trade or business, Jack can deduct his expenses. [Treas. Reg. 1.162-5(b)(3).]

Example Doris, a junior high school assistant principal, has a master's degree. She takes additional courses toward a doctorate which is required for appointment as a high school principal. Doris can deduct her education expenses leading to a doctorate. Even though Doris will now be a high school principal, for tax purposes, she is still considered to be performing the same general work. [Treas. Reg. 1.162-5(b)(3).]

Example Sarah, a high school history teacher, attended law school at night. She does not plan to practice law. She is attending law school because she believes it will improve her teaching skills. Sarah cannot deduct her law school expenses. Even though Sarah does not intend to practice law, her legal education still qualifies her for a new trade or business. [Reed v. Commissioner, 37 T.C.M. (CCH) 1508 (1978).]

Minimum Educational Requirements

With regard to educators, minimum educational requirements mean the minimum total college credit hours or the degree normally required of a person hired for that job. If there are no such requirements, you will have met the minimum educational requirements when you become a member of the faculty. Generally, you will be considered a member of the faculty when you have tenure, your years of service count toward obtaining tenure, you have a vote in faculty decisions, or your school is contributing to your retirement plan.

Example State "A" has a law which requires beginning school teachers to have a minimum of a bachelor's degree, including 30 credits in education. Because of a shortage of qualified applicants, the school district hired Vicki. At the time of hire, Vicki held a bachelor's degree but only 18 credits in education. During 1984, Vicki completed the additional 12 credits in education. Vicki can deduct her expenses incurred in 1984. For tax purposes, a bachelor's degree meets the minimum requirements for qualification as a teacher in State "A." Even though Vicki did not have 30 credits in education at the time she was hired, she did have a bachelor's degree. Thus, Vicki met the minimum educational requirements of State "A" and she can deduct her expenses. [Treas. Reg. 1.162-5(b)(2)(iii).]

Example State "B" has a law which requires beginning school teachers to have a minimum of a bachelor's degree. Because of a shortage of qualified applicants, the school district hired Julie, who had only 90 college credits (3/4 of a B.A. degree). During 1984, Julie attended college at night, completing an additional 15 credits. Julie cannot deduct the incurred expenses. For tax purposes, a bachelor's degree is the minimum requirement for qualification as a teacher in State "B." At the time she was hired, Julie did not meet this requirement. The fact that she was working as a teacher in 1984 does not, in and of itself, prove that she had met the minimum educational requirements. [Treas. Reg. 1.162-5(b) (2)(iii).]

Example Catherine had a bachelor's degree plus nine hours of graduate education when she was hired as a teacher last year. At the time she was hired, State "C" required each teacher to have a minimum of a bachelor's degree. Subsequently, State "C" decided that each teacher would be required to have a minimum of a bachelor's degree, plus 15 hours of graduate education. Catherine then enrolled in six hours of graduate education at night. Catherine can deduct her education expenses. For tax purposes, the minimum educational re-

quirement rule is measured at the time the teacher is hired. When Catherine was originally hired, she met the minimum educational requirements for qualification as a teacher in State "C," since she already possessed a bachelor's degree. [Treas. Reg. 1.162-5(b)(2)(iii).]

A final requirement for deducting your education expenses is that you must have a present teaching position. Thus, you may not deduct the cost of education taken to prepare you to return to teaching. There is, however, an exception to the "present teaching position" rule. If you take a temporary absence from teaching, take education courses, and return to teaching, you can still deduct your education expenses. The IRS considers a break of up to one year "temporary." However, the Tax Court recently allowed an education deduction for a Ph.D. degree even though the educator was away from teaching for three years.

Example Sheldon, a high school teacher, quit his teaching job to take a one year, full time graduate course in education. After completion of the course, Sheldon obtained a new teaching position. Sheldon can deduct his education expenses.

Where a teacher takes a "temporary" absence from teaching, takes education courses, and then returns to teaching, he or she can deduct education expenses incurred. It is the opinion of the IRS that a "temporary" absence is a period of one year or less.

Example During a ten-year period, Robert was both a teacher and an elementary school principal. Robert quit his position and enrolled in a three-year Ph.D. program. After completing the program, Robert began searching for a new position in the education field, although he was not able to find one. The IRS asserted that he was not entitled to a deduction since three years is not a "temporary" absence. However, the Tax Court allowed the deduction. The Court stated that it was not bound by an absolute one year time limitation. The court emphasized that Robert intended to resume his work in education. [Picknally v. Commissioner, 36 T.C.M. 1292 (1977).] In a 1981 decision, the Tax Court allowed an education deduction to a teacher who left teaching for two years to pursue a Ph.D. [Damm v. Commissioner, 41 T.C.M. 1359 (1981).]

If you have already met the minimum requirements to teach in one state and you then move to another state where you are not qualified, any education expenses you incur to meet new qualifications are deductible.

Example Phil, a teacher in New York, holds a teaching certificate in that state. Phil moved to San Diego and quickly secured a teaching position there. However, Phil is required to complete certain prescribed courses before he can get a California teaching certificate. Phil can deduct the costs of the additional education courses because the teaching position in San Diego involves the same general kind of work for which he was qualified in New York. [Rev. Rul. 58 1971-1 C.B. 55.]

Deductible Expenses

You can deduct expenditures for tuition, books, supplies, correspondence courses, lab fees and typing to prepare a paper. These expenses are deducted on line 22, Schedule A. You can also deduct certain travel and transportation costs related to education. You must also complete Part III, Form 2106, to show how the education relates to your present teaching position.

15 EDUCATOR-RELATED DEDUCTIONS

- ☐ Dues — Your membership dues for teacher organizations, societies and your union are deductible.
- ☐ Journals — Your subscription fees for magazines and journals connected with the teaching profession or your specific discipline are deductible.
- ☐ Books — Your expenditures for books specifically used in connection with your teaching assignments are deductible if their useful life is one year or less.
- ☐ Teaching License or Certificate — Your renewal fees are deductible.
- ☐ Teaching Supplies — Your cost for supplies and small tools, which you purchased because they were not supplied by the school, are deductible if they meet the previously discussed ordinary and necessary test.
- ☐ Uniforms and Special Clothing — Uniforms required for your teaching position are deductible if they are not suitable for everyday use and are required for your teaching position. This includes cost and upkeep.
- ☐ Legal Fees — Attorney's fees related to doing your job or keeping your job are deductible. Thus, if you incurred legal fees regarding a tenure dispute or for representation at a hearing, you can deduct them.
- ☐ Job Hunting Expenses — You can deduct expenses incurred in looking for a new teaching job, even if you do not get a new job. Such items would include employment agency fees, travel and transportation expenses, directories, telephone calls and resume preparation fees. If you are seeking your first teaching job, however, these job hunting costs are not deductible, even if you get the job.
- ☐ Telephone Expenses — If incurred for teaching-related purposes, they are deductible.
- ☐ Payments to Substitute Teacher — If you paid a substitute teacher to take your place, you can take a tax deduction.
- ☐ Entertainment Expenses — You may deduct entertainment expenses if you incurred them as a representative of your school or if they were directly related to your position. The tax law requires that you keep records and that records are supported by receipts. For 1985, these records must be prepared at the time of your expenditure.
- ☐ Performance Bond Fees — If you were required to post a performance bond during sabbatical leave, you can deduct the fee.
- ☐ Research Expenses of a College Professor — The IRS has ruled that research and related expenses, including travel costs, incurred by a college professor for the purpose of teaching, lecturing, or writing and publishing in his or her area, are deductible.
- ☐ Home Office Deduction — If you are an employee of a school system, you generally cannot deduct any expenses for maintaining an office in your home. However, if you are also self-employed and run a part time business out of your home, you may qualify for the deduction.
- ☐ Teaching Equipment — If you use equipment to assist you in carrying out your teaching assignments, you may be able to deduct it. Examples of such teaching equipment include reference books, musical instruments, camera equipment, audio-visual equipment, tape recorders, movie projectors, typewriters, microscopes and home computers.

1984 Tax Law Change

The Tax Reform Act of 1984 has imposed new depreciation and investment tax credit elegibility rules. These rules apply to "listed" property, including automobiles, home computers and related equipment, and any property of a type generally used for purposes of entertainment, recreation or amusement. This would seem to include camera equipment, audio-visual equipment, tape recordes and musical instruments. The new law considers whether the "listed" property is used more than 50 percent for business purposes and whether such use is for the convenience of the employer and required as a condition of employment.

Example Steve is a science teacher. He subscribes to "The Instructor" magazine, as well as to a scientific journal. Steven can take a tax deduction. The magazines are used by Steve to improve his teaching skills and knowledge. [Treas. Reg. 1.162-6.]

Example During the year Alice, a public school teacher, spent $125 for educational supplies which she used in the classroom. Unfortunately, Alice did not save her receipts. The Tax Court allowed Alice to take the deduction. The Court stated that, although Alice provided no documentation, her testimony as to the amount and its reasonableness was credible enough. [Gudmundsson, 37 T.C.M. 1249 (1978).]

Example Burnice is a high school science teacher. During the year, she purchased two lab coats which she wears exclusively in the school lab. Burnice can deduct both the cost and the cleaning of the lab coats. The coats were purchased for use in the school lab and they are not adaptable to everyday general wear. [Treas. Reg. 1.162-6.]

Example Mary is a teacher. In trying to secure a new teaching position in another city, Mary incurred expenses for preparing her resume, long distance telephone calls and airfare to this city for an interview. Even though Mary did not get the job, she is still entitled to take a tax deduction. Since Mary already had a teaching job, she is entitled to deduct her expenses in seeking a new teaching job, even though she did not get the new position. [Rev. Rul. 16, 1977-1 C.B. 37.]

Example Susan recently received a B.A. degree. She incurred $175 in job hunting expenses, trying to secure her first teaching job. Susan was successful and next month she will begin teaching at the local high school. Susan cannot take a $175 tax deduction. Even though Susan obtained a teaching job, she is still not permitted to take a deduction because this was her first teaching position.

Example Bill is a teacher in a small private school. It was Bill's turn to hold the school's PTA meeting in his home. Bill incurred $117 in expenses for food. Bill can take a deduction for entertainment. The PTA meeting was directly related to Bill's teaching responsibilities. Note, however, that the tax law requires Bill to keep a record of his expenses, a listing of who attended the PTA meeting, and to save his receipts. For 1985, Bill's records must be prepared at the time of the meeting. [I.R.C. §§162 and 274.]

Example Nancy, a professor at the local university, was required to publish a scholarly research paper in order to be considered for tenure. She incurred expenses in researching and writing the article. Nancy can take a tax deduction. The IRS has ruled that Nancy is entitled to deduct her expenses. [Rev. Rul. 275, 1963-2 C.B. 85.]

MISCELLANEOUS DEDUCTIONS

☐ Tax Counsel and Assistance Fees — The cost of this tax manual, as well as any fees paid to someone for tax advice or for preparing your income tax returns, are deductible.

☐ IRA Fees charged by banks or financial institutions are deductible.

☐ Investment Counseling Fees, as well as financial investing books and publications are deductible.

☐ Safe Deposit Box Rental Fees are deductible if you keep stocks, bonds or other investment-related papers and documents in them.

☐ Adoption Expenses — You can deduct up to $1,500 of qualified adoption expenses if you legally adopt a child with "special needs" as described in the Social Security Act Adoption Assistance Program and as determined by your state.

☐ Expenses of Producing Income — You can deduct any expenses you paid to produce or collect taxable income.

☐ Gambling Losses are deductible to the extent of gambling winnings you reported on line 22, Form 1040.

Example Michael opens an IRA account at his bank and the bank charges him a fee of $15. Since the IRS has recently announced that IRA fees charged by banks or financial institutions are deductible, Michael can deduct the $15.

Example Sheryl, who owns stocks in several companies, subscribes to the Wall Street Journal so she can follow their progress. Sheryl can deduct her subscription fees. [I.R.C. §212.]

Example Betty pays an attorney $125 to assist her in collecting back alimony. Betty can deduct the $125. You can deduct any expenses you paid to produce or collect taxable income. Since the alimony payments are taxable to Betty, she can deduct her expenses.

Example Jim occasionally goes to the local race track. One day he won $485 on the daily double. While the $485 is taxable income to Jim, he can deduct his race track losing bets, but not more than his total gambling winnings. [I.R.C. §165(d).]

SPECIAL TAX DEDUCTIONS FOR HOMEOWNERS

If you own a home, are about to buy a home or are about to build a home, you should consider these special tax deductions. If you are a homeowner, you are allowed a Schedule A deduction for interest and real estate taxes paid. If you own a condominium, you can deduct mortgage interest payments. You can also deduct real estate taxes on (1) your separate dwelling unit, (2) any other separate interest you own (e.g., storage or parking), and (3) your interest in the structure and land that is owned in common. And if you are a tenant-stockholder in a co-op, you can deduct, on your Form 1040—Schedule A, your proportionate share of interest and real estate taxes paid by the co-op corporation.

Tax-Free Rental Income

Under a special provision of the Internal Revenue Code, if you rent out your residence or vacation home for up to 14 days per year, you do not have to include this income in your tax return. Thus, you can receive 14 days of rental income tax-free each year. With regard to this year's rental period, your deductions for expenses are limited to real estate taxes, interest and casualty losses.

Example Phil and Arlene own a vacation home in a recreational area. During 1984, they rented this home to third parties for six days at Easter and seven days at Christmas. They received $1,300 in rent. They also made repairs to the home at a cost of $2,000, paid interest on their mortgage of $4,800, and real property taxes of $1,500.

Since Phil and Arlene rented their vacation home for only 13 days, none of the $1,300 is taxable to them. Additionally, they can deduct their interest payments and real property taxes on Schedule A. The repair expenses, however, are not deductible.

Home Office Deduction

If, in addition to your teaching position, you operate a part-time business in your home, you may be able to deduct part of the operating expenses and depreciation on your home. In order to qualify for these deductions, a specified part of your home must be regularly and exclusively used for business purposes, and the home office must be your principal place of conducting that business. An exception to the second requirement is applicable where the home office is a separate structure not attached to your home or the home office is used by your patients, clients or customers to meet or deal with you in the normal course of your trade or business. If you do not have a second business (i.e., something besides your classroom teaching job), it is likely that home office expenses will not be deductible because your principal place of business is school, not your home office.

Exclusive And Regular Requirement You must set an identifiable area of your home aside for the office and use it regularly. It does not have to be an entire room and a lack of physical separation between your office and the rest of the room will not jeopardize the deduction if you can establish that the area is used only for your business activity.

Principal Place Requirement This requirement can be satisfied if you are conducting another trade or business in addition to your employment in the educational field. You cannot claim a deduction if your secondary business activity centers around the management of your investments. You must be able to demonstrate active involvement in a trade or business.

Deductible Expenses If you qualify, you can deduct a pro rata share, based on the percentage of the home used for business, of the expenses attributable to the maintenance and upkeep of your home. Deductible expenses include electricity, gas, heating fuel, water, sanitation service, cleaning, repairs, insurance premiums, mortgage interest and property taxes. If you own your home, you can deduct an allowance for depreciation of the portion of your home devoted to the home office. And if you rent your home, you can deduct a portion of the rent.

There is a limitation on the deductibility of these home office expenses. The expenses you deduct cannot produce a loss for your business. After deducting business expenses other than home office expenses from your business income, you can proceed to deduct home office expenses, starting with interest and taxes, then operating expenses such as repairs, utilities, insurance, cleaning, and finally, depreciation. The total expenses, however, may not exceed business income. If you deduct interest and taxes attributable to your home office on Schedule C, only the portion of interest and taxes not previously deducted on Schedule C can be deducted on Schedule

A, Itemized Deductions. Also, if you move to a new home, do not overlook deducting the costs of moving your office.

Example Ralph operates a consulting business out of his home. His office is set up in a spare room which he regularly uses exclusively in his consulting business. His house has eight rooms and the office takes up 75 square feet of his 2,000 square foot house. To determine the percentage of Ralph's expense deduction for the office use of his home, the first step is to determine the pro rata business use of the home. One method of doing this is to divide the area of the entire home by the area occupied by the home office — 75/2000 = 3.8%. An alternate method is to divide the number of rooms in the house by the number of rooms occupied by the home office — 1/8 = 12.5%. This method is available where the rooms in the home are approximately the same size.

The second step is to determine the total housing expenses. In this example they would be computed as follows:

Depreciation of area attributable to home office	$2,000
Gas and electric bills	1,200
Repairs	1,000
Property Insurance	$ 500
Interest	1,500
Taxes	1,500
Cleaning	800
	$8,500

The final step is to multiply this amount ($8,500) by the business use percentage (3.8%) determined in Step 1. The net result is the home office deduction.

RESIDENTIAL ENERGY CREDITS

A tax credit of 15 percent is allowed on the first $2,000 you spend on "qualified" items to save energy in your home. Also, a tax credit of 40 percent is allowed on the first $10,000 you spend for solar, wind and geothermal energy items that heat or cool your principal residence or provide hot water or electricity for it.

Example During 1984, Larry insulated the attic in his home. He had been living in this home since 1976. Larry also installed storm windows and doors. He purchased these windows and doors new. They are expected to last seven to ten years. The total cost of these items was $1,400. Larry can claim a 1984 tax credit of $210 ($1,400 x 15% = $210).

DEDUCTIBLE HOME PURCHASE AND CONSTRUCTION EXPENSES

If you will be required to pay points or loan origination fees on a mortgage for the purchase of your principal residence, you can deduct the total amount in the year you buy the home. After you become a homeowner, you can take a Schedule A deduction for mortgage interest paid and real estate taxes paid.

If you decide to buy a home, make a commitment to record all future home improvement expenditures. While these expenditures are not currently deductible, you are permitted to increase your income tax basis and thus lower your gain when you eventually sell the home.

If you will be the general contractor for the construction of your principal residence, you may qualify for two special tax deductions. First, you are permitted to deduct the interest on your construction loan on your Schedule A. Secondly, you can deduct the sales tax paid on building materials.

OBTAINING THE FULL TAX BENEFITS FROM CHARITABLE CONTRIBUTIONS

You can deduct charitable contributions to qualified organizations. In most cases, you may deduct up to 50 percent of your adjusted gross income. Although, in certain cases, the deduction is limited to 20 or 30 percent, the tax benefits can be substantial.

By adhering to a few simple guidelines, you can be sure that you will never forget to take a charitable contribution deduction; and you will be able to substantiate your deductions to the IRS if you are ever required to do so. The first rule is to retain your cancelled checks for a minimum of three years. Secondly, you should record all cash contributions in a diary. Substantiating cash contributions to the satisfaction of the IRS is difficult. You have a much better chance of succeeding if you keep a contemporaneous written record.

Next, you should obtain written receipts from charities. Banks have been known, on occasion, to misplace cancelled checks. By obtaining a written receipt, you are establishing additional proof of your contribution. You should also list all property donated to charity. Many educators donate used clothing and other used property to charity. By making a list of such items and their fair value at the time of your donation, you can be sure to obtain the full tax benefits from such contributions.

Finally, you should record out-of-pocket expenses and transportation mileage while doing charitable work in a diary. While you are not permitted to deduct the estimated value of your volunteered services, you may deduct out-of-pocket costs of supplies, postage and uniforms. Transportation is deductible at 9 cents per mile (12 cents per mile in 1985) plus parking and tolls. You can also deduct meals and lodging if you are away from home.

If your taxable income has a tendency to be high one year and low another, you will obtain a greater tax benefit by saving up your contributions and making them in the year you are in the higher tax bracket. Contribution deductions are allowed only in the year you pay them, regardless of when they were pledged. However, if you made a contribution using your credit card during the year, it is currently deductible, even if you did not pay the credit card company until January of the following year.

Double Tax Benefit

If you contribute stocks, securities, real estate, or other similar items which increased in value during the time you owned them, and you held them for the minimum period required for long term treatment, you will derive a double tax benefit. Your contribution deduction will be the full appreciated fair market value; and the appreciation in value during the time you owned it will completely escape taxation.

Example On April 13, 1984, Ed and Mary contributed 200 shares of ABC stock to the American Cancer Society. They acquired the stock in 1982. The 200 shares originally cost them $1,200. At the time of their donation, the stock was worth $9,750.

Their contribution deduction is $9,750, the full appreciated fair market value of the shares contributed. And the $8,550 appreciation in value during the time they owned the stock ($9,750—$1,200 = $8,550) will completely escape taxation.

Because of 1984 tax law changes, there are two different minimum holding periods required for long term treatment. Property acquired before June 22, 1984, must be held for one year. Property acquired after that date need only be held for six months before it qualifies for long term capital gains treatment.

If you own stocks, securities, real estate or other similar items which decreased in value during the time you owned them, and you owned them for the minimum period required for long term treatment, such property should not be contributed to charity. Instead, you should sell the asset to obtain a tax loss and then contribute the sales proceeds to the charity.

If you pay more than fair market value to a qualified organization for tickets (e.g., tickets for fundraising show/sporting event), or goods (e.g., box lunch at church event), you may deduct the excess amount as a contribution.

Example Richard purchased two tickets to a concert. Because this was a special fundraiser and proceeds went to the American Heart Association, the tickets cost $300, instead of the usual $50. Richard can take a contribution deduction of $250.

New Appraisal Requirements For 1985

Beginning with the 1985 tax year, you will have to obtain a written appraisal if you contribute to charity a single item of property in excess of $5,000 or $10,000 in the case of stock not publicly traded. This appraisal must be written, contain a description of the property, contain the fair market value of the property, be performed by a qualified appraiser, contain the qualifications of the appraiser, be signed by the appraiser, and be attached to your return. The donee (recipient) will be required to report to the IRS any disposition of donated property with a value in excess of $5,000 which is made within two years of the date of transfer.

DEDUCTION FOR TRAVEL AND TRANSPORTATION EXPENSES

You, as an educator, are in an especially unique position when it comes to deducting travel and transportation expenses, since traveling, in many instances, can be a form of education. If your travel is directly related to your duties as an educator and is for the purpose of maintaining or improving your skills, you can deduct unreimbursed expenses from gross income, even if you do not itemize. The mere fact that you derive personal satisfaction from the travel will not jeopardize the deduction so long as you keep records and can establish the direct relationship with your work.

For purposes of this deduction, transportation is the cost of getting from one place to another, e.g., by airplane, bus, cab or automobile. Travel expenses, on the other hand, include living costs in addition to transportation expenses. Living costs can be meals, lodging, baggage charges, cleaning and laundry expenses, business telephone calls and tips. Living costs are only deductible if you are away from home overnight. If you are not away from home overnight, only your transportation expenses are deductible.

Travel To Obtain An Education

Travel and transportation expenses relating to your duties as an educator, and primarily for the purpose of maintaining or improving your skills, are deductible. You are entitled to select an institution which best serves your needs. The mere fact that attendance at the institution of your choice is more expensive than if you attended another will not jeopardize the deductibility of your expenses. This rule also applies if you decide to attend a university located outside of the United States. If you travel to a distant place while on sabbatical leave in order to study or do research in your field, your travel costs will be deductible.

If you attend courses at night school, you may deduct transportation expenses incurred in traveling between your job and school. However, you cannot deduct transportation costs to a course on a non-working day. The same rules apply to trips to the library.

Example Clark travels from the high school where he teaches to a local college where he is taking a course related to his teaching. Clark's costs of transportation from work to the college where the course is offered are deductible. Since the course is related to his teaching, it serves a business purpose. [Carlucci v. Commissioner, 37 T.C. 695 (1962).]

Example John is an English professor at a college in the South. During his summer vacation he attends an English course at a California university. John can deduct his expenses if he took the course to improve or maintain his teaching skills, and it was the primary reason for his trip to California. He can deduct his transportation costs to California and living costs while attending the course.

Travel As A Form Of Education

The act of traveling itself can be a form of education if your trip is properly planned. Be prepared to show a direct relationship between your travel and skills required in your teaching position. The major portion of your travel activities must be of a type which maintains or improves the skills required for your job. It is not sufficient that the primary purpose of the trip was business related.

Example Sally, a Spanish teacher, spends one month each summer traveling through Mexico. She tours historic sites and museums. She stays in the homes of Mexican teachers and works hard to improve her knowledge of Mexico and her language skills. Her travel expenses are probably deductible in full. [Smith v. Commissioner, 36 T.C. Memo 1407 1967.]

Transportation Expense To A Second Job

If you travel from one job location to another within the same day, be sure to deduct transportation expenses incurred for travel between your two jobs. The costs of going from your residence to your first job and the costs of returning home from the second job are non-deductible commuting costs. If you go home between jobs, the cost of going to your second job from home is a non-deductible commuting cost. An exception to this rule is available if you travel to a job location outside the general area of your principal place of work.

Example Jack, a high school science teacher, frequently arranges for field trips to local museums. He will often take several students in his car. Jack can deduct his expenses. He is traveling to a second job location and can deduct the costs of transportation between school and the museums. [Gudmundsson v. Commissioner, 37 T.C. Memo 1249 1978.]

Example Sylvia works as an elementary school teacher Monday through Friday. On Saturdays she works in her father's shoe store. Sylvia cannot deduct the transportation expenses to her second job because she is not traveling between two jobs in the same day. Commuting costs are non-deductible.

Travel To A Temporary Job Away From Home

You may deduct travel expenses to your temporary job away from home if you can establish that the job will end within a reasonably short time, generally one year. The purpose of this rule is to eliminate the hardship of maintaining homes in two places. If your job is temporary, you can also deduct your living expenses and commuting costs between your lodging and work. Trips back and forth between your principal residence and temporary home are also deductible.

Example Ted, a political science professor at a Wisconsin university, accepts a 6-month position as a Congressional aide in Washington, D.C. Ted can deduct his transportation costs to and from Washington, his living costs while residing in Washington and his costs of commuting from his Georgetown apartment to Capitol Hill. His family expenses are non-deductible.

Travel To Professional Meetings

All travel and living costs while attending conventions or seminars that require you to remain away from home overnight, and which are directly connected with your profession, are deductible.

Seeking New Employment

You may deduct travel expenses if your trip had, as its primary focus, the seeking of new employment in your current profession.

Example Betty, a high school principal in the midwest, traveled to Oregon for a job interview for a similar position. She did not get the job. Betty is currently employed and her travel and transportation expenses incurred in seeking new employment in a similar position are deductible even though she was unsuccessful. [Rev. Rul. 16, 1977-1 CB 37.]

Accompaniment By Spouse Or Family Members

Ordinarily, travel expenses of family members accompanying you on your business travel will not be deductible unless you are able to establish a bona fide business purpose for their presence. However, the mere fact that family members accompany you will not compromise your deduction. If you take along a family member, you are not required to split expenses equally among all family members. You can deduct the full amount of what it would have cost you to travel alone. Only the incremental amount attributable to the companionship of a family member is not deductible.

Example Melissa travels to Hawaii for a teacher's convention and takes her husband along. The room rate is $90 per night for a single and $100 per night for double occupancy. Melissa can deduct the $90 per day cost of the room.

Combined Business And Pleasure Travel

If your domestic trip was primarily for business reasons, travel expenses other than those specifically connected with personal activities are deductible. To determine whether business or pleasure was the primary purpose of the trip, look at the length of time spent on each. Even if business was not the primary reason for your trip, your non-travel business expenses may be deductible as an itemized deduction on Schedule A or as a business deduction on Schedule C, Profit or Loss From Business.

If you travel outside the United States for a week or less, or if you traveled for longer than one week and spent less than 25 percent of the time on non-business activities, you may deduct all of your transportation costs and your travel expenses attributable to business activities. [I.R.C. $_2$274(c).] If your trip lasted more than one week and you spent more than 25 percent on personal activities, you may deduct only in proportion to the time spent on business.

Example Janet traveled to New York to attend a week-long teachers' convention. Her husband accompanied her. After the convention was over they spent three days driving around upstate New York. Janet's round trip transportation costs between her home and New York City are deductible as are her living expenses while in the city. Her husband's expenses and the expenses of their side trip are not deductible.

Example Larry traveled to Paris primarily to attend a six-week course at the Sorbonne. When not in class he toured the city on sightseeing trips which supplemented his course work. After the course ended, he returned home. Larry's traveling expenses, including meals and lodging, are deductible if he spent less than 25 percent on personal activities while in Paris. If he spends more than 25 percent on personal activities he must allocate his expenses between business and non-business activities.

The Importance Of Current And Complete Records

You should retain your receipts and maintain, on a current basis, a diary of travel related expenses that identifies the date, type of expense, amount and business purpose for the expense.

The Tax Reform Act of 1984 imposes more stringent record keeping rules with respect to travel expenses. Under the old rules you were required to keep adequate records to substantiate your travel deductions. If you did not have adequate records, you could offer other corroborating evidence. Beginning in 1985, the new Act requires that your travel expense deductions be supported by adequate records that are made at the time that travel expenses are incurred.

The IRS gives you the option of using a per diem deduction for the cost of meals consumed on business trips. You may use the per diem rate in lieu of keeping track of your actual expenses. However, you still have to keep track of time, place and business purpose of the travel. For travel during 1984, the per diem meal allowance for a stay of less than 30 days in one general locality is $14 per day and $9 per day for a stay requiring 30 days or more in one locality. Clearly, it is to your advantage to keep records of actual expenses because the per diem allowances are low.

AUTO EXPENSES

If you use your car in your secondary self-employment business or in your primary job, you are entitled to a deduction for expenses relating to the business use of your car. There are two methods of figuring the amount of your deduction. You may use a standard mileage rate of 20.5 cents per mile, provided your car is not fully depreciated, for the first 15,000 miles of business use. After 15,000 miles and for all mileage if the car is fully depreciated, the rate is 11 cents per mile. This standard mileage rate may be used in lieu of calculating actual operating costs. However, you may deduct the business portion of automobile interest, state and local taxes, parking fees, tolls and available investment credit in addition to the standard mileage rate. If you use the standard mileage rate, you may not use the Accelerated Cost Recovery System for depreciation purposes.

Example Linda has driven her car over 19,000 miles in connection with her business. After the first 15,000 miles of business use, Linda must use a rate of 11 cents per mile.

If you use the standard mileage rate you must estimate the useful life of your auto. Next, you can calculate the applicable percentage for that useful life. The following table will assist you in making the required calculations.

Estimated Useful Life	Percent
Less than 3 years	0
3 years, but less than 5	33⅓
5 years, but less than 7	66⅔
7 or more years	100

Example Lisa buys a new car in 1984 for $10,000. She uses the auto 75 percent of the time in her business. During 1984, she drove the car 7,500 business miles and a total of 10,000 miles. Based on her experience, she estimates the useful life of the car to be four years. Lisa can take a deduction of $1,538 and an investment credit of $250, computed as follows:

Deduction: 7,500 miles x 20½ cents = $1,538

Investment Credit

$10,000 x 33⅓%	(percentage is based on estimated useful life)	= $3,333
$ 3,333 x 75%	(Percentage of business use)	= 2,500
$ 2,500 x 10%	(investment credit rate) . .	= $ 250

You can also compute the actual cost of operating your car and deduct the pro rata portion attributable to business use of your auto. If you use more than one vehicle in your business, you must figure your deductible costs using the actual expense method. Actual costs include gas and oil, repairs, insurance, car wash expenses, license fees, depreciation, interest, taxes, parking fees, tolls and the available investment tax credit. Although

the standard mileage rate may be the easiest method to use, you may save much more if you take the time to figure your actual costs.

The Tax Reform Act has eliminated some, but not all, of the advantages of computing your expenses based on actual costs. Under the Act, cars and trucks acquired after June 18, 1984, are referred to as "listed" property and new rules apply if listed property is used for both business and personal reasons. If you use your car for business more than 50 percent of the time, you can claim an investment tax credit of up to $1,000 depending on the percentage of business use. If you claim the full investment tax credit, you can depreciate 97 percent of the depreciable cost of the car over a three year period pursuant to the Accelerated Cost Recovery System (ACRS).

Alternatively, you may elect to claim a maximum investment tax credit of $667 (2/3 x $1,000) and depreciate 100 percent of the car's cost over the three-year ACRS period. Under both tax credit alternatives, the amount of depreciation you can take in any year is limited under the new Act. You can claim a maximum of $4,000 of depreciation the first year and $6,000 in each succeeding year.

If you are an employee, qualified business use occurs when you use the car for the convenience of your employer, and such use is required as a condition of your employment. These requirements are new and substantially more restrictive than the old rules.

If you are self-employed, the car must be used more than 50 percent of the time in your trade or business. If you use the car in connection with investment activities which do not amount to the conduct of a trade or business, this use will not count towards satisfying the more than 50 percent test. However, once you do satisfy the test, the investment activity use will be added to the amount of trade or business use to determine the percentage of the total amount of investment tax credit and allowable depreciation.

Example Jane is a high school teacher who also conducts a tutoring business. She and her husband own a piece of rental property. Jane uses her car in connection with her teaching and tutoring activities 60 percent of the time and 10 percent of the time in connection with the rental property. Jane has satisfied the 50 percent or more test because she uses the car 60 percent of the time in her trade or business. The use of the car 10 percent of the time in connection with the rental property does not count in determining whether the car is used in business more than 50 percent of the time. However, she can apply the investment tax credit percentage to 70 percent of the car's cost and, additionally, she can use ACRS to depreciate 70 percent of the car's cost over three years.

Cars or trucks used 50 percent or less in a trade or business do not qualify for the investment credit if purchased after June 18, 1984. Also, you must compute your depreciation using the straight line method and a half-year convention. Under the half-year convention, you are allowed one-half of the amount of the annual depreciation deduction, regardless of when the asset is placed in service during the year. Under this rule, the depreciation deduction will be the same whether the asset is acquired early or late in the year.

Example Gary purchased a car on August 1, 1984, for $20,000 and drove 10,000 miles by December 31, 1984. He used it for business 30 percent of the time. He can use either the standard mileage rate or the actual expense method of figuring his deductible costs. Using the standard mileage rate, he can deduct 3,000 x 20.5 cents or $615 in 1984. Using the actual expense method, he can deduct the following:

Operating Expenses

Gas and oil	$ 600
Repairs & parts	50
Insurance	400
License fees	50
Car wash	20
Total:	$1,120

x 30% business use = $336

In 1984, Gary can deduct $336 of operating expenses and $600 depreciation for a total of $936 if he uses the actual cost method of figuring his deduction. Next year, his deduction will be even larger because his depreciation deduction will jump to $1,200 as a result of having owned his car the entire year. He will be entitled to a full 20 percent deduction. Clearly, he should use the actual expense method. Gary will not be entitled to claim an investment credit because he does not use his car for business more than 50 percent of the time.

If you are self-employed, your deduction will be taken on Schedule C and will reduce the amount of income earned by your business. If you incur the expenses as an employee, they are deductible on line 25 and will also reduce your income regardless of whether you itemize or not. Form 2106, Employee Business Expenses, must be included with your return.

Depreciation must be figured using the straight line method over five years because the car is used for business less than 50 percent of the time.

The amount of depreciation deduction available is as follows:

Year	Straight Line Method	Deduction Available
1984	10%	$ 600
1985	20%	1,200
1986	20%	1,200
1987	20%	1,200
1988	20%	1,200
1989	10%	600
	100%	$6,000

Cars and trucks purchased before June 18, 1984, are subject to the old rules which required that adequate records be maintained to substantiate deductions for property used for both business and personal purposes. Adequate records could be supported by "other corroborating evidence." Under the Tax Reform Act of 1984, you will be required to keep adequate, contemporaneous records for property purchased after June 18, 1984, in order to substantiate your depreciation deductions and investment tax credit.

 SAMPLE TAX FORMS AND SCHEDULES

The forms which follow are based upon three hypothetical fact situations which cover many of the problems commonly encountered by educators who prepare their personal income tax returns. Also included are IRS forms and accompanying schedules. These have been filled in to illustrate many of the tax savings ideas that have been discussed in this manual.

The filled-in sample Form 1040EZ is based on the following information:

Sandy, a second grade teacher at DeWitt Elementary School, is single and has no dependents. During 1984 her income and expenses were:

Salary:	$18,000
Interest Income:	180
Charitable Contributions:	100

Discussion Of Important Points:

1. Sandy is using Form 1040EZ because she is single, has no dependents and her deductions did not exceed the $2,300 standard deduction available to single persons.

2. Even though Sandy is not itemizing her deductions, she can still deduct 25 percent of her charitable contributions on line 4.

Form 1040EZ Income Tax Return for Single filers with no dependents

1984

OMB No. 1545-0675

Name & address

Use the IRS mailing label. If you don't have one, please print:

▶ SANDY BROWN
Print your name above (first, initial, last)

1100 ELM STREET
Present home address (number and street)

ANYWHERE, USA 00000
City, town, or post office, State, and ZIP code

Please print your numbers like this.

1234567890

Social security number

010 00 0000

Presidential Election Campaign Fund
Check box if you want $1 of your tax to go to this fund. ▶ ☑

Dollars   Cents

Figure your tax

		Dollars	Cents
1	Total wages, salaries, and tips. This should be shown in Box 10 of your W-2 form(s). (Attach your W-2 form(s).) **1**	18,000	00
2	Interest income of $400 or less. If the total is more than $400, you cannot use Form 1040EZ. **2**	180	00
3	Add line 1 and line 2. This is your **adjusted gross income.** **3**	18,180	00
4	Allowable part of your charitable contributions. Complete the worksheet on page 21 of the instruction booklet. Do not enter more than $75. **4**	25	00
5	Subtract line 4 from line 3. **5**	18,155	00
6	Amount of your personal exemption. **6**	1,000	00
7	Subtract line 6 from line 5. This is your **taxable income.** **7**	17,155	00
8	Enter your Federal income tax withheld. This should be shown in Box 9 of your W-2 form(s). **8**	2,524	00
9	Use the **single** column in the tax table on pages 31-36 of the instruction booklet to find the **tax** on your taxable income on line 7. Enter the amount of tax. **9**	2,591	00

Attach Copy B of Form(s) W-2 here

Refund or amount you owe

Attach tax payment here

		Dollars	Cents
10	If line 8 is larger than line 9, subtract line 9 from line 8. Enter the **amount of your refund.** **10**	23	00
11	If line 9 is larger than line 8, subtract line 8 from line 9. Enter the **amount you owe.** Attach check or money order for the full amount, payable to "Internal Revenue Service." **11**		

Sign your return

I have read this return. Under penalties of perjury, I declare that to the best of my knowledge and belief, the return is true, correct, and complete.

Your signature   Date

Sandy Brown   4/14/85

For IRS Use Only—Please do not write in boxes below.

12345

The filled-in sample Form 1040A is based on the following information:

Bill and Nancy are married and have two small children, aged 4 and 6. Bill is an assistant junior high school principal. Nancy works part time as a secretary at the elementary school attended by their 6-year-old son.

Nancy received unemployment compensation for two months when her teaching position was eliminated. Also, Bill and Nancy provide over half of the support for Bill's mother who is in a rest home and whose only other income is a small amount of Social Security.

During 1984 their income and expenses were:

Income	Bill	Nancy	Total
Salary:	$28,000 ..	$7,000 ..	$35,000
Interest:			200
Dividends:			
ABC	200		
CDE	250	....	450
Unemployment Compensation:			1,000

Expenses

Charitable Contributions: ....$	200
Child Care:	3,000
Political Contributions	50
Individual Retirement Account Payments:	
Bill	500
Nancy	500

Discussion Of Important Points:

1. Bill and Nancy are using Form 1040A because their itemized deductions did not exceed the $3,400 standard deduction available to married persons filing a joint return.

2. For tax purposes, Bill's mother qualifies as their dependent — because they furnished over 50 percent of her support.

3. Because of their income level, Nancy's unemployment compensation is taxable.

4. On line 16, Bill and Nancy were permitted to deduct 25 percent of their ($200) charitable contributions.

5. On line 21a, Bill and Nancy qualified for a $600 credit for child care expenses.

6. On line 21b, Bill and Nancy claimed a tax credit for 50 percent of their ($50) political contributions.

1984

Department of the Treasury—Internal Revenue Service

Form 1040A US Individual Income Tax Return

OMB No. 1545-0085

Step 1
Name and address

Use the IRS mailing label. If you don't have one, print or type:

Your first name and initial (if joint return, also give spouse's name and initial) — Last name

WILLIAM F. AND NANCY M. WALTERS

Your social security no. — 000-000-001

Present home address (number and street)

5220 HILL ROAD

Spouse's social security no. — 000-000-002

City, town or post office, State, and ZIP code

ANYCITY, U.S.A. 00000

Presidential Election Campaign Fund

Do you want $1 to go to this fund?.................. ☑ Yes ☐ No

If joint return, does your spouse want $1 to go to this fund? ☑ Yes ☐ No

Step 2
Check your filing status
(Check only one)

1 ☐ Single (See if you can use Form 1040EZ.)

2 ☑ Married filing joint return (even if only one had income)

3 ☐ Married filing separate return. Enter spouse's social security number above and spouse's full name here.

4 ☐ Head of household (with qualifying person). If the qualifying person is your unmarried child but not your dependent, write this child's name here.

Step 3
Figure your exemptions

Attach Copy B of Form(s) W-2 here

Always check the exemption box labeled Yourself. Check other boxes if they apply.

5a ☑ Yourself ☐ 65 or over ☐ Blind

b ☑ Spouse ☐ 65 or over ☐ Blind

| Write number of boxes checked on 5a and b | 2 |

c First names of your dependent children who lived with you — JOHN, JEAN

| Write number of children listed on 5c | + 2 |

d Other dependents:

1. Name	2. Relationship	3. Number of months lived in your home.	4. Did dependent have income of $1,000 or more?	5. Did you provide more than one-half of dependent's support?
VIRGINIA WALTERS	MOTHER	0	NO	YES

| Write number of other dependents listed on 5d | + 1 |
| Add numbers entered on lines above | = 5 |

e Total number of exemptions claimed. (Also complete line 18.)

Step 4
Figure your total income

Attach check or money order here

6 Total wages, salaries, tips, etc. This should be shown in Box 10 of your W-2 form(s). (Attach Form(s) W-2.) — 6 — 35,000.—

7 Interest income. (If the total is over $400, also complete and attach Schedule 1 (Form 1040A), Part I.) — 7 — 200.—

8a Dividends. (If the total is over $400, also complete and attach Schedule 1 (Form 1040A), Part II.) — 8a — 450.—

b Exclusion. See the instructions on page 16. — 8b — 200.—

c Subtract line 8b from line 8a. Write the result. — 8c — 250.—

9a Unemployment compensation (insurance), from Form(s) 1099-G. Total received. — 9a — 1,000.—

b Taxable amount, if any, from the worksheet on page 17 of the instructions. — 9b — 1,000.—

10 Add lines 6, 7, 8c, and 9b. Write the total. This is your **total income**. — 10 — 36,450.—

Step 5
Figure your adjusted gross income

11a Individual retirement arrangement (IRA) deduction, from the worksheet on page 19. — 11a — 1,000.—

b Write IRA payments made in 1985 that you included on line 11a: ($ _____ . __)

12 Deduction for a married couple when both work. Complete and attach Schedule 1 (Form 1040A), Part III. — 12 — 650.—

13 Add lines 11a and 12. Write the total. These are your **total adjustments**. — 13 — 1,650.—

14 Subtract line 13 from line 10. Write the result. This is your **adjusted gross income**. — 14 — 34,800.—

Step 6
Figure your taxable income

15	Write the amount from line 14.	15	34,800.
16	Allowable part of your charitable contributions, from the worksheet on page 21 of the instructions.	16	50.
17	Subtract line 16 from line 15. Write the result.	17	34,750.
18	Multiply $1,000 by the total number of exemptions claimed on line 5e.	18	5,000.
19	Subtract line 18 from line 17. Write the result. This is your **taxable income.**	19	29,750.

Step 7
Figure your tax, credits, and payments

If You Want IRS to Figure Your Tax, See Page 21 of the Instructions.

20	Find the tax on the amount on line 19. Use the tax table, pages 31–36.	20	4,759.
21a	Credit for child and dependent care expenses. Complete and attach Schedule 1 (Form 1040A), Part IV.	21a	600.
b	Partial credit for political contributions for which you have receipts. See page 24 of the instructions.	21b	25.
22	Add lines 21a and 21b. Write the total.	22	625.
23	Subtract line 22 from line 20. Write the result (but not less than zero). This is your **total tax.**	23	4,134.
24a	Total Federal income tax withheld. This should be shown in Box 9 of your W-2 form(s). (If line 6 is more than $37,800, see page 24 of the instructions.)	24a	4,300.
b	Earned income credit, from the worksheet on page 26 of the instructions. See page 25 of the instructions.	24b	0.
25	Add lines 24a and 24b. Write the total. These are your **total payments.**	25	4,300.

Step 8
Figure your refund or amount you owe

26	If line 25 is larger than line 23, subtract line 23 from line 25. Write the result. This is the **amount of your refund.**	26	166.
27	If line 23 is larger than line 25, subtract line 25 from line 23. Write the result. This is the **amount you owe.** Attach check or money order for full amount payable to "Internal Revenue Service." Write your social security number and "1984 Form 1040A" on it.	27	.

Step 9
Sign your return

Under penalties of perjury, I declare that I have examined this return and accompanying schedules and statements, and to the best of my knowledge and belief, they are true, correct, and complete. Declaration of preparer (other than the taxpayer) is based on all information of which the preparer has any knowledge.

Your signature   Date   Your occupation

X _William F. Walters_   14 April 1985   PRINCIPAL

Spouse's signature (if joint return, both must sign)   Date   Spouse's occupation

X _Nancy N. Walters_   4/14/85   SECRETARY (P.T.)

Paid preparer's signature

X

Firm's name (or yours, if self-employed)   Employer identification no.

Address and ZIP code   Check if self-employed ☐

For **Privacy Act and Paperwork Reduction Act Notice,** see page 41.

Schedule 1 (Form 1040A)

OMB No. 1545–0085

Part I—Interest Income
Part II—Dividend Income
Part III—Deduction for a Married Couple When Both Work
Part IV—Credit for Child and Dependent Care Expenses

Name(s) as shown on Form 1040A.

WILLIAM F. AND NANCY M. WALTERS

Your social security number
000-000-001

You MUST complete and attach Schedule 1 to Form 1040A if you:

- Have over $400 of interest income (complete Part I)
- Have over $400 of dividend income (complete Part II)
- Claim the deduction for a working married couple (complete Part III)
- Claim the credit for child and dependent care expenses (complete Part IV)

Part I

Interest income (See page 15)

Complete this part and attach Schedule 1 to Form 1040A if you received over $400 in interest income. If you received any interest from an All-Savers Certificate (ASC), use Form 1040 instead of Form 1040A.

1 List name of payer	Amount
FIRST SAVINGS	$ 200.—
	$.
	$.
	$.
	$.
	$.
	$.
	$.
	$.
	$.

2 Add amounts on line 1. Write the total here and on Form 1040A, line 7. **2** | 200.—

Part II

Dividend income (See page 16)

Complete this part and attach Schedule 1 to Form 1040A if you received over $400 in dividends.

1 List name of payer	Amount
ABC	$ 200.—
CDE	$ 250.—
	$.
	$.
	$.
	$.
	$.
	$.
	$.

2 Add amounts on line 1. Write the total here and on Form 1040A, line 8a. **2** | 450.—

Part III

Deduction for a married couple when both work (See page 20)

Complete this part to figure the amount you can deduct on Form 1040A, line 12. Attach Schedule 1 to Form 1040A.

		(a) You	(b) Your spouse
1	Wages, salaries, tips, etc., from Form 1040A, line 6. **1**	28,000.—	7,000.—
2	IRA deduction, from Form 1040A, line 11a. **2**	— 500.—	— 500.—
3	Subtract line 2 from line 1. Write the result. **3**	= 27,500.—	= 6,500.—
4	Write the amount from line 3, column (a) or (b) above, whichever is smaller. **4**	6,500.	
5	Percentage used to figure the deduction (10%). **5**		× .10
6	Multiply the amount on line 4 by the percentage on line 5. Write your answer here and on Form 1040A, line 12. **6**	= 650.—	

Name(s) as shown on Form 1040A. (Do not complete if shown on other side.)   Your social security number

WILLIAM F. AND NANCY M. WALTERS   *000-000-001*

Part IV   **Credit for child and dependent care expenses** (See pages 22–24)

Complete this part to figure the amount of credit you can take on Form 1040A, line 21a. Attach Schedule 1 to Form 1040A.

1   Write the number of qualifying persons who were cared for in 1984. (See the instructions for the definition of a qualifying person.)   1   *2*

2   Write the amount of expenses you incurred and actually paid in 1984, but DO NOT write more than $2,400 ($4,800 if you paid for the care of two or more qualifying persons).   2   *3,000*

3   ● If **unmarried** at the end of 1984, write your earned income on line 3, OR
     ● If **married,** filing a joint return for 1984,
       a. Write your earned income $ *28,000* , and
       b. Write your spouse's earned income $ *7,000* , and
       c. Compare the amounts on lines 3a and 3b, and write the **smaller** of the two amounts on line 3.   3   *7,000*

4   Compare the amounts on lines 2 and 3. Write the **smaller** of the two amounts here.   4   *3,000*

5   Write the percentage from the table below that applies to the amount on Form 1040A, line 15.

If line 15 is:		Percentage is:	If line 15 is:		Percentage is:
Over—	But not over—		Over—	But not over—	
0—$10,000		30% (.30)	$20,000—22,000		24% (.24)
$10,000—12,000		29% (.29)	22,000—24,000		23% (.23)
12,000—14,000		28% (.28)	24,000—26,000		22% (.22)
14,000—16,000		27% (.27)	26,000—28,000		21% (.21)
16,000—18,000		26% (.26)	28,000		20% (.20)
18,000—20,000		25% (.25)			

5   × *20*

6   Multiply the amount on line 4 by the percentage on line 5. Write the result here and on Form 1040A, line 21a.   6 =   *600*

The filled-in sample Form 1040 is based on the following information:

Ed is a high school principal and his wife, Mary, is an elementary school teacher. They have three children, ages 16, 14 and 4.

During 1984, their income and expenses were:

1. **W-2 Information:**

	Ed	Mary	Total
Gross Wages	$31,070	$20,640	$51,710
Federal Withholding Taxes	3,462	2,308	5,770
FICA Taxes	2,082	1,383	3,465
State Withholding Taxes	1,243	826	2,069

2. **Other Income:**
   Interest (bank) $807
   Dividend Income (jointly held) 306
   1983 State Income Tax Refund 76

3. **Business Income (Schedule C):**
   Mary purchased a used piano on 7/1/84.
   Cost: .... $ 2,000
   From 7/5/84 to 12/31/84, Mary gave piano lessons after school hours and on weekends.
   Income: .... $ 1,785
   The piano is used 60% of the time for teaching purposes. The piano is kept in their living room.

4. **Stock Transaction (Schedule D):**
   On 8/4/84, Ed and Mary sold 100 shares of ABC stock. Amount received from sale: . $ 5,720
   They had originally purchased the stock on 4/2/79. Purchase price 2,085

5. **Rental Property (Schedule E):**
   Rent Received .... $ 7,200
   Expenses Paid
      Real Estate Taxes 900
      Mortgage Interest 1,900
      Insurance 300
      Repairs 650
      Yard work done by Ed
      and Mary's son 480

6. **Retirement Plan Deduction:**
   Ed's IRA .... $ 2,000
   Mary's IRA 2,000
   Mary's Keogh Account ($1,555 x 15%) 233

7. **Auto Expenses (A-Form 2106/B-Schedule C):**
   Ed used his car to attend graduate education classes
   (794 miles x 20½¢) .... $ 163
   Mary used her car to pick up and drive home her piano students
   (290 miles x 20½¢) 59

8. **Convention Expenses:**
   Ed attended a convention of high school principals in Hawaii. The convention lasted 4 days. Ed stayed a total of 6 days. (Mary did not attend.)
   Form 2106: Airfare .... $ 690
             Hotel 600
             Meals 195
   Schedule A: Convention Fee 275

9. **Itemized Deductions:**
   A) **Medical/Dental**
      Prescription Medicines & Drugs ..... $ 182
      Doctors/Dentists 371
      Contact Lenses 295
      Medical Insurance Premiums 591
      Transportation Expenses —
      (91 miles x 9¢) .. $ 8
      Parking 17 25

   B) **Taxes**
      State Income Taxes (See W-2)
      Real Estate Taxes
        (personal residence) .... $ 1,117
      Sales Tax - IRS tables used
      Sales Tax - Purchase of new car 642

   C) **Interest Paid**
      Home Mortgage .... $ 2,109
      Bank Credit Cards 486
      Student Loans 317
      Auto Loan 332

   D) **Contributions**
      Church .... $ 490
      American Heart Association 60
      Used Clothing to Salvation Army 48

   E) **Miscellaneous Potential Deductions**
      Teacher Association Dues -
        Ed: .... $ 250
        Mary: 250
      Professional Journals 148
      Certificate Renewal Fee 15
      IRA Fees 30
      Tax Manual 7
      Legal Expenses for drafting wills
        ($100 each) 200
      Safe Deposit Box 15
      Teaching Supplies 124
      Education Expenses For -
       Ed's graduate education classes:
        Tuition $800
        Books 117
        Supplies 41
        Registration Fees 35 993

10. **Child Care Expenses:**
Day Care Expenses for Ed and Mary's
4 Year Old Daughter .... $ 3,060

11. **Energy Conservation Expenses:**
Insulated Home and Weatherstripped
Doors and Windows .... $ 985

12. **Political Contributions:** ....$ 50

Discussion Of Important Points.

The 1983 state income tax refund of $76 is taxable income to Ed and Mary in 1984. This is because on their 1983 Federal income tax return, they took an itemized deduction with respect to these taxes.

Mary's Piano Lesson Business:

1. The piano was purchased after 6/1/84; thus, the new depreciation and investment credit rules apply.

2. Since the piano is used for business purposes over 50 percent of the time, investment tax credit can be taken and ACRS depreciation can be used. Also, Ed and Mary could elect the Section 179 deduction and forego the investment credit. (They choose to use ACRS and take the investment credit.)

3. For investment credit purposes, the unadjusted basis of the piano is $1,200. The original $2,000 cost was reduced by 40 percent — to reflect the amount of time that the piano is not used for teaching purposes.

4. For depreciation purposes, the unadjusted basis of the piano is $1,140. The original $2,000 cost was reduced by $800 (40 percent personal use) and by $60 (½ of the $120 investment credit).

5. A deduction for utility expenses and depreciation of their home cannot be taken because the piano is kept in their living room. Their living room is not used exclusively for piano lessons.

6. Mary's net income from this business is subject to self-employment tax ($1,555 x 11.3%).

7. Mary elects to make a contribution to her Keogh retirement plan ($1,555 x 15% = $233).

Rental Property:

Ed and Mary paid their 16-year-old son $480 to do yard work. Even though the money was paid to their son, Ed and Mary can still deduct it. (Note: Compensation for services performed by a child under 21 in the employ of his parents is not subject to Social Security (FICA) tax or Federal unemployment tax.

Auto Expenses:

Ed and Mary elect to use the standard rate of 20½ cents per mile.

Convention Expenses:

Ed's convention expenses are deductible because they relate to his school administration position.

Miscellaneous Potential Deductions:

The legal expenses incurred by Ed and Mary for drafting their wills are not deductible.

Ed's education expenses are deductible because he has already met the minimum educational requirements for his present position and they do not qualify him for a new trade or business. Also, they help improve skills which he uses in his present education position.

Child Care Expenses:

Ed and Mary paid day care expenses of $3,060 for their 4 year old daughter. The maximum amount of expenses eligible for the credit is $2,400 (since there was only one qualifying child).

Political Contribution Credit:

$$\$50 \times \tfrac{1}{2} = \$25$$

Department of the Treasury—Internal Revenue Service

U.S. Individual Income Tax Return 1984

For the year January 1-December 31, 1984, or other tax year beginning ____, 1984, ending ____, 19 ____ OMB No. 1545-0074

Use IRS label. Other-wise, please print or type.	Your first name and initial (if joint return, also give spouse's name and initial)	Last name	Your social security number
	EDWARD J. AND MARY	SMITH	111 11 1111
	Present home address (Number and street, including apartment number, or rural route)		Spouse's social security number
	100 HOME AVE.		222 27 2222
	City, town or post office, State, and ZIP code	Your occupation EDUCATOR	
	MAINTOWN, USA 00000	Spouse's occupation EDUCATOR	

Presidential Election Campaign ▶ Do you want $1 to go to this fund? . . . . [X] Yes [ ] No
If joint return, does your spouse want $1 to go to this fund?. . . [X] Yes [ ] No

Note: Checking "Yes" will not change your tax or reduce your refund.

For Privacy Act and Paperwork Reduction Act Notice, see Instructions.

Filing Status

Check only one box.

1 [ ] Single
2 [X] Married filing joint return (even if only one had income)
3 [ ] Married filing separate return. Enter spouse's social security no. above and full name here. ____
4 [ ] Head of household (with qualifying person). (See page 5 of Instructions.) If the qualifying person is your unmarried child but not your dependent, write child's name here. ____
5 [ ] Qualifying widow(er) with dependent child (Year spouse died ▶ 19 ____). (See page 6 of Instructions.)

Exemptions

Always check the box labeled Yourself. Check other boxes if they apply.

6a [X] Yourself [ ] 65 or over [ ] Blind
b [X] Spouse [ ] 65 or over [ ] Blind

Enter number of boxes checked on 6a and b ▶ **2**

c First names of your dependent children who lived with you MATTHEW, JOHN, ANN

Enter number of children listed on 6c ▶ **3**

d Other dependents: (1) Name	(2) Relationship	(3) Number of months lived in your home	(4) Did dependent have income of $1,000 or more?	(5) Did you provide more than one-half of dependent's support?

Enter number of other dependents ▶

e Total number of exemptions claimed (also complete line 36).

Add numbers entered in boxes above ▶ **5**

Income

Please attach Copy B of your Forms W-2, W-2G, and W-2P here.

If you do not have a W-2, see page 4 of Instructions.

7	Wages, salaries, tips, etc.	7	51710
8	Interest income (also attach Schedule B if over $400) . . .	8	807
9a	Dividends (also attach Schedule B if over $400) 306 , 9b Exclusion 200		
c	Subtract line 9b from line 9a and enter the result . . .	9c	106
10	Refunds of State and local income taxes, from the worksheet on page 9 of Instructions (do not enter an amount unless you itemized deductions for those taxes in an earlier year—see page 9) . . .	10	76
11	Alimony received	11	
12	Business income or (loss) (attach Schedule C)	12	1555
13	Capital gain or (loss) (attach Schedule D)	13	1454
14	40% of capital gain distributions not reported on line 13 (see page 9 of Instructions)	14	
15	Supplemental gains or (losses) (attach Form 4797) . . .	15	
16	Fully taxable pensions, IRA distributions, and annuities not reported on line 17 . . .	16	
17a	Other pensions and annuities, including rollovers. Total received 17a ____		
b	Taxable amount, if any, from the worksheet on page 10 of Instructions . . .	17b	
18	Rents, royalties, partnerships, estates, trusts, etc. (attach Schedule E) . . .	18	⟨1530⟩
19	Farm income or (loss) (attach Schedule F)	19	
20a	Unemployment compensation (insurance). Total received 20a ____		
b	Taxable amount, if any, from the worksheet on page 10 of Instructions . . .	20b	
21a	Social security benefits. (see page 10 of Instructions) 21a ____		
b	Taxable amount, if any, from the worksheet on page 11 of Instructions . . .	21b	
22	Other income (state nature and source—see page 11 of Instructions) ____	22	
23	Add lines 7 through 22. This is your total income . . . . ▶	23	54178

Adjustments to Income

(See Instructions on page 11.)

24	Moving expense (attach Form 3903 or 3903F) . . .	24	
25	Employee business expenses (attach Form 2106) . .	25	1648
26a	IRA deduction, from the worksheet on page 12 . .	26a	4000
b	Enter here IRA payments you made in 1985 that are included in line 26a above ▶ ____		
27	Payments to a Keogh (H.R. 10) retirement plan . .	27	233
28	Penalty on early withdrawal of savings	28	
29	Alimony paid	29	
30	Deduction for a married couple when both work (attach Schedule W)	30	1996
31	Add lines 24 through 30. These are your total adjustments . . . ▶	31	7877

Adjusted Gross Income

32 Subtract line 31 from line 23. This is your adjusted gross income. If this line is less than $10,000, see "Earned Income Credit" (line 59) on page 16 of Instructions. If you want IRS to figure your tax, see page 12 of Instructions. . . . ▶

| 32 | 46301 |

Tax Computation

(See Instructions on page 13.)

33	Amount from line 32 (adjusted gross income)	33	46301
34a	If you itemize, attach Schedule A (Form 1040) and enter the amount from Schedule A, line 26	34a	6749
	Caution: If you have unearned income and can be claimed as a dependent on your parent's return, check here ▶ ☐ and see page 13 of the Instructions. Also see page 13 if:		
	• You are married filing a separate return and your spouse itemizes deductions, OR		
	• You file Form 4563, OR • You are a dual-status alien.		
34b	If you do not itemize deductions, and you have charitable contributions, complete the worksheet on page 14. Then enter the allowable part of your contributions here	34b	
35	Subtract line 34a or 34b, whichever applies, from line 33	35	39552
36	Multiply $1,000 by the total number of exemptions claimed on Form 1040, line 6e	36	5000
37	Taxable Income. Subtract line 36 from line 35	37	34552
38	Tax. Enter tax here and check if from ☒ Tax Table, ☐ Tax Rate Schedule X, Y, or Z, or ☐ Schedule G	38	6099
39	Additional Taxes. (See page 14 of Instructions.) Enter here and check if from ☐ Form 4970, ☐ Form 4972, or ☐ Form 5544	39	
40	Add lines 38 and 39. Enter the total . . . . ▶	40	

Credits

(See Instructions on page 14.)

41	Credit for child and dependent care expenses *(attach Form 2441)*	41	480		
42	Credit for the elderly and the permanently and totally disabled *(attach Schedule R)*	42			
43	Residential energy credit *(attach Form 5695)*	43	148		
44	Partial credit for political contributions for which you have receipts	44	25		
45	Add lines 41 through 44. These are your total personal credits			45	653
46	Subtract line 45 from 40. Enter the result (but not less than zero) . . .			46	5446
47	Foreign tax credit *(attach Form 1116)*	47			
48	General business credit. Check if from ☐ Form 3800, ☐ Form 3468, ☐ Form 5884, ☐ Form 6478	48	120		
49	Add lines 47 and 48. These are your total business and other credits			49	120
50	Subtract line 49 from 46. Enter the result (but not less than zero). . . . . . . ▶			50	5326

Other Taxes

(Including Advance EIC Payments)

51	Self-employment tax *(attach Schedule SE)*	51	176
52	Alternative minimum tax *(attach Form 6251)*	52	
53	Tax from recapture of investment credit *(attach Form 4255)*	53	
54	Social security tax on tip income not reported to employer *(attach Form 4137)*	54	
55	Tax on an IRA *(attach Form 5329)*	55	
56	Add lines 50 through 55. This is your **total tax** . . . . ▶	56	5502

Payments

Attach Forms W-2, W-2G, and W-2P to front.

57	Federal income tax withheld	57	5770	
58	1984 estimated tax payments and amount applied from 1983 return.	58		
59	Earned income credit. If line 33 is under $10,000, see page 16 .	59		
60	Amount paid with Form 4868	60		
61	Excess social security tax and RRTA tax withheld (two or more employers)	61		
62	Credit for Federal tax on gasoline and special fuels *(attach Form 4136)* . . .	62		
63	Regulated Investment Company credit *(attach Form 2439)* . .	63		
64	Add lines 57 through 63. These are your **total payments** . . . . ▶			64	5770

Refund or Amount You Owe

65	If line 64 is larger than line 56, enter amount **OVERPAID** . . . . ▶	65	268
66	Amount of line 65 to be **REFUNDED TO YOU** . . . . ▶	66	268
67	Amount of line 65 to be applied to your 1985 estimated tax . . ▶	67	
68	If line 56 is larger than line 64, enter **AMOUNT YOU OWE**. Attach check or money order for full amount payable to "Internal Revenue Service." Write your social security number and "1984 Form 1040" on it . . . ▶	68	
	(Check ▶ ☐ if Form 2210 (2210F) is attached. See page 17 of Instructions.) $		

Please Sign Here

Under penalties of perjury, I declare that I have examined this return and accompanying schedules and statements, and to the best of my knowledge and belief, they are true, correct, and complete. Declaration of preparer (other than taxpayer) is based on all information of which preparer has any knowledge.

▶ *Edward J. Smith* Your signature | *4/14/85* Date | ▶ *Mary Smith* Spouse's signature (if filing jointly, BOTH must sign)

Paid Preparer's Use Only

Preparer's signature ▶		Date	Check if self-employed ☐	Preparer's social security no.
Firm's name (or yours, if self-employed) and address ▶			E.I. No.	
			ZIP code	

SCHEDULES A&B (Form 1040)
Department of the Treasury
Internal Revenue Service

Schedule A—Itemized Deductions
(Schedule B is on back)
▶ Attach to Form 1040. ▶ See Instructions for Schedules A and B (Form 1040).

OMB No. 1545-0074
1984
07

Name(s) as shown on Form 1040: **EDWARD AND MARY SMITH**

Your social security number: 111 11 1111

Medical and Dental Expenses
(Do not include expenses reimbursed or paid by others.)
(See Instructions on page 19)

1 Prescription medicines and drugs; and insulin	1	182
2 a Doctors, dentists, nurses, hospitals, insurance premiums you paid for medical and dental care, etc.	2a	462
b Transportation and lodging	2b	25
c Other (list—include hearing aids, dentures, eyeglasses, etc.) ▶ CONTACT LENSES $295	2c	295
3 Add lines 1 through 2c, and write the total here	3	1464
4 Multiply the amount on Form 1040, line 33, by 5% (.05)	4	2315
5 Subtract line 4 from line 3. If zero or less, write -0-. **Total medical and dental** ▶	5	0

Taxes You Paid
(See Instructions on page 20)

6 State and local income taxes	6	2069
7 Real estate taxes	7	1117
8 a General sales tax (see sales tax tables in instruction booklet)	8a	372
b General sales tax on motor vehicles	8b	642
9 Other taxes (list—include personal property taxes) ▶	9	
10 Add the amounts on lines 6 through 9. Write the total here. **Total taxes** ▶	10	4200

Interest You Paid
(See Instructions on page 20)

11 a Home mortgage interest you paid to financial institutions	11a	2109
b Home mortgage interest you paid to individuals (show that person's name and address) ▶	11b	
12 Total credit card and charge account interest you paid	12	486
13 Other interest you paid (list) ▶ STUDENT LOANS $317 AUTO LOAN 332	13	649
14 Add the amounts on lines 11a through 13. Write the total here. **Total interest** ▶	14	3244

Contributions You Made
(See Instructions on page 20)

15 a Cash contributions. (If you gave $3,000 or more to any one organization, report those contributions on line 15b.)	15a	550
b Cash contributions totaling $3,000 or more to any one organization. (Show to whom you gave and how much you gave.) ▶	15b	
16 Other than cash (attach required statement)	16	48
17 Carryover from prior year	17	
18 Add the amounts on lines 15a through 17. Write the total here. **Total contributions** ▶	18	598

Casualty and Theft Losses

19 Total casualty or theft loss(es). (You must attach Form 4684 or similar statement.) (see page 21 of Instructions) ▶	19	0

Miscellaneous Deductions
(See Instructions on page 21)

20 Union and professional dues	20	500
21 Tax return preparation fee	21	
22 Other (list type and amount) ▶ SEE ATTACHED SCHEDULE	22	1607
23 Add the amounts on lines 20 through 22. Write the total here. **Total miscellaneous** ▶	23	2107

Summary of Itemized Deductions
(See Instructions on page 22)

24 Add the amounts on lines 5, 10, 14, 18, 19, and 23. Write your answer here.	24	10,149
25 If you checked Form 1040 { Filing Status box 2 or 5, write $3,400 / Filing Status box 1 or 4, write $2,300 / Filing Status box 3, write $1,700 }	25	3,400
26 Subtract line 25 from line 24. Write your answer here and on Form 1040, line 34a. (If line 25 is more than line 24, see the Instructions for line 26 on page 22.) ▶	26	6,749

EDWARD J. AND MARY SMITH
SCHEDULE A
MISCELLANEOUS DEDUCTIONS

PROFESSIONAL JOURNALS	$148
CERTIFICATE RENEWAL FEE	15
IRA FEES	30
TAX MANUAL	7
SAFE DEPOSIT BOX	15
TEACHING SUPPLIES	124
CONVENTION FEES	275
TUITION & FEES	835
BOOKS	117
EDUCATION SUPPLIES	41
	$1,607

Schedule B—Interest and Dividend Income

08   OMB No. 1545-0074   Page **2**

Name(s) as shown on Form 1040 (Do not enter name and social security number if shown on other side.) | Your social security number

EDWARD J. AND MARY SMITH   111 11 1111

Part I Interest Income

(See Instructions on pages 8 and 22)

Also complete Part III.

If you received more than $400 in interest income, you must complete Part I and list ALL interest received. If you received interest as a nominee for another, or you received or paid accrued interest on securities transferred between interest payment dates, or you received any interest from an All-Savers Certificate, see page 22.

Interest income		Amount
1 Interest income from seller-financed mortgages. (See Instructions and show name of payer.) ▶	1	
2 Other interest income (list name of payer) ▶		
MAINTOWN USA SAVINGS BANK		807
	2	
3 Add the amounts on lines 1 and 2. Write the total here and on Form 1040, line 8 . ▶	3	807

Part II Dividend Income

(See Instructions on pages 8 and 22)

Also complete Part III.

If you received more than $400 in gross dividends (including capital gain distributions) and other distributions on stock, or you are electing to exclude qualified reinvested dividends from a public utility, complete Part II. If you received dividends as a nominee for another, see page 22.

Name of payer		Amount
4	4	
5 Add the amounts on line 4. Write the total here	5	
6 Capital gain distributions. Enter here and on line 15, Schedule D.*	6	
7 Nontaxable distributions. (See Schedule D Instructions for adjustment to basis.)	7	
8 Exclusion of qualified reinvested dividends from a public utility. (See page 23 of Instructions.)	8	
9 Add the amounts on lines 6, 7, and 8. Write the total here	9	
10 Subtract line 9 from line 5. Write the result here and on Form 1040, line 9a . . . ▶	10	

*If you received capital gain distributions for the year and you do not need Schedule D to report any other gains or losses, do not file that schedule. Instead, enter 40% of your capital gain distributions on Form 1040, line 14.

Part III Foreign Accounts and Foreign Trusts

(See Instructions on page 23)

If you received more than $400 of interest or dividends, OR if you had a foreign account or were a grantor of, or a transferor to, a foreign trust, you must answer both questions in Part III.

	Yes	No
11 At any time during the tax year, did you have an interest in or a signature or other authority over a bank account, securities account, or other financial account in a foreign country? (See page 23 of the Instructions for exceptions and filing requirements for Form TD F 90-22.1.)		X
If "Yes," write the name of the foreign country ▶		
12 Were you the grantor of, or transferor to, a foreign trust which existed during the current tax year, whether or not you have any beneficial interest in it? If "Yes," you may have to file Forms 3520, 3520-A, or 926 . . .		X

For Paperwork Reduction Act Notice, see Form 1040 Instructions.

SCHEDULE C
(Form 1040)

Department of the Treasury
Internal Revenue Service

Profit or (Loss) From Business or Profession
(Sole Proprietorship)
Partnerships, Joint Ventures, etc., Must File Form 1065.
▶ Attach to Form 1040 or Form 1041. ▶ See Instructions for Schedule C (Form 1040).

OMB No. 1545-0074

19 84
09

Name of proprietor **MARY SMITH**

Social security number **222 22 2222**

A Main business activity (see Instructions) ▶ **MUSIC LESSONS** Product or Service ▶

B Business name and address ▶ **MARY SMITH'S PIANO LESSONS**
100 HOME AVE, MAINTOWN USA 00000

C Employer ID number **N/A**

D Method(s) used to value closing inventory:
(1) ☐ Cost (2) ☐ Lower of cost or market (3) ☐ Other (attach explanation) **N/A**

E Accounting method: (1) ☐ Cash (2) ☐ Accrual (3) ☐ Other (specify) ▶ .... **N/A**

	Yes	No
E		N/A
F Was there any change in determining quantities, costs, or valuations between opening and closing inventory?. . . . . If "Yes," attach explanation.		N/A
G Did you deduct expenses for an office in your home?		X

Part I Income

1 a Gross receipts or sales	1a	1,785
b Less: Returns and allowances	1b	0
c Subtract line 1b from line 1a and enter the balance here	1c	1,785
2 Cost of goods sold and/or operations (from Part III, line 8)	2	0
3 Subtract line 2 from line 1c and enter the **gross profit** here.	3	1,785
4 a Windfall Profit Tax Credit or Refund received in 1984 (see Instructions)	4a	0
b Other income	4b	0
5 Add lines 3, 4a, and 4b. This is the **gross income** . . . . ▶	5	1,785

Part II Deductions

6 Advertising		**23** Repairs		
7 Bad debts from sales or services (Cash method taxpayers, see Instructions)		**24** Supplies (not included in Part III below)		
8 Bank service charges.		**25** Taxes (Do not include Windfall Profit Tax here. See line 29.) . . .		
9 Car and truck expenses	59	**26** Travel and entertainment		
10 Commissions		**27** Utilities and telephone		
11 Depletion		**28 a** Wages . .		
12 Depreciation and Section 179 deduction from Form 4562 (not included in Part III below).	171	**b** Jobs credit		
		c Subtract line 28b from 28a . .		
		29 Windfall Profit Tax withheld in 1984		
13 Dues and publications		**30** Other expenses (specify):		
14 Employee benefit programs		**a**		
15 Freight (not included in Part III below) .		**b**		
16 Insurance		**c**		
17 Interest on business indebtedness . .		**d**		
18 Laundry and cleaning		**e**		
19 Legal and professional services . . .		**f**		
20 Office expense.		**g**		
21 Pension and profit-sharing plans . . .		**h**		
22 Rent on business property		**i**		

31 Add amounts in columns for lines 6 through 30i. These are the **total deductions** . . . . ▶	31	230
32 Net profit or (loss). Subtract line 31 from line 5 and enter the result. If a profit, enter on Form 1040, line 12, and on Schedule SE, Part I, line 2 (or Form 1041, line 6). If a loss, you **MUST** go on to line 33	32	1,555

33 If you have a loss, you **MUST** answer this question: "Do you have amounts for which you are not at risk in this business (see Instructions)?" ☐ Yes ☐ No
If "Yes," you **MUST** attach **Form 6198.** If "No," enter the loss on Form 1040, line 12, and on Schedule SE, Part I, line 2 (or Form 1041, line 6).

Part III Cost of Goods Sold and/or Operations (See Schedule C Instructions for Part III)

1 Inventory at beginning of year (if different from last year's closing inventory, attach explanation)	1	
2 Purchases less cost of items withdrawn for personal use	2	
3 Cost of labor (do not include salary paid to yourself)	3	
4 Materials and supplies	4	
5 Other costs	5	
6 Add lines 1 through 5	6	
7 Less: Inventory at end of year	7	
8 Cost of goods sold and/or operations. Subtract line 7 from line 6. Enter here and in Part I, line 2, above.	8	N/A

For Paperwork Reduction Act Notice, see Form 1040 Instructions.

Schedule C (Form 1040) 1984

SCHEDULE D (Form 1040)

Department of the Treasury
Internal Revenue Service

Capital Gains and Losses

(Also reconciliation of sales of stocks, bonds, and bartering income from Forms 1099-B)

▶ Attach to Form 1040.   ▶ See Instructions for Schedule D (Form 1040).

OMB No. 1545-0074

1984

12

Name(s) as shown on Form 1040   **EDWARD J. AND MARY SMITH**

Your social security number   111 11 1111

Part I — Short-term Capital Gains and Losses-Assets Held One Year or Less (6 months if acquired after 6/22/84)

a. Description of property (Example, 100 shares 7% preferred of "Z" Co.)	b. Date acquired (Mo., day, yr.)	c. Date sold (Mo., day, yr.)	d. Gross sales price	e. Cost or other basis (see instructions)	f. LOSS If column (e) is more than (d) subtract (d) from (e)	g. GAIN If column (d) is more than (e) subtract (e) from (d)
1						

2 Short-term gain from sale or exchange of a principal residence from Form 2119, lines 7 or 11 . . . . **2**

3 Short-term gain from installment sales from Form 6252, lines 22 or 30 **3**

4 Net short-term gain or (loss) from partnerships, S corporations, and fiduciaries **4**

5 Add lines 1 through 4 in columns f and g . . . . **5** ( )

6 Combine columns f and g of line 5 and enter the net gain or (loss) **6**

7 Short-term capital loss carryover from years beginning after 1969 . . . . **7** ( )

8 Net short-term gain or (loss), combine lines 6 and 7 . . . . **8**

Part II — Long-term Capital Gains and Losses-Assets Held More Than One Year (6 months if acquired after 6/22/84)

a. Description of property	b. Date acquired	c. Date sold	d. Gross sales price	e. Cost or other basis	f. LOSS	g. GAIN
9 100 Shs ABC Co.	4/2/79	8/1/84	5720	2085		3635

10 Long-term gain from sale or exchange of a principal residence from Form 2119, lines 7, 11, 16, or 18 . . . . **10**

11 Long-term gain from installment sales from Form 6252, lines 22 or 30 . . . . **11**

12 Net long-term gain or (loss) from partnerships, S corporations, and fiduciaries . **12**

13 Add lines 9 through 12 in columns f and g . . . . **13** ( )   3635

14 Combine columns f and g of line 13 and enter the net gain or (loss) **14** 3635

15 Capital gain distributions **15**

16 Enter gain from Form 4797, line 6(a)(1) **16**

17 Combine lines 14 through 16 . . . . **17** 3635

18 Long-term capital loss carryover from years beginning after 1969 . . . . . . **18** ( )

19 Net long-term gain or (loss), combine lines 17 and 18 . . . . **19** 3635

Note: *Complete the back of this form. However, if you have capital loss carryovers from years beginning before 1970, do not complete Parts III or IV. See Form 4798 instead.*

For Paperwork Reduction Act Notice, see Form 1040 instructions.

Schedule D (Form 1040) 1984

Name(s) as shown on Form 1040 (Do not enter name and social security number if shown on other side)	Your social security number
EDWARD J. AND MARY SMITH	*111 11 1111*

Part III — Summary of Parts I and II

20	Combine lines 8 and 19, and enter the net gain or (loss) here	20	*3635*
	Note: *If line 20 is a loss, skip lines 21 through 23 and complete lines 24 and 25. If line 20 is a gain complete lines 21 through 23 and skip lines 24 and 25.*		
21	If line 20 shows a gain, enter the smaller of line 19 or line 20. Enter zero if there is a loss or no entry on line 19. . . . . **21** *3635*		
22	Enter 60% of line 21	22	*2181*
	If line 22 is more than zero, you may be liable for the alternative minimum tax. See Form 6251.		
23	Subtract line 22 from line 20. Enter here and on Form 1040, line 13	23	*1454*
24	If line 20 shows a loss, enter one of the following amounts:		
	a If line 8 is zero or a net gain, enter 50% of line 20;		
	b If line 19 is zero or a net gain, enter line 20; or		
	c If line 8 and line 19 are net losses, enter amount on line 8 added to 50% of the amount on line 19 .	24	
25	Enter here and as a loss on Form 1040, line 13, the smallest of:		
	a The amount on line 24;		
	b $3,000 ($1,500 if married and filing a separate return); or		
	c Taxable income, as adjusted.	25	

Part IV — Computation of Post-1969 Capital Loss Carryovers from 1984 to 1985
(Complete this part if the loss on line 24 is more than the loss on line 25)

26	Enter loss shown on line 8; if none, enter zero and skip lines 27 through 30, then go to line 31 . . .	26	
27	Enter gain shown on line 19. If that line is blank or shows a loss, enter zero	27	
28	Reduce any loss on line 26 to the extent of any gain on line 27	28	
29	Enter smaller of line 25 or line 28	29	
30	Subtract line 29 from line 28. This is your short-term capital loss carryover from 1984 to 1985 . .	30	
31	Subtract line 29 from line 25. (Note: If you skipped lines 27 through 30, enter amount from line 25)	31	
32	Enter loss from line 19; if none, enter zero and skip lines 33 through 36	32	
33	Enter gain shown on line 8. If that line is blank or shows a loss, enter zero	33	
34	Reduce any loss on line 32 to the extent of any gain on line 33	34	
35	Multiply amount on line 31 by 2	35	
36	Subtract line 35 from line 34. This is your long-term capital loss carryover from 1984 to 1985 . . .	36	

Part V — Complete this Part Only If You Elect Out of the Installment Method and Report a Note or Other Obligation at Less Than Full Face Value

☐ Check here if you elect out of the installment method.
Enter the face amount of the note or other obligation. ▶ --------------------------------
Enter the percentage of valuation of the note or other obligation. ▶ --------

Part VI — Reconciliation of Forms 1099-B With Tax Return (Complete this part if you received one or more Forms 1099-B or equivalent statement reporting sales of stock, bonds, etc. or bartering income.)

SECTION A.—Reconciliation of Sales of Stocks, Bonds, etc.

37	Total sales of stock, bonds, etc. from Forms 1099-B or equivalent statement received from your brokers	37	
38	Proceeds from sale or exchange of capital assets reported on Schedule D, but not included in line 37	38	
39	Add lines 37 and 38.	39	
40	Part of line 37 not reported on Schedule D this year, attach explanation	40	
41	Subtract line 40 from line 39	41	
	Note: *The amount on line 41 should be the same as the total of all amounts on page 1, lines 1 and 9 of column d.*		

SECTION B.—Reconciliation of Bartering Income
Indicate below the amount of bartering income reported on each form or schedule

		Amount of bartering from Form 1099-B or equivalent statement
42	Form 1040, line 22.	42	
43	Schedule C (Form 1040)	43	
44	Schedule D (Form 1040)	44	
45	Schedule E (Form 1040)	45	
46	Schedule F (Form 1040)	46	
47	Other (identify) (if not taxable, indicate reason—attach additional sheets if necessary) ▶ --------------	47	
48	Total (add lines 42 through 47)	48	
	Note: *The amount on line 48 should be the same as the total bartering on all Forms 1099-B or equivalent statements received.*		

Supplemental Income Schedule

(From rents and royalties, partnerships, estates, and trusts, etc.)
▶ Attach to Form 1040. ▶ See Instructions for Schedule E (Form 1040).

OMB No. 1545-0074

1984
13

Name(s) as shown on Form 1040	Your social security number
EDWARD J. AND MARY SMITH	111 11 1111

Part I Rent and Royalty Income or Loss

1 Did you or a member of your family use for personal purposes any rental property listed below for more than the greater of 14 days or 10% of the total days rented at fair rental value during the tax year? . . . . ☐ Yes ☒ No

2 **Description of Properties** (Show kind and location for each)

Property A ONE FAMILY RESIDENTIAL — MAINTOWN, USA

Property B

Property C

Rental and Royalty Income		A	B	C		Totals (Add columns A, B, and C)	
3 a Rents received		7200			} 3		
b Royalties received							

Rental and Royalty Expenses

		A	B	C			
4 Advertising	4						
5 Auto and travel	5						
6 Cleaning and maintenance . . .	6						
7 Commissions	7						
8 Insurance	8	300					
9 Interest	9	1900					
10 Legal and other professional fees . .	10						
11 Repairs	11	650					
12 Supplies	12						
13 Taxes (Do **not** include Windfall Profit Tax here. See Part III, line 37.) . . .	13	900					
14 Utilities	14						
15 Wages and salaries	15						
16 Other (list) ▶ YARD WORK		480					

17 Total expenses other than depreciation and depletion. Add lines 4 through 16	17	4,230			17		
18 Depreciation expense (see Instructions), or depletion	18	4,500			18		
19 Total. Add lines 17 and 18	19	8,730					
20 Income or (loss) from rental or royalty properties. Subtract line 19 from line 3a (rents) or 3b (royalties) .	20	⟨1,530⟩					

21 Add properties with profits on line 20, and write the total profits here . . . . | 21 | 0

22 Add properties with losses on line 20, and write the total (losses) here . . . . | 22 | (1530)

23 Combine amounts on lines 21 and 22, and write the net profit or (loss) here . . . . | 23 | ⟨1530⟩

24 Net farm rental profit or (loss) from Form 4835, line 49 . . . . | 24 |

25 Total rental or royalty income or (loss). Combine amounts on lines 23 and 24, and write the total here. If Parts II, III, and IV on page 2 do not apply to you, write the amount from line 25 on Form 1040, line 18. Otherwise, include the amount in line 39 on page 2 of Schedule E . . . . | 25 | ⟨1530⟩

For Paperwork Reduction Act Notice, see Form 1040 Instructions.

Schedule E (Form 1040) 1984

SCHEDULE SE (Form 1040)	Computation of Social Security Self-Employment Tax	OMB No. 1545-0074
Department of the Treasury Internal Revenue Service	▶ See Instructions for Schedule SE (Form 1040). ▶ Attach to Form 1040.	1984 18

Name of **self-employed** person (as shown on social security card)	Social security number of **self-employed** person ▶
MARY SMITH	222 22 2222

Part I Regular Computation of Net Earnings from Self-Employment

Note: *If you performed services for certain churches or church-controlled organizations and you are not a minister or a member of a religious order, see the instructions.*

1 Net profit or (loss) from Schedule F (Form 1040), line 56 or line 89, and farm partnerships, Schedule K-1 (Form 1065), line 17a .... | **1** | |

2 Net profit or (loss) from Schedule C (Form 1040), line 32, Schedule K-1 (Form 1065), line 17a (other than farming), and Form W-2 wages of $100 or more from an electing church or church-controlled organization (See instructions for other income to report.) . . . . . | **2** | *1555* |

Note: ☐ Check here if you are **exempt** from self-employment tax on your earnings as a minister, member of a religious order, or Christian Science practitioner because you filed **Form 4361**. See instructions for kinds of income to report. If you have other earnings of $400 or more that are subject to self-employment tax, include those earnings on this line.

Part II Optional Computation of Net Earnings from Self-Employment (See "Who Can Use Schedule SE")

Generally, this part may be used **only** if you meet any of the following tests:

A Your gross farm profits (Schedule F (Form 1040), line 31 or line 87) were not more than $2,400, or

B Your gross farm profits (Schedule F (Form 1040), line 31 or line 87) were more than $2,400 and your net farm profits (Schedule F (Form 1040), line 56 or line 89) were less than $1,600, or

C Your net nonfarm profits (Schedule C (Form 1040), line 32) were less than $1,600 and also less than two-thirds (⅔) of your gross nonfarm income (Schedule C (Form 1040), line 5).
See instructions for other limitations.

3 Maximum income for optional methods . . . . | **3** | $1,600 | 00 |

4 Farm Optional Method—If you meet test A or B above, enter: two-thirds (⅔) of gross profits from Schedule F (Form 1040), line 31 or line 87, and farm partnerships, Schedule K-1 (Form 1065), line 17b, or $1,600, whichever is smaller | **4** | |

5 Subtract line 4 from line 3 . . . . | **5** | |

6 Nonfarm Optional Method—If you meet test C, enter: the smaller of two-thirds (⅔) of gross nonfarm income from Schedule C (Form 1040), line 5, and Schedule K-1 (Form 1065), line 17c (other than farming), or $1,600, or, if you elected the farm optional method, the amount on line 5 . . . . | **6** | |

Part III Computation of Social Security Self-Employment Tax

7 Enter the amount from Part I, line 1, or, if you elected the farm optional method, Part II, line 4 . . . . | **7** | |

8 Enter the amount from Part I, line 2, or, if you elected the nonfarm optional method, Part II, line 6 . . | **8** | *1555* |

9 Add lines 7 and 8. If less than $400, you are not subject to self-employment tax. Do not fill in the rest of the schedule. (**Exception:** If this line is less than $400 and you are an employee of an electing church or church-controlled organization, complete the schedule unless this line is a loss. See instructions.) . . . . | **9** | *1555* |

10 The largest amount of combined wages and self-employment earnings subject to social security or railroad retirement tax (Tier I) for 1984 is . . . . | **10** | $37,800 | 00 |

11 a Total social security wages and tips from Forms W-2 and railroad retirement compensation (Tier I). **Note:** U.S. Government employees whose wages are only subject to the 1.3% hospital insurance benefits tax (Medicare) and employees of certain church or church-controlled organizations, should not include those wages on this line (see instructions) . . . . | **11a** | *20640* | |

b Unreported tips subject to social security tax from Form 4137, line 9, or to railroad retirement tax (Tier I) . . . . | **11b** | |

c Add lines 11a and 11b . . . . | **11c** | *20640* |

12 a Subtract line 11c from line 10 . . . . | **12a** | *17160* |

b Enter your "qualified" U.S. Government wages if you are required to use the worksheet in Part III of the instructions. | **12b** | |

c Enter your Form W-2 wages from an electing church or church-controlled organization. | **12c** | |

13 Enter the smaller of line 9 or line 12a . . . . | **13** | *1555* |

If line 13 is $37,800 or more, fill in $4,271.40 on line 14. Otherwise, multiply line 13 by .113 and enter the result on line 14 | | .113 |

14 Self-employment tax. Enter this amount on Form 1040, line 51 . . . . | **14** | *176* |

For Paperwork Reduction Act Notice, see Form 1040 Instructions. Schedule SE (Form 1040) 1984

Schedule W
(Form 1040)
Department of the Treasury
Internal Revenue Service

Deduction for a Married Couple When Both Work
▶ For Paperwork Reduction Act Notice, see Form 1040 Instructions.
▶ Attach to Form 1040.

OMB No. 1545-0074

1984
20

Names as shown on Form 1040 *EDWARD J. AND MARY SMITH*

Your social security number *111 11 1111*

Step 1 Figure your earned income

			(a) You		(b) Your spouse
1	Wages, salaries, tips, etc., from Form 1040, line 7. (Do not include nondisability pensions or annuities.)	1	31070	1	20640
2	Net profit or (loss) from self-employment (from Schedules C and F (Form 1040), Schedule K-1 (Form 1065), and any other taxable self-employment or earned income)	2	0	2	1555
3	Add lines 1 and 2. This is your total earned income.	3	31070	3	22195

Step 2 Figure your qualified earned income

			(a) You		(b) Your spouse
4	Adjustments from Form 1040, lines 25, 26a, 27, and any repayment of sub-pay included on line 31. (See instructions below.)	4	3648	4	2233
5	Subtract line 4 from line 3. This is your qualified earned income. (If the amount in column (a) or (b) is zero (-0-) or less, stop here. You may not take this deduction.)	5	27422	5	19962

Step 3 Figure your deduction

6	Compare the amounts in columns (a) and (b) of line 5. Write the smaller amount here. (Write either amount if 5(a) and 5(b) are exactly the same.) **Do not write more than $30,000**	6	19962
7	Percentage used to figure the deduction (10%)	7	x .10
8	Multiply the amount on line 6 by the percentage on line 7. This is the amount of your deduction. Write the answer here and on Form 1040, line 30 ▶	8	1996

Instructions

Complete this schedule and attach it to your Form 1040 if you take the deduction for a married couple when both work. You may take the deduction if both you and your spouse:

- work and have qualified earned income, and
- file a joint return, and
- do not file **Form 2555** to exclude income or to exclude or deduct certain housing costs, and
- do not file **Form 4563** to exclude income.

There are three steps to follow in figuring the deduction on Schedule W.

Step 1 (lines 1, 2, and 3).—Figure earned income separately for yourself and your spouse.

Step 2 (lines 4 and 5).—Figure qualified earned income separately for yourself and your spouse by subtracting certain adjustments from earned income.

Step 3 (lines 6, 7, and 8).—Figure the deduction based on the **smaller** of:

- the qualified earned income entered in column (a) or (b) of line 5, whichever is less, **OR**
- $30,000.

Earned income.—This is generally income you receive for services you provide. It includes wages, salaries, tips, commissions, certain disability income, sub-pay, etc. (from Form 1040, line 7). It also includes income earned from self-employment (from Schedules C and F of Form 1040 and Schedule K-1 of Form 1065), and net earnings and gains (other than capital gains) from the disposition, transfer, or licensing of property that you created. Earned income does not include interest, dividends, social security or tier 1 railroad retirement benefits, IRA distributions, unemployment compensation, deferred compensation, or nontaxable income. It also does not include any amount your spouse paid you.

Caution: Do not consider community property laws in figuring your earned income.

Qualified earned income.—This is the amount on which the deduction is based. Figure it by subtracting certain adjustments from earned income.

These adjustments (and the related lines on Form 1040) are:

- Employee business expenses (from line 25).
- Payments to an IRA (from line 26a).
- Payments to a Keogh plan (from line 27).
- Repayment of supplemental unemployment benefits (sub-pay) included in the total on line 31. See the instructions on repayment of sub-pay on page 12 of the Form 1040 Instructions.

Enter the total of any adjustments that apply to your or your spouse's earned income in the appropriate column of line 4.

Example.—You earned a salary of $20,000 and had $3,000 of employee business expenses (line 25 of Form 1040). Your spouse earned $17,000 and put $1,000 into an IRA (line 26a of Form 1040). Your qualified earned income is $17,000 ($20,000 minus $3,000) and your spouse's is $16,000 ($17,000 minus $1,000). Because your spouse's qualified earned income is less than yours, the deduction is figured on your spouse's income. Therefore, the deduction is $1,600 ($16,000 x .10).

Form 2106

**Department of the Treasury
Internal Revenue Service**

Employee Business Expenses

(Please use Form 3903 to figure moving expense deduction.)

▶ Attach to Form 1040.

OMB No. 1545-0139

1984

54

Your name	Social security number	Occupation in which expenses were incurred
EDWARD J. SMITH	111 11 1111	HIGH SCHOOL PRINCIPAL

Part I — Employee Business Expenses Deductible in Figuring Adjusted Gross Income on Form 1040, Line 32

1 Reimbursed and unreimbursed fares for airplane, boat, bus, taxicab, train, etc	1	690
2 Reimbursed and unreimbursed meal, lodging, and other expenses while away from your tax home. . .	2	795
3 Reimbursed and unreimbursed car expenses from Part II.	3	163
4 Reimbursed and unreimbursed outside salesperson's expenses other than those shown on lines 1 through 3. **Caution:** *Do not use this line unless you are an outside salesperson (see instructions).*	4	
5 Reimbursed expenses other than those shown on lines 1 through 3 (see instructions).	5	
6 Add lines 1 through 5	6	1648
7 Employer's payments for these expenses only if not included on Form W-2	7	0
8 If line 6 is more than line 7, subtract line 7 from line 6. Enter here and on Form 1040, line 25 . .	8	1648
9 If line 7 is more than line 6, subtract line 6 from line 7. Enter here and on Form 1040, line 7.	9	

Part II — Car Expenses (Use either your actual expenses or the mileage rate.)

	Car 1	Car 2	Car 3
A Number of months you used car for business during 1984 .	12 months	months	months
B Total mileage for months on line A	12000 miles	miles	miles
C Business part of line B mileage	794 miles	miles	miles
D Date placed in service	/ /	/ /	/ /

Actual Expenses (Include expenses on lines 1 and 2 only for the months shown on line A, above.)

		Car 1	Car 2	Car 3
1 Gasoline, oil, lubrication, etc.	1			
2 Other	2			
3 Total (add lines 1 and 2)	3			
4 Divide line C by line B, above	4	%	%	%
5 Multiply line 3 by line 4	5			
6 Depreciation (see instructions)	6			
7 Business parking fees and tolls.	7			
8 Add lines 5 through 7. Also enter in Part I, line 3.	8			

Mileage Rate

9 Enter the smaller of (a) 15,000 miles or (b) the total mileage (Car 1+ Car 2+ Car 3) from line C, above	9	794 miles
10 Multiply line 9 by 20½¢ (.205) (11¢ (.11) if applicable, see instructions)	10	163
11 Enter the total mileage, if any (Car 1 + Car 2 + Car 3) from line C that is over 15,000 miles	11	0 miles
12 Multiply line 11 by 11¢ (.11) and enter here	12	0
13 Business part of car interest, parking fees, tolls, and State and local taxes (except gasoline tax) . . .	13	0
14 Total (add lines 10, 12, and 13). Enter here and in Part I, line 3.	14	163

Part III — Information About Educational Expenses Shown in Part I or on Schedule A (Form 1040)

1 Did you need this education to meet the minimum educational requirements for your business or profession? . . . . ☐ Yes ☒ No

2 Will this study program qualify you for a new business or profession? . . . . ☐ Yes ☒ No

Note: *If your answer to question 1 or 2 is "Yes," stop here. You cannot deduct these expenses, even if you do not intend to change your business or profession.*

3 If "No," list the courses you took and their relationship to your business or profession ▶ ⒶCONVENTION OF HIGH SCHOOL PRINCIPALS, HAWAII ⒷGRADUATE CLASSES IN EDUCATION ADMINISTRATION (MAINTAIN & IMPROVE SKILLS NEEDED IN JOB)

Changes You Should Note

New rules apply that may limit the amount of your recovery deduction for depreciation and investment credit for certain property used in your trade or business and placed in service after June 18, 1984.

- For calendar year 1984, the recovery deduction for a "passenger automobile" may not exceed $4,000, and the investment credit may not exceed $1,000. In figuring your recovery deduction, for purposes of this limitation, the section 179 expense deduction is treated as a recovery deduction. These amounts are reduced if your business use is less than 100%.

- The section 179 expense deduction and investment credit are not allowed for certain property such as "passenger automobiles" and other transportation property used 50% or less in your trade or business. Additionally, if you use the property 50% or less in a trade or business, you must use the straight-line method of depreciation.

- No deduction for recovery depreciation or investment credit will be allowed for an employee's "passenger automobile" or other transportation property unless such use is for the convenience of the employer and required as a condition of employment.

- New recordkeeping rules for trade or business expenses will apply beginning in 1985. See **Important Tax Law Changes** on page 2 of your 1984 Form 1040 Instructions.

  See **Publications 572**, Investment Credit and **534**, Depreciation, for more detail on the kinds of property to which the above limitations apply. Also, see **Forms 3468**, Computation of Investment Credit, and **4562**, Depreciation and Amortization, for additional information.

For Paperwork Reduction Act Notice, see instructions on back.

Form **2106** (1984)

Form **2441**

Department of the Treasury
Internal Revenue Service

Credit for Child and Dependent Care Expenses

▶ Attach to Form 1040.
▶ See Instructions below.

OMB No. 1545-0068

1984
23

Name(s) as shown on Form 1040

EDWARD J AND MARY SMITH

Your social security number

111 11 1111

1 Write the number of qualifying persons who were cared for in 1984. (See the instructions below for the definition of qualifying persons.) . . . . ▶ | **1** | *1*

2 If payments listed on line 3 were made to an individual, complete the following: *N/A*

		Yes	No
a If you paid $50 or more in a calendar quarter to an individual, were the services performed in your home?	**2a**		
b If "Yes," have you filed appropriate wage tax returns on wages for services in your home (see instructions for line 2)?	**2b**		

c If the answer to **b** is "Yes," write your employer identification number. . . . . ▶ | **2c** |

3 Write the amount of qualified expenses you incurred and actually paid in 1984, but **do not** write more than $2,400 ($4,800 if you paid for the care of two or more qualifying persons) . . . . | **3** | *2400*

4 You **must** write your earned income on line 4. See the instructions for line 4 for the definition of earned income.

- If you were **unmarried** at the end of 1984, write your earned income on line 4, **OR**
- If you are **married,** filing a joint return for 1984,

  a write your earned income $ *27,422*, and

  b write your spouse's earned income $ *19,962*, and

  c compare amounts on lines 4a and 4b, and write the **smaller** of the two amounts on line 4. . . . | **4** | *19962*

5 Compare amounts on lines 3 and 4, and write the **smaller** of the two amounts on line 5 . . . . | **5** | *2400*

6 Write the percentage from the table below that applies to the adjusted gross income on Form 1040, line 33. . . . . | **6** | *20%*

If line 33 is:		Percentage is:	If line 33 is:		Percentage is:
Over—	But not over—		Over—	But not over—	
0–$10,000		30% (.30)	$20,000–22,000		24% (.24)
$10,000–12,000		29% (.29)	22,000–24,000		23% (.23)
12,000–14,000		28% (.28)	24,000–26,000		22% (.22)
14,000–16,000		27% (.27)	26,000–28,000		21% (.21)
16,000–18,000		26% (.26)	28,000		20% (.20)
18,000–20,000		25% (.25)			

7 Multiply the amount on line 5 by the percentage shown on line 6, and write the result. . . . . . | **7** | *480*

8 Multiply any child and dependent care expenses for 1983 that you paid in 1984 by the percentage that applies to the adjusted gross income on Form 1040, line 33, for 1983. Write the result. (See line 8 instructions for the required statement.) . . . . | **8** |

9 Add amounts on lines 7 and 8. Write the total here and on Form 1040, line 41. This is the maximum amount of your credit for child and dependent care expenses. . . . . | **9** | *480*

General Instructions

Paperwork Reduction Act Notice.—We ask for this information to carry out the Internal Revenue laws of the United States. We need it to ensure that taxpayers are complying with these laws and to allow us to figure and collect the right amount of tax. You are required to give us this information.

What Is the Child and Dependent Care Expenses Credit?

You may be able to take a tax credit for amounts you paid someone to care for your child or other qualifying person so you could work or look for work in 1984. The credit will lower the amount of your tax. The credit is based on a percentage of the amount you paid during the year. The most you may take as a credit is $720 if you paid for the care of one qualifying person, or $1,440 if you paid for the care of two or more qualifying persons.

Additional information.—For more information about the credit, please get **Publication 503**, Child and Dependent Care Credit, and Employment Taxes for Household Employers.

Who Is a Qualifying Person?

A qualifying person is any one of the following persons:

- Any person under age 15 whom you claim as a dependent (but see the special rule later for **Children of divorced or separated parents**).
- Your disabled spouse who is mentally or physically unable to care for himself or herself.
- Any disabled person who is mentally or physically unable to care for himself or herself and whom you claim as a dependent, or could claim as a dependent except that he or she had income of $1,000 or more.

Children of divorced or separated parents.—If you were divorced, legally separated, or separated under a written agreement, you may be able to claim the credit even if your child is not your dependent. Your child is a qualifying person if **all four** of the following apply:

1. You had custody for the longer period during the year; and

2. The child received over half of his or her support from one or both of the parents; and

3. The child was in the custody of one or both of the parents over half of the year; and

4. The child was under age 15, or was physically or mentally unable to care for himself or herself.

(Continued on back)

Form **2441** (1984)

Form **3468**	**Computation of Investment Credit**	OMB No. 1545-0155
Department of the Treasury Internal Revenue Service	▶ Attach to your tax return. ▶ Schedule B (Business Energy Investment Credit) on back.	**19 84** 24

Name(s) as shown on return **EDWARD J. AND MARY SMITH**   Identifying number **111-11-1111**

Part I Elections (Check the box(es) below that apply to you (See Instruction D).)

A I elect to increase my qualified investment to 100% for certain commuter highway vehicles under section 46(c)(6) . . . . ☐

B I elect to increase my qualified investment by all qualified progress expenditures made this and all later tax years . . . . ☐
   Enter total qualified progress expenditures included in column (4), Part II ▶ - - - - - - - - - - - - - - - -

C I claim full credit on certain ships under section 46(g)(3) (See **Instruction B** for details.) . . . . ☐

Part II Qualified Investment (See instructions for new rules on automobiles and certain property with any personal use)

1 Recovery Property

		Line	(1) Class of Property	(2) Unadjusted Basis	(3) Applicable Percentage	(4) Qualified Investment (Column 2 x column 3)
Regular Percentage	New Property	(a)	3-year		60	
		(b)	Other		100	
	Used Property	(c)	3-year		60	
		(d)	Other	1200	100	1200
Section 48(q) Election to Reduce Credit (instead of adjusting basis)	New Property	(e)	3-year		40	
		(f)	Other		80	
	Used Property	(g)	3-year		40	
		(h)	Other		80	

2 Nonrecovery property—Enter total qualified investment (See instructions for line 2)	**2**	
3 New commuter highway vehicle—Enter total qualified investment (See **Instruction D(1)**)	**3**	
4 Used commuter highway vehicle—Enter total qualified investment (See **Instruction D(1)**)	**4**	
5 **Total qualified investment in 10% property**—Add lines 1(a) through 1(h), 2, 3, and 4 (See instructions for special limits)	**5**	1200
6 Qualified rehabilitation expenditures—Enter total qualified investment for:		
a 30-year-old buildings	**6a**	
b 40-year-old buildings	**6b**	
c Certified historic structures (You must attach NPS certification—see instructions)	**6c**	

Part III Tentative Regular Investment Credit

7 10% of line 5	**7**	120
8 15% of line 6a	**8**	
9 20% of line 6b	**9**	
10 25% of line 6c	**10**	
11 Credit from cooperatives—Enter regular investment credit from cooperatives	**11**	
12 Regular investment credit—Add lines 7 through 11	**12**	120
13 Business energy investment credit—From line 11 of Schedule B (see back of this form)	**13**	
14 Current year investment credit—Add lines 12 and 13	**14**	

Note: If you have a 1984 jobs credit (Form 5884), credit for alcohol used as fuel (Form 6478), or employee stock ownership plan (ESOP) credit (Form 8007), in addition to your 1984 investment credit, you must stop here and go to new **Form 3800**, General Business Credit, to claim your 1984 investment credit. If you have only the investment credit (which may include business energy investment credit) or an investment credit carryforward from 1983, you may continue with lines 15 through 22 to claim your credit.

15 Carryforward of unused regular or business energy investment credit from 1983	**15**	120
16 Total—Add lines 14 and 15.	**16**	6099

Part IV Tax Liability Limitations

17 a Individuals—From Form 1040, enter amount from line 46		
b Estates and trusts—From Form 1041, enter tax from line 26a, plus any section 644 tax on trusts .	**17**	480
c Corporations—From Form 1120, Schedule J, enter tax from line 3 (or Form 1120-A, Part I, line 1).		
d Other filers —Enter tax before credits from return		
18 a Individuals—From Form 1040, enter credits from line 47, plus any orphan drug, nonconventional source fuel, and research credits		
b Estates and trusts—From Form 1041, enter any credits from line 27d	**18**	5619
c Corporations—From Form 1120, Schedule J, enter credits from lines 4(a) through 4(e) (Form 1120-A filers, enter zero)		
d Other filers—See instructions for line 18d		
19 Income tax liability as adjusted (subtract line 18 from line 17). . . .	**19**	5619
20 a Enter smaller of line 19 or $25,000. (See instructions for line 20)	**20a**	5619
b If line 19 is more than $25,000—Enter 85% of the excess.	**20b**	
21 Investment credit limitation—Add lines 20a and 20b	**21**	120
22 Total allowed credit—Enter the smaller of line 16 or line 21. This is your **General Business Credit** for 1984. Enter here and on Form 1040, line 48; Form 1120, Schedule J, line 4(f); Form 1120-A, Part I, line 2 ; or the proper line of other returns	**22**	

For Paperwork Reduction Act Notice, see separate instructions.   Form **3468** (1984)

Form **4562**

Department of the Treasury
Internal Revenue Service

Depreciation and Amortization

▶ See separate instructions.
▶ Attach this form to your return.

OMB No. 1545-0172

1984

67

Name(s) as shown on return
EDWARD J. AND MARY SMITH

Identifying number
111-11-1111

Business or activity to which this form relates
SCHEDULE C — MUSIC LESSONS

Part I Depreciation

For transportation equipment (e.g. autos), amusement/recreation property, and computer/peripheral equipment placed in service after June 18, 1984, and used 50% or less in a trade or business, the section 179 deduction is not allowed and depreciation must be taken only on line 2(h).

Section A.—Election to expense recovery property (Section 179)

A. Class of property	**B.** Cost	**C.** Expense deduction

1	Total (not more than $5,000). (Partnerships or S corporations—see the Schedule K and Schedule K-1 Instructions of Form 1065 or 1120S)	*0*

Section B.—Depreciation of recovery property

A. Class of property	**B.** Date placed in service	**C.** Cost or other basis	**D.** Recovery period	**E.** Method of figuring depreciation	**F.** Deduction
2 Accelerated Cost Recovery System (ACRS) (see instructions): *For assets placed in service ONLY during taxable year beginning in 1984*					
(a) 3-year property					
(b) 5-year property		*1140*	*5*	*ACRS*	*171*
(c) 10-year property					
(d) 15-year public utility property					
(e) 15-year real property— low-income housing					
(f) 15-year real property other than low-income housing					
(g) 18-year real property					
(h) Other recovery property				S/L	
				S/L	

3	ACRS deduction for assets placed in service prior to 1984 (see instructions)	*0*

Section C.—Depreciation of nonrecovery property

4	Property subject to section 168(e)(2) election (see instructions)	
5	Class Life Asset Depreciation Range (CLADR) System Depreciation (see instructions) . . .	
6	Other depreciation (see instructions)	

Section D.—Summary

7	Total (Add deductions on lines 1 through 6). Enter here and on the Depreciation line of your return (Partnerships and S corporations—DO NOT include any amounts entered on line 1.)	*171*

Part II Amortization

A. Description of property	**B.** Date acquired	**C.** Cost or other basis	**D.** Code section	**E.** Amortization period or percentage	**F.** Amortization for this year

Total. Enter here and on Other Deductions or Other Expenses line of your return	*0*

See Paperwork Reduction Act Notice on page 1 of the separate instructions.

Form **4562** (1984)

Form **4562**

Department of the Treasury
Internal Revenue Service

Depreciation and Amortization

▶ See separate instructions.
▶ Attach this form to your return.

OMB No. 1545-0172

1984

67

Name(s) as shown on return: *EDWARD J. AND MARY SMITH*

Identifying number: *111-11-1111*

Business or activity to which this form relates: *SCHEDULE E — RENTAL PROPERTY "A"*

Part I Depreciation

For transportation equipment (e.g. autos), amusement/recreation property, and computer/peripheral equipment placed in service after June 18, 1984, and used 50% or less in a trade or business, the section 179 deduction is not allowed and depreciation must be taken only on line 2(h).

Section A.—Election to expense recovery property (Section 179)

A. Class of property	B. Cost	C. Expense deduction

1 Total (not more than $5,000). (Partnerships or S corporations—see the Schedule K and Schedule K-1 Instructions of Form 1065 or 1120S) . . . . | |

Section B.—Depreciation of recovery property

A. Class of property	B. Date placed in service	C. Cost or other basis	D. Recovery period	E. Method of figuring depreciation	F. Deduction
2 Accelerated Cost Recovery System (ACRS) (see instructions): *For assets placed in service ONLY during taxable year beginning in 1984*			/////	/////	/////
(a) 3-year property	/////				
(b) 5-year property	/////				
(c) 10-year property	/////				
(d) 15-year public utility property	/////				
(e) 15-year real property— low-income housing					
(f) 15-year real property other than low-income housing					
(g) 18-year real property					
(h) Other recovery property				S/L	
				S/L	

3 ACRS deduction for assets placed in service prior to 1984 (see instructions) . . . . | *4500* |

Section C.—Depreciation of nonrecovery property

4 Property subject to section 168(e)(2) election (see instructions)	
5 Class Life Asset Depreciation Range (CLADR) System Depreciation (see instructions)	
6 Other depreciation (see instructions)	

Section D.—Summary

7 Total (Add deductions on lines 1 through 6). Enter here and on the Depreciation line of your return (Partnerships and S corporations—DO NOT include any amounts entered on line 1.) . . . . | *4500* |

Part II Amortization

A. Description of property	B. Date acquired	C. Cost or other basis	D. Code section	E. Amortization period or percentage	F. Amortization for this year

Total. Enter here and on Other Deductions or Other Expenses line of your return . . . .

See Paperwork Reduction Act Notice on page 1 of the separate instructions.

Form **4562** (1984)

Form **5695**

Department of the Treasury
Internal Revenue Service

Residential Energy Credit

▶ Attach to Form 1040.   ▶ See Instructions on back.

▶ For Paperwork Reduction Act Notice, see Instructions on back.

OMB No. 1545-0214

1984

30

Name(s) as shown on Form 1040   EDWARD J. AND MARY SMITH

Your social security number   111 11 1111

Enter the address of your principal residence on which the credit is claimed if it is different from the address shown on Form 1040.

If you have an energy credit carryover from a previous tax year and no energy savings costs this year, skip to Part III, line 24.

Part I Fill in your energy conservation costs (but do not include repair or maintenance costs).

1 Was your principal residence substantially completed before April 20, 1977? (See instructions) ▶ [X] Yes [ ] No

Note: *You MUST answer this question. Failure to do so will delay the processing of your return. If you checked the "No" box, you CANNOT claim an energy credit under Part I and you should not fill in lines 2a through 12 of this form.*

2	**a**	Insulation	2a	800
	b	Storm (or thermal) windows or doors	2b	
	c	Caulking or weatherstripping	2c	185
	d	A replacement burner for your existing furnace that reduces fuel use	2d	
	e	A device for modifying flue openings to make a heating system more efficient	2e	
	f	An electrical or mechanical furnace ignition system that replaces a gas pilot light	2f	
	g	A thermostat with an automatic setback	2g	
	h	A meter that shows the cost of energy used	2h	
3		Total (add lines 2a through 2h)	3	985
4		Enter the part of expenditures made from nontaxable government grants and subsidized financing	4	
5		Subtract line 4 from line 3	5	985
6		Maximum amount of cost on which credit can be figured	6	$2,000 00
7		Enter the total energy conservation costs for this residence. Add lines 2 of your 1978, 1979, and 1980 Forms 5695 and line 3 of your 1981, 1982, and 1983 Forms 5695	7	500
8		Subtract line 7 from line 6. If line 7 exceeds line 6, enter zero here and on line 12	8	1500
9		Enter the total nontaxable grants and subsidized financing used to purchase qualified energy items for this residence. Add the amount on line 4 of this form and your 1981, 1982, and 1983 Forms 5695.	9	
10		Subtract line 9 from line 8. If zero or less, do not complete the rest of Part I	10	1500
11		Enter the amount on line 5 or line 10, whichever is less	11	985
12		Enter 15% of line 11 here and include in amount on line 23 below	12	148

Part II Fill in your renewable energy source costs (but do not include repair or maintenance costs).

13	**a** Solar _____ **13b** Geothermal _____ **13c** Wind _____ Total ▶		13d	
14	Enter the part of expenditures made from nontaxable government grants and subsidized financing		14	
15	Subtract line 14 from line 13d		15	
16	Maximum amount of cost on which the credit can be figured		16	$10,000 00
17	Enter the total renewable energy source costs for this residence. Add line 5 of your 1978 Form 5695, line 9 of your 1979 and 1980 Forms 5695, and line 13d of your 1981, 1982, and 1983 Forms 5695		17	
18	Subtract line 17 from line 16. If line 17 exceeds line 16, enter zero here and on line 22		18	
19	Enter the total nontaxable grants and subsidized financing used to purchase qualified energy items for this residence. Add the amount on line 14 of this form and your 1981, 1982, and 1983 Forms 5695		19	
20	Subtract line 19 from line 18. If zero or less, do not complete the rest of Part II		20	
21	Enter the amount on line 15 or line 20, whichever is less		21	
22	Enter 40% of line 21 here and include in amount on line 23 below		22	

Part III Fill in this part to figure the limitation.

23	Add lines 12 and 22. If less than $10, enter zero	23	148
24	Enter your energy credit carryover from a previous tax year. **Caution**—Do not make an entry on this line if your 1983 Form 1040, line 49, showed an amount of more than zero.	24	
25	Add lines 23 and 24	25	148
26	Enter the amount of tax shown on Form 1040, line 40	26	6099
27	Add lines 41, 42, and 44 from Form 1040 and enter the total	27	625
28	Subtract line 27 from line 26. If zero or less, enter zero	28	5474
29	Residential energy credit. Enter the amount on line 25 or line 28, whichever is less. Also, enter this amount on Form 1040, line 43. Complete Part IV below if this line is less than line 25	29	148

Part IV Fill in this part to figure your carryover to 1985 (complete only if line 29 is less than line 25).

30	Enter amount from Part III, line 25	30	
31	Enter amount from Part III, line 29	31	
32	Credit carryover to 1985 (subtract line 31 from line 30)	32	

I N D E X